The Social Determinants of Health

The Social Determinants of Health

Looking Upstream

Kathryn Strother Ratcliff

polity

First published in 2017 by Polity Press

Polity Press
65 Bridge Street
Cambridge CB2 1UR, UK

Polity Press
101 Station Landing
Suite 300,
Medford, MA 02155
USA

ISBN-13: 978-1-5095-0431-2
ISBN-13: 978-1-5095-0432-9(pb)

A catalogue record for this book is available from the British Library.

Library of Congress Cataloging-in-Publication Data

Names: Ratcliff, Kathryn Strother, 1944- author.
Title: The social determinants of health : looking upstream / Kathryn
    Strother Ratcliff.
Description: Cambridge, UK ; Malden, MA : Polity, [2017] | Includes
    bibliographical references and index.
Identifiers: LCCN 2017000625 (print) | LCCN 2017009267 (ebook) | ISBN
    9781509504312 (hardback) | ISBN 9781509504329 (pbk.) | ISBN 9781509504343
    (Mobi) | ISBN 9781509504350 (Epub)
Subjects: LCSH: Social medicine. | Public health.
Classification: LCC RA418 .R336 2017 (print) | LCC RA418 (ebook) | DDC
    362.1--dc23
LC record available at https://lccn.loc.gov/2017000625

Typeset in 10.5 on 12 pt Plantin by
Servis Filmsetting Ltd, Stockport, Cheshire
Printed and bound in Great Britain by CPI Group (UK) Ltd, Croydon, CR0 4YY

For further information on Polity, visit our website: www.politybooks.com

Contents

Preface

Improving the health of our world requires knowledge of the principal determinants of our health and the ways to address them effectively. Fortunately many scholars, activists, community residents, and organizations like the World Health Organization, as well as various professional organizations, people, and groups have worked hard to understand and change what has become known as the social determinants of health (SDoH).

The task of understanding the SDoH is not easy, as our social world is a complicated and ever-changing place. Our understanding of the significance and long-term impact of human activity on our health and on the environment evolves with research and experience. Furthermore, the upstream triggers that affect our health downstream through conditions of daily life such as work, water, air, food, and transportation are subject to the vagaries of politicians, policy makers, industry advocates, lobbyists, and activists. These players necessarily change as public sentiment and the political climate shifts.

I am writing this during a particularly dramatic shift in health-related influences in the United States. With new industry-friendly occupants in the White House and a Republican Party that has vowed to replace the Affordable Care Act in control of both houses of Congress, what had been a growing commitment to addressing the SDoH was dramatically turned on its head. The promise of a "cleaner, greener" future seems at odds with the new administration's aim to grow our economy by deregulating industry and by pursuing policies that threaten negative impacts on the SDoH. For example, in his first month in office, President Trump signed an order that would roll back a whole host of Environmental Protection Agency (EPA) regulations needed to protect the environment, including a regulation that restricted coal companies from dumping mining waste into waterways. The man he appointed director of the EPA, Scott Pruitt, has had close working ties with fossil fuel industries, worked to block President Obama's climate change agenda, and, as Attorney General of Oklahoma, sued the EPA 14 times.

While business and industry leaders applaud the new president's assault on protective regulation, science-based agencies throughout the government, from the National Science Foundation (NSF) to the Department of Energy (DOE), have been rattled by White House requests for information on scientists engaged in climate and other environmental research; many are concerned that this is a first step to eliminating from the government anyone with these views. The National Forest Service made headlines defying orders to suspend the distribution of public information about climate change during the transition of the new administration, and scientists scheduled an unprecedented march on Washington. How will these activities factor into society's ability and desire to reduce poverty, clean up our environment, reduce emissions that contribute to climate change, provide safe and healthy jobs, and eliminate health disparities?

While the examples highlighted in this book predate the current changes, they illustrate precisely the mechanisms that have connected and continue to connect our political, economic, and social institutions to our health. Indeed, the issues remain the same, regardless of politics. As members of a society, we are all responsible for identifying the drivers of systemic public health problems and for working to correct them. Looking "upstream" is the first step in our collective progress. That is where this book begins. It ends optimistically, with examples of both government action and corporate social responsibility that illustrate a fundamental common ground: the importance of an environment in which we should be able not only to survive, but to thrive as a healthy, productive society.

This book is an attempt to reach out to college audiences in public health, sociology, political science, and environmental science as well as to the general public that has not yet joined the conversation but needs to, if we are to make substantial progress. By providing an accessible overview of the SDoH and some of the possible solutions, this book hopes to ignite interest and informed activism. Our communities, nations, and the world are not healthy. We cannot continue down our current path. Doing so is not sustainable.

Kathryn Strother Ratcliff
March 2017
Storrs, Connecticut

1

Introduction

America is a rich nation with an abundance of highly sophisticated and to-be-envied healthcare technology. It has well-trained, sophisticated healthcare providers and spends much more per person on healthcare than other nations do: it spends about $8,700 a year, while most peer countries spend less than $5,000, the average being $3,453 (OECD Health Statistics 2015). Its health expenditures aren't just a little bit more; they are a lot more.

With all of this going for them, it would seem that Americans are healthier than the citizens of other countries; but they are not. Two typical health outcomes used to measure the health status of a population are telling: infant mortality and life expectancy. On these two measures, the United States does not rank highly; it is about thirtieth on both. This means that in almost thirty other countries babies are more likely to survive and people are more likely to live longer than in the United States.

Many people would find the juxtaposition of the high health expenditures and poor health outcomes puzzling. But there is a good reason for this seemingly illogical pairing: healthcare is only one contributor to health, and it is a small one. The quality of the US healthcare system, the amount that Americans spend on it, and the ever more impressive medical advances are not the main contributors to population or individual health. Lester Breslow, a US public health leader, said it succinctly: "In the long run, housing may be more important to health than hospitals" (quoted in Richmond 2012). Or, stated differently, "in creating its way of life, each society creates its way of death," disease and injury (quoted in Freund and McGuire 1999: 2). A classic article (McKinlay and McKinlay 1977) provides a focused piece of evidence for this idea by analyzing the

contributions of medical interventions to the declining death rate for
nine common infectious diseases: measles, scarlet fever, tuberculo-
sis, typhoid, pneumonia, influenza, whooping cough, poliomyelitis,
and diphtheria. All are diseases associated with effective vaccines
or other medical measures (e.g., the administration of penicillin).
Many people believe that the decline of those diseases was due to
such medical interventions, but the analysis showed that most of
the decline in the death rate for each disease actually came *before*
the medical measure had been introduced, and was often the result
of improved sanitation. Clearly these observations suggest that
medical measures are important, but not the *most* important cause
of improved health. When Centers for Disease Control (CDC) looks
at the contributors to health, it reports that only about 20 percent of
the nation's health is the result of medical care, while 5 percent is the
result of biology and genetics, 20 percent is the result of individual
actions, and over 50 percent is caused by the "social determinants
of health" (CDC 2011). To improve America's health statistics,
Americans need to better understand these other determinants of
poor health and to design and fund initiatives that tackle them. These
social determinants are the focus of this book.

But what are "social determinants"? The Robert Wood Johnson
Foundation (2010) found that these words did not resonate easily
with most people. In chapter 2 we will explore important social
determinants in greater depth, but here let me define them simply
as (1) *conditions of life* people are exposed to because of the way their
society is built—how we live, how we work, how we move from place
to place, and what we eat and drink; and (2) the *causes or triggers of
those conditions of life*—such as government policies, social structure,
and the actions of powerful actors and organizations.

A growing consensus in many academic fields, in the World Health
Organization (WHO), and among human rights spokespeople is that
we need to take the social determinants of health more seriously. We
have long focused on the biological causes of poor health (genes,
germs, viruses) and on the contribution of the healthcare system to
better health. But the focus is now changing. Examining social determinants is often referred to as an "upstream" approach, so named
from the oft-used image of people drowning in a river. This image
is typically credited to John McKinlay, author of a classic article in
which he quotes his friend Irving Zola:

> There I am standing by the shore of a swiftly flowing river and I hear
> the cry of a drowning man. So I jump into the river, put my arms

around him, pull him to shore and apply artificial respiration. Just when he begins to breathe, there is another cry for help. So I jump into the river, reach him, pull him to shore, apply artificial respiration, and then just as he begins to breathe, another cry for help. So back in the river again, reaching, pulling, applying, breathing and then another yell. Again and again, without end, goes the sequence. You know, I am so busy jumping in, pulling them to shore, applying artificial respiration, that I have *no* time to see who the hell is upstream pushing them all in. (McKinlay 1979: 9)

Although both efforts—saving people in immediate danger and discovering why they are in danger—are important, this book is focused on the latter and examines the society's infrastructure (our conditions of life), why it is built as it is (the causes or triggers of these conditions) and the resulting consequences for health.

An important aspect of the upstream perspective is that it makes sure that the analysis of these upstream root causes takes the race, ethnic, and class structure of society and the power of institutional racism into account. Continuing with the river imagery, there are disparities among people that determine who is pushed into the river, and hence who has the worst health consequences. Or, moving from the image to real examples, corporate decisions on the advertising and availability of tobacco, alcohol, and healthy food in rich white neighborhoods versus poor minority neighborhoods have disparate health impacts. The enduring racism in our society, combined with government policies such as discriminatory housing or with practices like redlining (see chapter 3), have encouraged the development of segregated neighborhoods, African American ones being at a considerable disadvantage in terms of air pollution, dampness, dust, and pests (all of which contribute to asthma), and the residents being exposed to stress from the living conditions and discrimination. The combination of these upstream determinants leads to major disparities in asthma, black children being more likely to suffer than white ones (Williams et al. 2009). Such differences are well documented in a substantial literature on health disparities. Some researchers cast this health disparity information in a social injustice or human rights framework, so that the lenses they use go beyond recounting disparities in health to offering an evaluative statement: these differences shouldn't exist—they are unjust.

The social justice perspective used in this book is more inclusive. I argue that some structural features affect *the health of everyone*, and a focus limited to health disparities between specific social groups glosses over this general impact. In this view, social injustice is not just about differences but also examines conditions that affect us all—conditions no one should experience (see Hofrichter 2003a and Levy and Sidel 2013). Thus it is an injustice if we all live in a world that assaults our health by preventable means (e.g., inadequate clean water, lack of sustainable methods to grow food, or pollution that effects climate change). A focus on disparities alone could easily miss the full impact of these conditions on our health. Since some of the causes of disparities—such as discrimination, at both the individual and the institutional level—are not the same as the causes of population health (Krieger 2008a: 1100), I will not attempt to cover the full complexity of such disparities, which is reflected in the important literature. That said, this book will clearly note that health disparities exist in almost all situations, which means that the people most likely to be exposed to unhealthy conditions of living—poor air and water quality, limited food choices, dangerous work environments, and so on—are lower-class individuals and people of color. Likewise, I won't fully cover gender disparities in health, although I will offer some important examples. Due to discrimination and cultural values, women face very different kinds of assault on their health from the ones men do. They are more likely to be victims of domestic violence and of stress from discrimination, they are disproportionately poor, and they face atypical occupational hazards as a result of gender-based division of labor (Ratcliff 2002).

While the social determinants of health as a topic refers to society in general, this book supports the viewpoint that people matter and social justice is paramount (Marmot 2005). Throughout the book you will encounter not just a social justice and human rights perspective, but also a strong critique of situations of differential power in which democracy seems to be forgotten. Our government "of the people, by the people, and for the people" has in many situations been overrun by those with enormous economic and political power. Each chapter documents instances of this trend—which is the result of weak public regulatory efforts, strong private interests, or both—and reveals the alarming health hazards that have resulted. Where possible, I also look for positive trends, social activism, reform, or legislation that might prevent, mitigate, or reverse negative health outcomes.

Chapter 2 will discuss social determinants in greater detail, then six substantive chapters will explore various aspects of how we live (chapters 3, 4, and 5), how we move from place to place and in our built environment (chapter 6), how we work (chapter 7), and how we eat (chapter 8). Topics fully deserving similar coverage but that are not covered due to space include the pharmaceutical industry and the firearms industry: the power of each has changed the conditions of life for millions. The reader is referred in particular to Freudenberg's (2014) excellent coverage in *Legal but Lethal*.

In every chapter of this book I will examine the associated conditions of life, the causes of those conditions, and the resulting consequences for health. To limit my scope, I will focus on physical health more than on mental health and on the United States more than on other countries. While several health problems will constitute the clear "dependent variable" in each chapter, the discussion of disease and injury will include neither a technical description (the understanding of which would require a background in biology, biochemistry, and endocrinology), nor a technical discussion of appropriate treatments. Rather, each chapter will present descriptive information designed to educate the reader on the impact of a disease (e.g., how asbestosis reduces the quality of one's life) and on the extent or seriousness of the health problem in question. The focus throughout will be on the social determinants of health (SDoH).

In examining many conditions, we will discover that the evidence that a particular toxic agent has caused a particular health hazard is not as robust as we might like. In those situations, when strong but less than conclusive evidence exists, I suggest that delays in reducing exposure to a potential health hazard in order to allow the collection of additional information is ill advised. The long history of unhealthy conditions of living is so alarming that immediate action to reduce exposure is often warranted. I will invoke the precautionary principle (discussed in chapter 4), which states that, when there is serious potential for harm, even if proof is not definitive, society has an obligation to act. Finally, I will argue that we can't just focus on remedying existing unhealthy situations but must prevent the next ones from happening. The trajectory we are on is not a healthy one, and we need to change course.

The concluding chapter will suggest some of the ways in which we can look upstream and begin to reduce the root causes of ill health, often by drawing on creative ideas from entrepreneurs, community residents, and social justice networks (among others). In addition, I will refer back to examples from the chapters, especially ones that draw upon the important "popular epidemiology" work of Phil Brown and the community activism it inspired. Finally, the last chapter will examine the importance of healthcare providers' looking upstream and thereby doing a better job of saving people from drowning in the river.

2

Social Determinants of Health

In the past two decades, the World Health Organization (WHO) as well as numerous researchers and authors have emphasized the importance of the social determinants of health (SDoH). Investigators describe the SDoH in distinctive ways and focus on different aspects in their research. The commonality among these views is the idea that the *conditions of life* people are exposed to as a result of the way their society is built affect their health. Such conditions concern how we live (e.g., the fact that many of us live in poverty, the quality of our housing and our neighborhoods, the amount of pollution in our environment); how we work (e.g., safety, stress, availability of work); how we move from place to place and how that affects our built environment (e.g., use of cars, building of highways, need for gasoline, lack of walkable space); and what we eat and drink (e.g., availability and affordability of healthy food and clean water).

A focus on conditions of life takes us away from looking at germs and viruses or at disruptions in the normal biochemistry or hormone activity of the human body—away from the biological causes of health and toward the larger social, political, and economic environment of the larger society. While some writers stop at conditions of life when they talk about the SDoH, I will be more comprehensive in this book: the SDoH discussed here will include not just the conditions of life, but also what others call the "drivers" (Marmot and Allen 2014)—the causes or triggers of these conditions of life. Doing so means that our focus will move further upstream.

So what are the drivers of the conditions of life? They are complex, intertwined, and numerous. They include the power and actions of groups—in particular large industries and corporations—and sometimes of individuals; the structure of society—its race-, ethnicity-, class-based organization and the inequalities in wealth, income, and power; and government policies that provide healthy housing, clean air and water, and safe employment. This description attempts to capture the *forces behind the conditions of life* in very broad strokes. The diagram in Figure 2.1 brings them under three big concepts: political economy, power, and policies. Others have labeled these "drivers" in similar ways: "poor social policies and programmes, unfair economic arrangements, and bad politics" (WHO 2008a); "inequities in power, money and resources" (Marmot 2010: 10); "decisions made by executives" in various industries (Freudenberg 2014: 3); institutional racism, government support for the public sector (Hofrichter 2003b: 16–17); "economic, political, legal, religious and cultural structures that stop individuals, groups, and societies from reaching their full potential" (Farmer et al. 2006: 1686); the "social, economic, political, and physical environments humans create" (Markowitz and Rosner 2013b: xiv); "structures of power and privilege" (Hofrichter 2003b: 7); "how power—both *power over* and *power to do*, including constraints on and possibilities for exercising each type—structures people's engagement with the world and their exposures to material and psychosocial health hazards" (Krieger 2008b: 223); "the political determinants of health: ... power constellations, institutions, processes, interests, and ideological positions" (Kickbusch 2015: 1); "economic and political institutions and decisions that create, enforce, and perpetuate economic and social privilege and inequality" (Krieger 2003: 434), including policies on education, childcare, community revitalization, and land use (Woolf and Braveman 2011: 1855); political traditions that show a commitment to redistributive policies (Navarro and Shi 2003: 195); and, quite specifically, federal policies like redlining, which lead to segregated neighborhoods (Williams and Sternthal 2010). Missing from all these enumerations is the impact of culture on health, which is explored below.

 In this book, both the conditions of life and the drivers of those conditions are considered SDoH and I will discuss both, as well as the links between them. To do so, I will use a decidedly sociological lens, informed by an interdisciplinary literature, drawing particularly on sociology, public health, and history. I will illustrate how particular conditions of life came to be by providing specific examples in each chapter. For instance, race and ethnicity have long been, tragically, an organizing principle of American life that produced prejudice and discrimination at the individual level. Importantly for our purposes, this has also meant government policies and institutional practices that have produced an unequal society, with unfavorable conditions

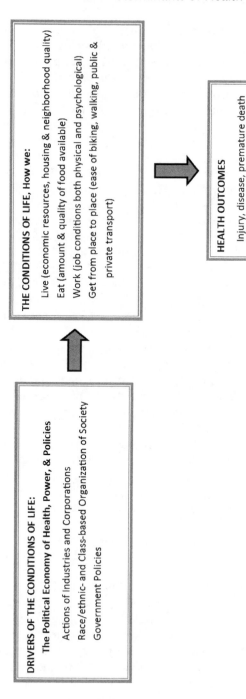

Figure 2.1   Drivers of the conditions of life

Culture and Health

Although not entirely separable from our focus on power, political economy, and societal organization, culture is also a strong determinant of health. People adopt behaviors because of their culture—the beliefs, values, practices, and material objects in their society—and some of these behaviors have consequences for health. For instance, for over 1,000 years, women in China hobbled around in extreme pain. Their feet were bound, their toes bent inward under their sole, and their arch was crushed. It took several years of binding for the feet to take the desired shape, and the process was excruciatingly painful (Chang 1991). This practice came from a cultural belief that bound feet made women more erotic. The effects on health included severe lifelong disabilities, greater risk of falling, a reduced ability to squat (important in a country with squat toilets), and increased chances of social isolation, as the women were more likely to stay indoors, away from the gaze of others (Cummings et al. 1997). Culture created a way of life that in turn created a health problem.

One could argue that a parallel cultural practice exists today in the United States and other countries of the industrialized world: stiletto heels. Our cultures want women in high heels because high heels are perceived to make a woman look more feminine and alluring. Yet high heels impose an abnormal body posture and put unusual pressure on the foot, causing possible nerve damage, back problems, and bunions. In fact women in our culture are subject to serious body image scrutiny, and this sometimes leads to a medical "solution" for something that is not a medical problem at all. Consider breast augmentation. Before the American Society of Plastic and Reconstructive Surgeons (ASPRS) used its power to declare the female breast a suitable object of concern, small breasts exposed women to ridicule ("can't tell if you are coming or going"), but not to surgery. That changed when the ASPRS decreed: "There is a substantial and enlarging body of medical information and opinion to the effect that these deformities [small breasts] are really a disease" (quoted in Ehrenreich 1992: 88). With some humor, one observer noted: "Not a fatal disease, perhaps, to judge from the number of sufferers who are still hobbling around untreated, but a disease nonetheless" (Ehrenreich 1992: 88). Never once did the ASPRS indicate that micromastia presented any physical health risk. Rather, just by having "statistically small" breasts, the woman had a problem that medicine could and should address (Haiken 1997: 272). Women responded by eagerly seeking out doctors who could augment their breasts through implants. The procedure became controversial as a result of reports of problems with the implants, particularly the ones that ruptured. The data on the health effects of breast implants suggest that such implants decrease the chances that a nursing mother will have sufficient lactation, reduce the accuracy of mammograms, and cause or exacerbate autoimmune diseases (Zuckerman 2010). Our culture allowed the medicalization of a normal condition and then caused a health problem through its surgical solution.

Men are not exempt from cultural expectations that can lead to the medicalization of normal differences. Culture favors tall men, which has led some parents to accept the idea that shortness is a disease to be addressed with human growth hormone (HGH). Evidence on the effectiveness of HGH for "normally short" children—that is, for children with no known pituitary problem—is lacking. Some argue that diagnosing a child with the "disease" of shortness not only exposes him/her unnecessarily to potent drugs with possible effects on health, but also has mental health consequences, since that child's stature is officially labeled "abnormal" (Cohen and Cosgrove 2009).

We can also see the health impact of cultural "norms" on class and race. Cultures tend to privilege higher social-class groups over others, allowing differential access to safety and health. The sinking of the *Titanic* in 1912 is a classic example. While access to its lifeboats could have been more or less random, it was anything but. People in steerage (the cheapest section of the ship) were much more likely to be denied a space on a lifeboat. Seventy-five percent of them died, versus only 38 percent of the first-class passengers. Women and children in the first and second class were particularly favored: only 10 percent of them died (Gregson 2008: 273).

The racial structure of society causes and reinforces racism, which can become a powerful cultural script: it permits differential and deadly treatment administered by police to people of color, prejudicial actions that limit one's opportunities for a healthy life, and exposure to constant micro aggressions that cause stress and poor mental health. Racism as a cause of health disparities is understudied, yet extremely important (Bassett 2015: 1086).

I'll give just a couple more brief examples of health outcomes driven by culture. Our love of football has blinded us for decades to possible health problems that come from the head and neck traumas endemic in football. Our cultural designation of gold, diamonds, and flowers as symbols of affection for suitors, lovers, and others has fostered industries that are harmful to both humans and the environment. Practices like using toxic chemicals to cut flowers in the floral industry or leaching gold with cyanide in the metallurgy of gold extraction contaminate our ground water. Meanwhile diamond workers and gold miners are increasingly exposed to HIV from sex slaves in camps (Donohoe 2008)—all because our cultures value the treasures produced.

of life for many race and ethnic groups. Such practices represent institutional racism, in other words they are practices of whole institutions and their employees, often codified in law or unquestioningly incorporated in behavior. They impact vulnerable groups of people differentially. Thus federal redlining policies (chapter 3), government segregation policies for public housing, siting of harmful industries, and waste dumps (chapter 4), and highway construction through black neighborhoods (chapter 6) have all meant poorer conditions of life for African Americans and poor people. Government tax policy and accepted political ideologies that resist the redistribution of income have produced huge inequities in wealth and income in the United States. Currently there are historic highs in income disparity in this country and the gap between rich and poor is widening. Emblematic of that disparity is the top 1 percent of the population, which now receives 20 percent of the total annual income—an increase from 9 percent in 1976 (Alvaredo et al. 2013). This kind of inequity has medical consequences, as studies of "the social gradient of health" have documented (e.g., Marmot et al. 1991; Marmot 2006). The more unequal the distribution of wealth and income in a country, the worse the country's health; and within a country there is a gradient of health in which people in a given category of income have better health than people in the category immediately below. Thus, in an unequal society, it is not just that poverty has consequences for health, but people at all levels of income below the top one have diminished health outcomes. Social structure matters.

Given that so many researchers and writers are talking about SDoH and there are so many excellent examples of how to approach the matter of "drivers," it is significant that most of the discussion, research, and action revolves around the conditions of life.

Discussions have neglected the causes—the part that power, politics, ideology, and conflict play in health and health inequities (Hofrichter 2003b: 2)—and produced a literature on the SDoH that doesn't engage the political economy (Raphael 2003: 68). We rarely study the impact of political forces and public policies on social inequalities and health (Navarro and Shi 2003: 196). When it comes to improving health, researchers have focused almost exclusively on the conditions of life. They have implemented various successful social reforms designed to change those conditions: sewage systems, drinking-water standards, the chlorination of water, the abolition of child labor, a shortened working day, occupational health-and-safety standards, minimum wages, safer food regulations. Indeed, these measures have dramatically improved our health. Yet reformers focus on them not just because the results are predictable but also because they are easier to implement. They are not as political, and hence not as controversial as other factors—which is a major reason why they have been in the focus; but the conditions of life are only one part of the picture. Why are we ignoring the factors that trigger these conditions? Why do we refuse to look upstream?

The Neglect of the Political Economy: The Healthcare System

There are several other, interrelated reasons why the causal factors behind the conditions of life are neglected. First, when Americans consider what it means to be healthy, they often think of the health-care system first. Why? Clearly the healthcare system has direct, very observable, and undeniably positive effects on health. We all know people who have been saved through medical care, people who would not be alive today had modern medicine not existed or modern medication not been available. The Center for Disease Control (CDC) figures given in the introductory chapter attest to the value of a robust healthcare system; yet they account for only about 20 percent of our health, while SDoH account for more than 50 percent.

The Neglect of the Political Economy: Individualism and the Biomedical Model

Second, Americans often cite individual actions as a primary contributor to our health. We are all aware of various things that individuals can do for themselves in order to become healthier: eat nutritious food, exercise regularly, sleep well, not smoke, avoid stress. Among Americans, that individual-level thinking is quickly reinforced by a tendency to think more at the psychological level than at the societal level. Rothman puts it well:

> Americans are good at seeing the individual. We think individualistically, we think psychologically and not sociologically. We can see the person; in sophisticated, nuanced ways we can understand individuals, their motives, concerns, actions, behaviors. What we are less good at, as a people, is seeing a people: seeing the whole, seeing the social, the system within which individuals move. (Rothman 2001: 162)

Or, stated slightly differently: "We live in the Western cultural tradition, which has exploited the cultural values of individualism. As children of that tradition, we are most comfortable taking the individual person as the starting point of analysis" (Smelser 1997: 29).

If the individual is your analytical starting point, it is much easier for you to think that genetics or some individual action would produce good or poor health. Tell someone that people should stop smoking because it is bad for their health, and you will receive little argument. Tell them that the political economy has a major impact on smoking and health, and the reaction will likely contain confusion or disbelief. We easily accept the idea that people make an individual decision to smoke or not smoke; but we don't think about the seductive power of the tobacco industry, with its centuries-old connections to powerful political people, and how it can convince people to smoke. We all want to believe that we have complete control over our choices and our behavior, despite evidence that we are all subject to external forces. As individuals trying to understand health, we don't tend to look upstream.

Closely aligned with, and reinforcing, Americans' individualistic tendencies is the power of the biomedical model, which has long dominated the discourse about health, the training of healthcare providers, and the funding of health initiatives (Ratcliff 2002). Although the model has been revised over the years (for instance we no longer believe the doctrine of specific etiology—the idea that each disease has one and only one cause), the power of the perspective that privileges individuals, finds disease in individuals, and treats individuals persists. Doctors learn to look deep down into the individual when seeking answers about health. The "holy grail of modern medicine remains the search for the molecular basis of disease" (Farmer et al. 2006: 1686). When the biomedical model guides the analysis of health, one looks at cells, body organs, and bodily systems. When the individual is the unit of analysis, one doesn't see the individual in the context of the community and one misses many of the important SDoH: the conditions of life and the drivers of those conditions. A recent National Institute of Health (NIH) report illustrates this all too well. The 441-page report titled "Minority Health and Health Disparities" used terms such as *genome*, *genomic*, *genetic*, and *gene* 457 times, while using *discrimination* and *poverty* twice, *socioeconomic* 12 times, and *racism* not at all. All this was noted by New York City Health Commissioner Mary Bassett in her acceptance of the Frank A. Calderone prize (Bassett 2016). Clearly the authors of the report tried to understand the causes of health disparities at the individual, biological level, not at the level of SDoH.

The Neglect of Political Economy: Resistance and the Tobacco Playbook

Another reason why we don't focus on political economy, power, and policies is a strong resistance to doing so. The nature of this resistance will provide the bulk of the discussion, here and in subsequent chapters. On the other hand, there is less or no resistance to focusing on causal factors when the conditions of living are designated as causes of health, or when the remedies for the identified poor conditions of living become the object of social reforms—such as sanitation, safety on the job, or health education that encourages people to change their individual choices or habits. Why is resistance so minimal when the analysis is at the individual level—when the fault lies in our genes, or in viruses, or in individuals who need to change their behavior, such as by reducing their smoking? Resistance is minimal in such cases because there is *no organized group* to protest and say that genes, viruses, or individual actions could *not* be the cause of disease. But when we look upstream and identify a structural cause such as the actions of the tobacco industry, there will often be an organized group that resists that identification. The discourse about structural causes is contested by those who have vested interests in deflecting debate from a particular industry or set of organizations. By identifying the trigger of a condition of life as a determinant of poor health, we are often pointing fingers at organizational behaviors and threatening the profits of investors (Rothman 2001). Resistance can be strong and is often successful.

In each chapter I will illustrate and discuss this resistance, which frequently includes corporate strategies that turn the public's attention away from political economy and connections to political power and toward individual responsibility, in order to delay actions that would hold the real drivers of the conditions of life accountable. In this chapter I provide an overview of such strategies, primarily by using the tobacco industry as an example. I do this for several reasons. First, the actions of the tobacco industry have had devastating effects on health. In the United States, there were 17.7 million smoking-attributable deaths between 1964 and 2012 (Holford et al. 2014). The WHO (2012) estimates that worldwide 5 million people die each year from smoking. The health impact is indeed staggering. Second, tobacco was the earliest industry to systematically cover up the fact that it was *manufacturing disease*—that using its product *as intended* was a health hazard. Third, the literature documents the large number of other industries that have followed the "tobacco playbook," including the food industry (Brownell and Warner 2009), the sugar industry (Le Bodo et al. 2015), the soda industry (Dorfman et al. 2012), and various chemical industries (Michaels 2008b). Fourth, the tobacco playbook is particularly well documented because litigation between the tobacco industry and the federal government, which led to the Tobacco Master Settlement Agreement in 1998, uncovered 14 million internal documents that are now publicly available through the UCSF Library and Center for Knowledge Management (https://industrydocuments.library.ucsf.edu/tobacco) and detail various corporate resistance techniques.

So how did tobacco companies resist attempts to find their industry responsible for poor health? Over sixty years ago, the tobacco industry found itself under attack, as credible researchers and government agencies began to document the health hazards of tobacco. A publication in the *Journal of the American Medical Association* and a summary of it in a 1952 issue of the then popular *Reader's Digest* entitled "Cancer by the Carton" created a huge amount of concern. The industry's first response was the 1954 "Frank Statement" newspaper advertisement, which stated that its customers' health was "a basic responsibility, paramount to every other consideration in our business" (quoted in Proctor 2011: 258). Thus began a "half-century-long campaign to mislead Americans about the catastrophic effects of smoking and to avoid public policy that might damage sales" (Brownell and Warner 2009: 260)—a campaign veiled in the antithetical claim that the industry cared about smokers' health. The centerpiece of this resistance campaign was stated very clearly by a tobacco industry executive in a private memo that became public: "*Doubt is our product* since it is the best means of competing with the 'body of fact' that exists in the minds of the general public. It is also the means of establishing controversy" (quoted in Michaels 2008a: 11; italics added). To cast doubt was to attack the science that documented the health risk of smoking, to label it "junk science," and to fund research that came to different conclusions. Repeatedly the tobacco industry stated its supposed desire for better information about health through "sound science."

> **The Advancement of Sound Science Coalition (TASSC)**
> TASSC was established in 1993, with funding from Philip Morris channeled through APCO, a public relations firm, in an attempt to hide the organization's connection to the tobacco company (Michaels 2008a: 85). The mission of TASSC "was not to advance science, but to discredit it" (Oreskes and Conway 2010: 150). The first executive director, Steven J. Milloy, created "Junk Science. com that freely attacked science related to health and environmental issues" (Oreskes and Conway 2010: 151). One tactic was to promulgate supposedly sound science principles, which in fact altered the standards of proof to make them advantageous to the "corporate interests of their clients" (Ong and Glantz 2001: 1754). For instance they pushed for a statistical standard that would not allow evidence if the "relative risk" was smaller than 2; this meant that the exposed people had to have twice, or more than twice, the chance of an impact. While at a glance this might seem reasonable, in conditions of gathering community-based epidemiological data on a disease with a long latency period the standard becomes unreasonably and irresponsibly high (Cranor 2008: 234–8). Such a standard "would have made it impossible to conclude that secondhand smoke, as well as many other environmental toxins, is dangerous" (Ong and Glantz 2001: 1754).

The strategy was brilliant in concept, because it seemed to show that the industry *wanted to know* what the health impact of tobacco was—after all, they were funding research. But the industry-funded research program was actually a red herring (Proctor 2011: 260), so called because it moved the conversation away from concern about smoking and health. The tobacco industry made sure that the research was *not* relevant to whether smoking cigarettes increased one's risk of lung cancer. To achieve this goal, its program-supported research focused not on smoking but on the mechanisms of disease, for example on how heredity, infection, nutrition, hormones, nervous strain, or environmental factors like humidity and temperature could increase the risk of lung disease (Proctor 2011: 261–2). No matter how the data turned out, smoking could not be implicated as a cause of lung cancer. By the mid-1980s the industry had spent over $100 million on research, exceeding the amount "given for research by any other source except the federal government" (industry document quoted by Oreskes and Conway 2010: 210), and as a big player in research it was able to shape the discourse about smoking and health for decades. Also important to the industry's strategy was having funded researchers to become willing experts who offered testimony in many venues, including courtrooms when smokers' lawsuits against the tobacco industry came to trial. To meet the needs of industry, "a lucrative business of science for hire has emerged" (Michaels and Monforton 2005: S43). Two historians commented on the invitation they received from a talent-search company that specialized in expert witnesses, when they were asked whether they wanted to be vetted as possible experts for a trial on lead. The invitation indicated that they "need not be a subject matter expert" but just someone who could "easily communicate a story to a jury" (Rosner and Markowitz 2009: 273). The tactic of using credentialed researchers as expert witnesses was so effective that the tobacco industry lost no legal cases between 1954 and 1979, despite being in court 117 times (Oreskes and Conway 2010: 14).

The evidence available in 1950 could have convinced people that smoking was a health hazard, but the tobacco industry's "doubt is our product" campaign put a damper on that knowledge, prolonging and exacerbating negative health outcomes for millions. The data on the percentage of people who believed throughout the years that smoking was bad is telling. In 1954 only 41–6 percent (depending on income level) believed that smoking was harmful. By the early 1970s, the percentage increased to 63–85 percent; by 1977–85 it was 72–92 percent; and by 1990–7 it was 87–97 percent (Link 2008: 377). Thus it took fifty years for people to learn and accept the truth—that smoking led to lung cancer—because the tobacco industry resisted the attack against it so successfully and disseminated doubt about its product, so people would be confused about the life-threatening consequences of smoking.

The industry's strategy was not just to fund research that would muddy the waters and create doubt, but to develop sophisticated ways to spread the false word, which, as we will see in later chapters, has become commonplace in other industries. The tobacco industry created newsletters, journals, and magazines that appeared to be independent peer-reviewed or quality publications when in fact they were none of these things. One such journal was *Tobacco and Health Research.* Its publication criterion was straightforward, as stated by the editors: "The most important type of story is that which casts doubt on the cause and effect theory of disease and smoking." Editorial guidelines for headlines were even more explicit: the headlines "should strongly call out the point—Controversy! Contradiction! Other Factors! Unknowns!" (quoted in Michaels 2008b: 92). The existence of such journals allowed the publication of industry-friendly research and its distribution to targeted audiences, such as doctors (Oreskes and Conway 2010: 244).

The tobacco industry also turned to a public relations firm, Hill+Knowlton, whose other clients included oil, chemical, asbestos, and vinyl chloride industries (Michaels and Monforton 2005) and which helped it develop general strategies for swaying public opinion. As the industry got more sophisticated, it learned that names matter; hence in 1964 tobacco changed the name of its research-funding organization from "the Tobacco Industry Research Committee" to "the Council for Tobacco Research" (Proctor 2011: 260), promising that "the new organization would be wholly dedicated to health research, and not to 'industry or commercial studies'" (Oreskes and Conway 2010: 22). I explore in this book other industries that have funded various front groups and suggested an exclusive interest in health and good science through authoritative names, which offer no indication of ties with an industry. Such tactics make it easier and easier for people to fall prey to misinformation and bias.

Rhetorical strategies also included developing grassroots support among the public for industry views. The tobacco industry in the United States was particularly clever at this: it appealed to feelings of patriotism during World War II and produced an advertisement that showed how many battleships, destroyers, and bombers the government could buy using the tax revenues from tobacco sales. Clearly, being anti-tobacco was tantamount to being anti-American (Proctor 2011: 372 ff.). Another strategy was to find a theme that would resonate politically. Freedom of choice is a cherished American value, and it was expertly exploited by US tobacco companies "to emphasize liberty, as well as the lack of a need for government regulation." Internal tobacco industry memos called "freedom of choice (read: smoking) 'an American birthright.'" Horace Kornegay, president of the Tobacco Institute, said: "Let us tell the American people— smokers and non-smokers—that the real issue is freedom of choice. Once the government can control our smoking behavior it can turn the thumbscrews and control other behavior as well" (Friedman et al. 2015: 252). More broadly, the industry used a "personal responsibility" rhetoric that resonates in a culture where individualism is so highly regarded. What it failed to disclose is that smoking behavior *was* being controlled, not by individual choice or by the government, but by a calculated, industry-driven narrative designed to promote a product through powerful democratic ideals.

In other chapters we will see how the personal responsibility frame is used in occupational settings to counter the idea that the workplace is to blame for injuries and disease. The industry, clearly pushing for a downstream view, will claim that the worker is careless or fails to use protection and that these individual failures are the cause of occupational health hazards. In chapter 8 readers will find the food industry argument that obesity comes not from the seductive advertising of unhealthy high-caloric foods, but from people's poor choices and failure to exercise. The oft-repeated refrain will be that people's poor health is caused by their own bad choices rather than by structural limitations on choice—limitations that are, in turn, the intended result of strategic industry decisions made far upstream.

In the world of tobacco, grassroots support was also engineered by targeting particular communities, for instance African American and Hispanic ones. The tobacco industry analyzed market research in order to determine social values that would allow its salespeople to tailor advertisements, then "through philanthropy curried favor with minority organizations in the hope of defusing opposition to pro-tobacco policies," and finally hired local influential African Americans in its workforce, including a youth director for outreach to colleges and universities with predominantly African American student bodies (Shelley et al. 2014: e10).

More recently these grassroots support tactics have evolved into *fake* grassroots support, cleverly named by some as "astroturfing" (Beder 1998). An industry's organization can generate the appearance of considerable support for a product by buying online tweets and friends. There is even a site (buycheapfollowers.com) that will sell 3,000 Twitter followers for $15 (Kessler 2015). The grassroots specialist has the task of drawing the attention of politicians by making it look as if millions of people supported the industry's position (Beder 1998).

The tobacco playbook also mentioned the strategic funding of good causes in the name of corporate responsibility; this had the purpose of silencing potential critics of smoking. For instance, tobacco funded women's groups for sporting events such as the Virginia Slim Tennis Tour, and then these groups "were silent on the rapidly escalating epidemic of lung cancer in women, focusing instead on breast cancer and other problems" (Brownell and Warner 2009: 268). Sometimes the money sent to the cause was *less* than the money spent on advertising the company's good deed. In 2000 Philip Morris spent $115 million on social causes, and then turned around and spent another $150 million "on a national TV advertising campaign touting its beneficence" (Brownell and Warner 2009: 269).

Corporations have also seen the value of doing good deeds at a local level. They have served on community boards and built parks, golf courses, and other local amenities. These and other corporate strategies will be explored in other chapters. The big point here is that corporations do feel threatened when questioned about the health impact of their manufacturing process or final product and deflect that argument by documenting the value of their economic contribution and their becoming a vital part of the community.

The Neglect of Political Economy: Government, Politics, and the Lack of Political Will

Muddying public perception and stimulating "doubt is our product" discourse, however, was not reassuring enough for big tobacco. The industry also worked hard to be more closely and more effectively involved in government policy and regulation discussions. They were successful early on in obtaining "veto power over the membership of the advisory committee that eventually produced the first surgeon general's report on smoking and health" (Brownell and Warner 2009: 269). They lobbied hard to get exclusions from regulations. Thus a variety of federal acts that protect consumers, such as the Controlled Substances Act, the Consumer Product Safety Act, and the Toxic Substances Control Act, contain specific statements that *exclude* tobacco from their regulation (Emmons et al. 1997). A profitable industry is able to make huge campaign contributions and assemble large lobbying teams, smoothing the way to industry-friendly legislation.

This kind of political power is not limited to the United States. The European Union (EU) found the power of the tobacco industry too great to ignore. In 1999, massive lobbying by the company British American Tobacco (BAT) resulted in a change in EU policy that mandated a business-friendly form of cost–benefit analysis: "BAT and other large companies operating in Europe have fundamentally altered EU policymaking by ensuring that all decisions are passed through an economic framework that provides business with a range of advantages" (Smith et al. 2010: 9). For instance, the lobbying resulted in an increased burden of proof on the EU when there was indication of possible harmful results from the proposed business. The tobacco industry responded to a proposal to limit tobacco advertising in the EU with "the most ferocious lobbying campaign seen in Europe" (Bitton et al. 2002: 7), resulting in a ten-year delay. Similar tactics continue today. The US Chamber of Commerce aggressively advocates for tobacco worldwide, having recently attacked "an excise tax in the Philippines, cigarette advertising bans in Uruguay and restrictions on smoking in public places in Moldova" (Hakim 2015: A1).

The tobacco industry (like other industries, as we will see) was in part successful in limiting national and state actions that would have required more healthful corporate actions. In these cases opposition from politicians can generate career-ending publicity and would require from the public a strong "sense of social solidarity" against corporate offenses, which is often lacking in our culture of individualism (Braveman, Egerter, and Williams 2011: 392). Ironically, pro-corporate solidarity was more likely to emerge within communities dependent on various industries, despite the health problems that those industries might cause. Economic benefits to tobacco-growing regions were regularly used as a reason to be supportive of the industry. In subsequent chapters I will explore how corporations (a) stress the contribution of their new or continued business to the economic health of the region or local community and (b) argue that economic growth is more important than any harm to health. I will note that unions have sometimes agreed with this logic, assessing the harm to health as a reasonable price to pay for jobs in the area. Sometimes the offending corporation provides the best jobs in the region, which makes its argument particularly compelling. Entire communities have been convinced that the siting of a polluting industry or toxic waste dump is worth the health hazards involved, though later on many of them decide that they were not fully informed and that a "jobs or our health" choice is not a fair one.

It is just plain hard to mobilize a community before the consequences manifest themselves, especially when a corporation has campaigned to "manufacture doubt" and to establish economic dependence. The amount of time needed to organize people, gather evidence, and develop a legal or political strategy to contest actions is typically overwhelming, and the expertise required is often not available in the community. If the case ends up in court, the odds of community health winning over economics are slim to none, given the disproportionate resources of the corporation. The lack of a strong regulatory mandate for health and the limited size of government agency staff that monitors health problems compound the difficulty of addressing such cases appropriately and in a timely manner. I will examine all of these issues in later chapters.

Conclusion

The task of this book is to clarify the SDoH. The present chapter has given an overview that defines the SDoH as more than conditions of life, which have been the focus of most inquiries and attempts at remedy so far. Here I have emphasized that most literature does not go "upstream" enough to hold the drivers of the conditions of life accountable for egregious health outcomes. Recalling the river analogy, the task is not just to save people from drowning but to determine who or what is pushing them into the river. In order to provide a framework for looking upstream in future chapters, this chapter has examined the tobacco playbook, trying to reveal how industry actions have had negative effects on our health and how various strategies deliberately employed by the tobacco industry have been used to deflect criticism. Central to the industry's plan (and well documented in internal papers made public during litigation) was its skill at "manufacturing doubt," its power to control the narrative around smoking, and its role as an economic engine in the community.

In what follows we will examine a variety of substantive areas (poverty, the environment, water, automobiles, occupations, and food) and will analyze how decisions and policies about each have threatened our health. Each chapter will describe a group of health-threatening conditions of life (e.g., unhealthy working conditions) and then look upstream to find how power, the political economy, and policies have made those conditions the way they are (e.g., the power of a business to ignore safety regulations). In most chapters the strategies of the tobacco playbook will factor in my explication, but each chapter will emphasize slightly different aspects of the SDoH.

I will use well-documented examples, which will mean at times highlighting industrial and governmental actions from decades ago. The main reason for adopting this historical perspective is that solid research into an unhealthy condition of life requires time to identify it, investigate it, and find an answer that can link its cause to its impact on health. Often it takes an egregious health problem or a well-crafted lawsuit to draw attention to a situation. Even identifying the problem can be delayed, since many health problems have a latency period of a decade or more. Once the problem has been identified, the research may require years to complete—but only to come to tentative conclusions. Sadly, today's examples are still in the making. One needs only to read the news headlines to find unhealthy practices. As this chapter was being written, the world found that Volkswagen had manipulated the emission systems in cars so that they could promote better gas mileage; but in the meantime they were making our air unhealthy. This same time period has also witnessed a fresh example of strategic corporate investment. Coke had a six-year relationship with the American Academy of Pediatrics, providing nearly $3 million dollars for the Academy's healthy children website, as well as multi-million-dollar relationships with other medical groups, including the American College of Cardiology, the American Academy of Family Physicians, and the Academy of Nutrition and Dietetics. These "soda grants appear to have, in some cases, won the company allies in anti-soda initiatives, wielded influence over health recommendations about soft drinks, and shifted scientific focus away from soda as a factor in the causes of obesity" (O'Connor 2015: D1). Just as we will need to wait for a full investigation before we can measure the environmental fallout from automobile emissions tampering, we will need more time before we can determine the extent of Coke's influence on the process of deflecting concerns about the link between soda consumption and obesity. In the meantime, however, our health is being affected everyday by those who influence or drive the conditions of our lives—for good or bad.

My coverage begins with a chapter on poverty, a topic that requires a slightly different emphasis. I have already noted that income is correlated to overall health; and those in the top 1 percent enjoy the best outcomes. While each lower income level experiences a downward trend in health, those who live in poverty are exposed to a myriad of severely unhealthy conditions. Before turning to specific drivers like limited access to healthy food, exposure to a risky built environment, or a narrow range of occupational choices (which are addressed in later chapters), I will examine the health impact of simultaneous exposure to these multiple conditions. I will also look at how impoverished individuals have too few choices to avoid the unhealthy conditions that accompany poverty. Thus the core of the next chapter will be describing these interconnected conditions and understanding the power of poverty in determining one's health.

3
Poverty and Health

The idea that economic health, and in particular poverty, is an important determinant of physical and mental health is not new. Rudolph Virchow, a nineteenth-century physician often referred to as the father of social medicine, argued that poverty increased people's susceptibility to disease and resulted in a reduced life expectancy. More recent times have seen the accumulation of a substantial literature documenting not just the impact of poverty, but also the power of the "social gradient of health." These findings show significant health disparities in acute and chronic disease, self-reports of health, and life expectancy according to social class, such that each higher step up the economic ladder is associated with better health (e.g., Marmot et al. 1984; Geronimus 2000; Sapolsky 2005; Wilkinson 2006). Thus a graph of earning deciles (the bottom 10 percent, the next 10 percent, and so on, up to the top 10 percent) indicates a systematic increase in life expectancy for each decile over the one immediately below. And these differences in life expectancy are increasing over time. The cohort born in 1940 presents a larger life-expectancy gap between deciles than the cohort born in 1920 (Bosworth et al. 2014: 87). The fact that inequality is growing, the top 1 percent now controlling 40 percent of the country's wealth, reveals a tragic trajectory (Abramsky 2013: 32). Economic inequality has serious health implications. In addition, if we compare countries, we find that countries with a higher level of economic inequality have worse health outcomes than countries with less economic inequality (Pickett and Wilkinson 2015). The relationship persists even in countries with universal healthcare (such as the United Kingdom)—yet again, testimony to the importance of the social determinants of health (Tyler 2013).

This chapter explores the low end of the social gradient of health, poverty, as a condition of life with grave health outcomes. Looking upstream to see what causes poverty in our society would require in this case a lengthy discussion about a broad array of economic policies and practices: the existence (or absence) of various social and economic welfare policies of the government and their impact, income redistribution and income supports such as anti-poverty programs, individual tax rates, the earned income tax credit, corporate taxation policies, and inheritance laws; employment and retraining programs, including facts about unemployment benefits (e.g., their length and adequacy) and educational supports; safety nets such as child credits, maternity leave, health benefits, food programs, social security and disability benefits; and healthy housing supports such as affordable housing programs, policies outlawing racial bias in mortgages, and programs for the homeless. One would also need to examine corporate actions that have a direct effect on economic health, for example the wage and benefit structure and the sustainability of business plans. A full examination of all these social determinants of economic health is beyond the scope of this book; but they remain an important backdrop to its topic and will require further consideration.

By focusing on poverty, however, we can document how living at the low end of the economic spectrum increases people's chances of exposure to a host of conditions that lead to serious negative health outcomes. I will then explore in detail most of these conditions in future chapters: pollution of our environment (in chapters 4 and 5), unhealthy occupational conditions (in chapter 7), the unhealthy built environment derived in part from our car culture (in chapter 6), and the difficulty in obtaining healthy food (in chapter 8). In each case I will also examine the relevant drivers—the forces that trigger the conditions of life under consideration. For instance, in chapter 4 I will examine government policies and the actions of corporations—both being drivers that have led to poor environmental health (condition of life)—and how poor people suffer disproportionately as a result of it. Looking upstream in each chapter will provide useful pieces for the puzzle of economic-driven health outcomes introduced here. In other words, poverty is a condition of life so complex that it affects one's health at every turn, in every way imaginable.

As people unlikely to have ever been truly impoverished, most readers of this book will have seen little firsthand evidence of extreme poverty, even if we are familiar with economic struggle and occasional hardship. We live our lives among similarly privileged neighbors; we mix and mingle at work, in retail stores, and on vacation with people more like us than different from us. Yet, despite this invisibility, poverty exists in our world. In America, the US Census reports that 42.7 million people (14.3 percent of the entire population) have incomes below the poverty line (Macartney et al. 2013). Other researchers in the United States use a statistic that many of us can relate to—the amount spent each day—and report that 1.5 million households in 2011 with 3 million children spent less than $2 a day per person (Edin and Shaefer 2015: xvii).

Poverty is not just a matter of having very little money; poverty largely determines the conditions of living to which one is exposed on a daily basis. In the 1960s, Michael Harrington wrote an influential book, *The Other America*, which stimulated the legislation known as "the War on Poverty." He said that poverty is all-enveloping: "Everything about [poor people], from the condition of their teeth to the way in which they love, is suffused and permeated by the fact of their poverty" (Harrington 1962: 23). Poverty is still with us today, as one critic points out:

> It's everywhere: tent cities in municipal parks, under freeway overpasses, along river walks. Food lines stretching down city blocks. Foreclosure signs dotting suburban landscapes. ... Unemployed men and women looking for clothes for their kids at thrift stores and food for their families in pantries. Mothers begging for free turkeys from churches so they can at least partially partake in the national ritual of Thanksgiving. (Abramsky 2013: 9)

In this chapter I look at where people in poverty live and work and consider the general stress and impact of poverty, in particular on children. Ultimately poverty itself is a health hazard, primarily because it greatly increases the chances of exposure to a variety of unhealthy conditions. Although this book is not about healthcare per se, the failure of healthcare systems to look after poor and minority individuals is so significant that some coverage of poverty from this angle is warranted.

Healthcare

The task of this book is to examine the social determinants of health as distinct from the impact of our healthcare system on our health. For poor people in the United States, however, the greatly reduced access to healthcare and the lower quality of the healthcare they receive are so consequential that a brief note on healthcare is important. In the absence of a system of universal healthcare (which all other industrialized countries have), Americans end up treating "medical care as a market commodity, to be rationed by the ability to pay—rather than as (a) a social good to be distributed in response to medical need, (b) a responsibility of government, and (c) a fundamental right embodied in a social contract" (Geiger 2006: 207). The result is that poor people are often uninsured or underinsured because they cannot afford good—or sometimes any—health insurance. This is true despite Medicaid, a fifty-year-old federal state program for very poor people, and the new Affordable Care Act, the fate of which is being determined as this chapter is being written. Access to healthcare without insurance or with Medicaid is difficult because providers want to know that the patient will be able to pay for services rendered. Some providers perform a "pocket biopsy," checking the patient's insurance coverage before agreeing to provide care (Sered and Fernandopulle 2007: 83). Healthcare providers sometimes deny care to people with Medicaid because the program's reimbursement for services is stingy by comparison to that paid by private insurance, and sometimes the reimbursement is even below the cost of the service (Cunningham 2002). Service providers may try to discourage poor patients from using a service by making them wait, or by making the service inconvenient, uncomfortable, or too time-consuming (Cheung et al. 2012). Access to care is also difficult for the poorly insured and uninsured because US healthcare is not organized as an integrated system, with a coordinated set of services that would make access to different types of providers and resources as seamless and convenient as possible (Ratcliff, 2002). Rather it is a non-system—"a blotchy and frayed patchwork of unreliable and inconsistent programs, providers, and facilities" (Sered and Fernandopulle 2007: 10). All of these actions and characteristics clearly restrict access to healthcare for people in poverty.

If a poor person does receive care, it is less likely to be with a private doctor or in a private hospital and more likely to be in a city or county hospital, clinic, or emergency room. In an emergency room and in most public facilities, patients are seen by a healthcare provider who is a stranger, unaware of their medical history. Furthermore, public facilities and emergency rooms are poorly funded, overcrowded, and busy settings in which a good medical history is unavailable or difficult to construct in the limited time period allotted to individual patients. Under these conditions, and with no regular care provider, problems are missed, diagnoses are more likely to be incorrect, and chronic conditions are less likely to be monitored regularly (Grumbach and Bodenheimer, 2002; Hoffman and Paradise, 2008). In fact patients cared for in the emergency room are less likely to be aware of their significant chronic conditions (Ndumele et al. 2012). Failure to diagnose and treat chronic conditions early on greatly increases the health risk and the cost of treatment (Virnig et al. 2009). For instance, diabetes can be controlled if it is identified early on and managed regularly. But without consistent treatment a person's risk of amputation, blindness, and kidney failure due to diabetes increases dramatically (Wilper et al. 2009; Eslami et al. 2007; Henry et al. 2011). Thus inadequacies in access and quality dramatically affect the health of poor people. (See Ratcliff 2013 for further discussion and references.)

Neighborhoods and the Concentration of Poverty

Much of the all-encompassing impact of economics on health has to do with neighborhoods; and the differences among them are striking. Neighborhoods run the gamut from districts overrun by dilapidated homes, trash-filled yards, and unsafe public areas to gated communities filled with multimillion dollar McMansions. Because neighborhoods tend to be economically homogeneous, poor people find financially viable housing choices almost exclusively in inner-city neighborhoods or in older suburban areas (Katz and Turner 2006). As a result, poor people live in neighborhoods where they are likely to encounter many unhealthy conditions: street violence, illegal drugs, a dangerous environment for outdoor exercise, and high levels of noise and environmental pollutants (Braveman, Egerter, and Williams 2011; Diez Roux and Mair 2010). Neighborhood deterioration, for instance in the form of boarded-up housing, litter, broken windows, and vandalism, has an impact on health, partly due to the fear and social isolation that residents experience on a regular basis (Cohen et al. 2003). Even something as basic as the noise produced by speeding cars and rowdy neighbors has a significant effect on health: it induces sleep deprivation and high levels of stress (Passchier-Vermeer and Passchier 2000; Krieger and Higgins 2002). Health problems in poor neighborhoods have been exacerbated by the development of a transportation system dependent on private cars and trucks that burn oil and diesel. These vehicles rush through poor urban neighborhoods on highways that were built with little regard for their impact on the health of nearby residents. Pollution and limitations on safe walking, biking, and exercising are some of the consequences (see chapter 6 for further discussion).

Poor people are not only more likely to live in physically deteriorating circumstances; they also reside in areas where a large percentage of their neighbors live in poverty too. This concentration of poverty in whole neighborhoods is particularly harmful and appears to be on the increase. Between 2000 and 2009 the number of people living in "extreme-poverty neighborhoods" rose by a third (Kneebone et al. 2011). Concentrated poverty is associated with other aggregate characteristics such as percentage of people with poor education, lower rates of home ownership, less residential stability, higher eviction rate, and lower percentage of people with connections to resources, information, activism networks, powerful people, and decision makers. Although the mechanisms by which such neighborhood characteristics can affect health are not fully understood, research does suggest that moving a family from a high-poverty area can improve that family's health, even lowering the risk of obesity and diabetes (Ludwig et al. 2011). Some of the reasons why living in areas with high poverty rates is unhealthy might be related to the fact that residents in such areas do not have the time, money, or expertise to help each other solve health-related problems or to challenge unhealthy conditions in the neighborhood. In contrast, better-off neighborhoods have "social networks and voluntary affiliations [that] ... sustain health by reducing personal isolation and stress and increasing mutual trust. ... [Such networks] underpin local communities' ability to influence their own destiny through collective efficacy" (Miller et al. 2011: S50). Neighborhood protests against health hazards are known as Not in My Back Yard (NIMBY) protests. While such protests do spring up in poor neighborhoods—a good example is the effort of grassroots organizations in Chester, Delaware County, Pennsylvania to fight environmental injustice—they are more likely to occur in middle-class neighborhoods, where they are also more effective. Middle-class residents tend to have useful professional connections and expertise, for instance training or employment in research or in legal or medical fields, so it is easier for them to mount successful protests. Furthermore, local government is more responsive to residents from better-off neighborhoods when they request changes. A resident of a low-income neighborhood in Oakland, California put it simply: "We cannot get the attention of the elected officials" (Altschuler et al. 2004: 1226).

Housing

Poor health also comes from the conditions within the walls of one's home. Poor people have very limited residential choices, given that home ownership is typically out of the question and finding afford-able rentals is a big challenge. Housing that poor people can afford is very likely to be unsanitary and unsafe. Apartments and houses may lack adequate heating or plumbing; they tend to have unsafe stairs, old and dirty carpeting, dampness, mold, dust, allergens and mites, cockroaches or mice (Leventhal and Newman 2010; Krieger and Higgins 2002). These conditions are exacerbated by the differential enforcement of housing codes in poor neighborhoods (Tyler 2013) and produce respiratory, allergic, hematological, and neurological diseases (Krieger and Higgins 2002). Housing for poor people is also likely to be overcrowded, which leads to elevated blood pressure, elevated neuroendocrine hormone activity, spread of respiratory infections, and psychosocial distress (Evans and Saegert 2012). Poor people are more stressed and more ill than other income groups, often as a direct result of living where they do.

Inadequate housing options for those in poverty include homeless-ness. In the United States, in Chicago alone an estimated 92,000 people, including 14,000 school children, are homeless during the course of one year (Abramsky 2013: 101). Nationwide millions of Americans become homeless each year because landlords evict them, sometimes through legal channels, due to failure to pay rent, sometimes informally, on the grounds that particular residents are found to be too troublesome. A city might have a "nuisance prop-erty ordinance" with penalties for landlords when the police receive three or more 911 calls about an address during a thirty-day period (Desmond 2016: 191). Loud arguments, noise complaints, and domestic violence are the top three reasons for informal eviction. One study reports that, in 83 percent of instances when landlords are told there is a domestic violence problem at one of their properties, they respond by evicting or threatening to evict the resident(s) in question. As a result, many women who are subjected to violence at home face a choice between keeping quiet and enduring the abuse or calling the police and being evicted (Desmond 2016: 192). Eviction is a more likely fate for black women (1 in 5) and Hispanic women (1 in 12) than it is for white women (1 in 15) (Desmond 2016: 299).

Some homeless people live in emergency shelters or in transitional housing spaces. Not only are these accommodations temporary, but they are not healthy places for adults or families (Burt 2006).

Overcrowding and lack of privacy compromise a person's physical and mental health, for instance by elevating his or her blood pressure; thus they make homeless people sicker than individuals with stable housing (Sered and Fernandopulle 2007: 174). In most US cities, the number of homeless people far exceeds the capacity for even minimal accommodations. Those unable to be housed in shelters turn to the streets, setting up cardboard homes or sleeping on park benches, where the immediate health hazards are great and the prospects for future health are bleak. Homelessness and other inadequacies in housing for the poor are more than an economic problem; they quite definitely constitute "a public health crisis" (Bashir 2002: 733).

Pollution

In addition to living in low-quality housing and in neighborhoods with concentrated poverty and widespread physical deterioration, poor people reside in areas where they are more likely to get exposed to pollution. Air pollution is a huge health problem, with effects that include excess cardio-respiratory mortality, asthma complications, increased respiratory illness, decreased lung function, and lung inflammation (American Lung Association, 2001). The polluting of poor neighborhoods by industrial sites and by waste facilities (a phenomenon referred to in the literature as environmental injustice and discussed in chapter 4) is a persistent concern. Poor neighborhoods and polluting facilities seem to attract each other. On the one hand, poor people are more likely than those from higher income brackets to live in a neighborhood with a "dirty industry" because there the rents are cheaper and residents have better access to low-skill jobs (Bullard et al. 2008). On the other hand, the "dirty industry" is likely to move to a poor neighborhood or stay there because the cost of land is low, the labor pool is plentiful, and the residents are much less able to put up resistance to the industry.

Many studies have documented this association between neighborhood income (either percentage of low income or mean income) and dirty industries. The process by which an income-poor and environmentally dirty neighborhood comes into existence often takes many decades and involves racial and ethnic segregation and ghettoization. For instance, middle-class whites founded Phoenix, Arizona, but the development of the town year by year led to the formation of clear economic and ethnic segregation patterns and to dramatic differences in land use. Whites lived in Central Phoenix, where land use regulations maintained the residential quality of neighborhoods and permitted housing values to rise. South of the railway, South Phoenix became an industrial area with low rents affordable to low-income families and with a policy of accepting ethnic minorities. In consequence South Phoenix was totally unattractive to higher income families. The quality of life in South Phoenix spiraled downward, because the town of Phoenix encouraged industrial development in the area but provided minimal public services. Industry was attracted to South Phoenix for obvious reasons: the land was cheap, the appropriate (less well educated) labor supply was nearby, and residents were less likely to oppose industrial development or a toxic waste dump than were the residents of Central Phoenix (Bolin et al. 2005). The daily living conditions in such neighborhoods, as seen through the lens of residents themselves, are telling. A woman from a similar neighborhood in South Camden, New Jersey (which we'll also encounter in chapter 4) comments:

> I live in Waterfront South. We have so many industries, we have more than anywhere else in the state. We have co-gen, burning factory, cement factory, sewage plant ... We have so much air pollution because of all the industries. We have soot and we live in it, we eat it, we breathe it everyday, we breathe in mercury, lead, it's all in this community. ... We have children that are born too small, we have a high number of asthma and lung trouble, people are sick ... just because we are poor doesn't mean we don't have the right to fresh air and good health. (Testimony of Lula Williams, quoted in Arnold 2007)

Availability of unhealthy and healthy products and options

A variety of other health hazards in poor neighborhoods arise from the abundance of unhealthy products for sale. An obvious one is tobacco. Low-income neighborhoods are literally targeted by tobacco companies. Retail stores selling tobacco products are readily available in poor neighborhoods (Novak et al. 2006; Braveman, Egerter, and Mockenhaupt 2011). Storefront and point-of-sale (POS) advertising are more common in lower income neighborhoods (Laws et al. 2002), which is consequential: POS advertising has been growing since the 1998 agreement with the tobacco industry, which bans the use of many other kinds of advertisement. The findings for alcohol are similar. The density of liquor stores is greater in low-income neighborhoods than in more prosperous ones (Romley et al. 2007). Although some research findings show conflicting results when the measurement is done per capita, a more reliable measure seems to be the number of outlets per roadway mile, as it captures the individual's ability to purchase alcohol (Blumenthal et al. 2008).

While unhealthy products like tobacco and alcohol are readily available in poor neighborhoods, many healthy products are not. Barely able to afford enough food of any kind, residents of these neighborhoods face a dearth of good, healthy food options. Sometimes characterized as "food deserts," such areas have more small grocery stores, convenience stores, liquor stores, and fast-food establishments than well-off neighborhoods, but fewer well-stocked large and chain supermarkets. The result is a serious shortage of supermarkets in one's neighborhood—what is called a "grocery gap" (Powell et al. 2007). One recent study reported that less than one in five of the food stores in poor minority neighborhoods carried a selection of healthy foods, in contrast to over half of the stores in white areas (Moore and Diez-Roux 2006). Access to fresh produce and healthy choices is thus limited. Although there may be options in nearby neighborhoods, poor people are often confined to local stores through lack of time and of available transportation. Neighborhood differences in types of stores are consequential and shape the choices available to their residents. The local food environment is also associated with the risk of obesity and atherosclerosis (Morland et al. 2006; Morland and Evenson 2009).

Lack of cheap nutritious food is a more general problem in the United States because various food subsidies from the federal government actually make *less* nutritious food *more* affordable (more on this in chapter 8). For example, the US Farm Bill supports corn as an agricultural crop, and thus various products that include corn (corn syrup, starch, oil, flour, etc.) are inexpensive; on the other hand, these corn-based products tend not to be very healthy. Fresh fruit and vegetables, in contrast, get no such subsidy (Mortazavi 2011). Although these price differentials affect all Americans, poor people are obviously the ones who need most of all to take advantage of price breaks; and so they do—to the detriment of their health.

In addition to the fact that unhealthy products are more available and healthy ones less available, residents of poor neighborhoods have fewer opportunities to engage in healthy activities. Exercise is a good example. Not only is gym membership prohibitively expensive for poor people; even indoor recreational facilities are much less likely to be located in poor neighborhoods (Moore et al. 2008). Obviously the free alternative to exercise is walking around the block or using public parks. Walkable and safe areas allow for physical activity indispensable for one's health, hence having them is important (Doyle et al. 2006). But in poor neighborhoods walking in general is constrained: the built environment makes people feel unsafe due to abandoned buildings, poor street lighting, excessive traffic, and undesirable land use (Alfonzo et al. 2008; Cutts et al. 2009). Although research on public parks suggests that poor people are as likely as the rich or the well-off to live in geographic areas—specifically, census tracks—endowed with public parks (Moore et al. 2008), they are less likely to have easy and safe access to such places: the high crime rates and the heavy local traffic of the neighborhoods in which poor people live pose threats to walkers. These "disamenities" (Weiss et al. 2011) mean that *social access* (actual capacity to use the park) is much lower than *spatial access* (proximity) would imply. The parks are in the census track, but poor people feel discouraged from using them. Other research (Krieger et al. 2009) has looked at the quality of parks in poor neighborhoods and found other disamenities. In one neighborhood the staircase giving access to the park was "overgrown with invasive vegetation, steps were covered with moss, and handrails were in disrepair" (Krieger et al. 2009: S594–5). Once the community cleaned up the access route and other changes were made, usage increased. People need safe, accessible green space if they are to be healthy (Maas et al. 2009).

Jobs

People who are poor obviously do not have well-paying jobs, and often have jobs that do not even provide a living wage. Furthermore, these jobs are more likely to be associated with health hazards, as they involve heavy and repetitive physical labor, work with toxic chemicals, exposure to noise and air pollution, and low control over one's job (Benach et al. 2010; Clougherty et al. 2010; Braveman, Egerter, and Williams 2011; Baron et al. 2011; see chapter 7). A telling example of a job-related health risk is lead exposure. For adults, the most common exposure to lead occurs in the workplace, and data show a clear correlation between income and blood lead levels in men. Low-income men have six times the blood lead level of high-income men, and the health impacts include memory loss, kidney damage, and reproductive damage (Pamuk et al. 1999: 122). Not only are their jobs unhealthy, but low-wage earners are allowed fewer sick days, have less chance to take time off if they do need to see a doctor, and often do not have health insurance to cover the cost of medical care. Many do not speak up about the occupational hazards they face—fearing that they would be fired or punished in some other way (Human Rights Watch 2002; Baugher and Roberts 2004).

Unemployment is a threat to health not just by depriving people of wages but also by causing loss of connectivity to others, lack of purpose, and diminished self-worth. Unemployed people have a higher annual illness rate, poor mental health, and an increased risk of death (Athar et al. 2013). Becoming unemployed can be the start of a downward spiral from less money for healthy food and fewer lifestyle options to homelessness or poor housing, all of which makes the person so unhealthy as to be unemployable in the future. Like other poverty conditions, unemployment is more prevalent among African American and Hispanic populations, further compromising the health outcomes of these groups.

Stress

In the life of a poor person stress can come from all the sources discussed here and can be a daily fact of life. Reporting on one uninsured woman, researchers identified an interrelated set of stressors:

> Choosing between buying food and buying medicine, the stress of working in temporary and seasonal jobs, the stress of feeling trapped in circumstances of poverty that she cannot control, the stress of living with a man who is often angry and frustrated that he cannot provide for his family, and, above all, the stress of living with chronic illnesses and chronic pain that she does not have the resources to remedy. (Sered and Fernandopulle 2007: xxi)

Chronic stress in cases of this sort is conducive to particularly poor health outcomes. The cumulative burden weakens the immune system and causes adverse metabolic, vascular, and hormonal reactions (Thoits 2010; Braveman, Egerter, and Mockenhaupt 2011). Poor people suffering from stress can display diminished coping ability, self-efficacy, and perceived control, psychological attributes that support an improved health and are associated with high socioeconomic status (Fiscella and Williams 2004: 1142).

Because ethnicity and income are correlated in our society, poor people are more likely to suffer unhealthy levels of stress as a result of racial discrimination as well as of class. People of color face prejudice and discrimination in interpersonal encounters, in the work setting, and when they try to find housing. Predominantly black neighborhoods encounter "retail redlining," that is, chain stores (such as athletic stores, shoe stores, clothing stores, and pharmacies) not wanting to open an outlet nearby (Kwate et al. 2013). Despite laws to the contrary, African American families are still disadvantaged when it comes to obtaining a mortgage (when they do, their monthly payments are often higher than usual) and arranging foreclosure terms (Rugh et al. 2015). Eviction from one's rental home is twice or three times more likely to happen to African American women than to white women: in a study conducted in Milwaukee, Wisconsin, more than 20 percent of the black women reported an eviction, by comparison to less than 10 percent of the white women (Desmond 2016). The stress resulting from discrimination has major negative effects on health. It isn't hard to imagine that differences in stress levels between blacks and whites are an important factor that underpins the stubborn racial differences in health outcomes (Satcher et al. 2005).

Children in Poverty

The impact of poverty on children is particularly distressing, since children are so vulnerable. Our attention to the impact of poverty on children's health was heightened in the 1990s, when a prominent researcher reported that half of all "poor black children have elevated blood lead levels" (quoted in Markowitz and Rosner 2013b: 16). A more recent estimate related to dwellings finds that a third of all low-income housing is contaminated with lead-based paint (Jacobs et al. 2002), which causes neurodevelopmental abnormalities, reproductive dysfunction, as well as kidney, blood, and endocrine system problems (Sanborn et al. 2002; Evens et al. 2015). Despite sporadic enforcement efforts, lead paint continues to be a threat in many low-income neighborhoods. And lead from paint is not the only source of concern, as the news from Flint, Michigan made clear in early 2016. To save money, the government had switched water sources in this very poor community, and the new source corroded the old lead pipes, contaminating the water. Pediatricians who witnessed rising lead levels among Flint's youngest residents were among the first to sound the alarm.

> **Lead Paint and Children's Health**
> Suspicions that lead is harmful to our health have been around since the nineteenth century. In the first three decades of the twentieth century, Alice Hamilton, a doctor you will meet in chapter 7, expressed concerns. Afterwards scientific reports started to appear showing the impact of lead on workers and children. Poor, under-

nourished children are particularly vulnerable because their bodies lack the nutrients that could reduce the absorption of lead. Lead poisoning affects the brain and the central nervous system and can cause mental retardation.

Despite these warnings, the lead industry promoted several uses of lead that were not essential to the usefulness of the product laced with it. I already mentioned lead paint, and chapter 6 will discuss the unnecessary addition of lead to gasoline. Just as the fuel industry could have opted for a less harmful solution to knocking engines than lead additives, from the first decade of the twentieth century until the mid-1970s paint companies chose to put lead in paint for color and durability, although less toxic alternatives existed—for example zinc (Markowitz and Rosner 2013b: 8). The Lead Industries Association (LIA) not only promoted lead paint but also advertised it as healthy: "lead helps guard your health" (Markowitz and Rosner 2003a: 82).

As homes and their paint jobs aged, the lead paint peeled and chips fell on windowsills and floors. In poor neighborhoods the resources for removing this hazard were judged to be too expensive, so peeling paint in older homes was typical. Toddlers and other youngsters found the paint attractive, as it was sweet and, given the hand-to-mouth behavior typical of their age group, their exposure to lead paint was considerable. The lead industry did not acknowledge the problem as something it had caused; it blamed it instead on the children, their mothers, and poverty in general. Its representatives suggested that these children were engaged in "pathological behavior," namely eating non-nutritious substances—a diagnosable psychiatric problem called "pica" (Markowitz and Rosner 2003a: 43). The health and safety director of LIA commented that "paint eaters were a real headache" (Markowitz and Rosner 2013b: 32) and that there was "all too much 'gnaw-ledge' among Baltimore babies" (Markowitz and Rosner 2013b: 35). Since lead poisoning reduces the intelligence, this particular reference to eating paint from the window ledge was markedly insensitive. In addition to blaming the children themselves, the LIA blamed parents by declaring that they were "ineducable" (Markowitz and Rosner 2013b: 35). Clearly a good mother would figure out a way to keep curious children from putting their lead-covered fingers in their mouths.

Although many people think that lead paint is a thing of the past, lead paint health problems continue to appear. Many poor families live in housing built before 1978, when lead paint was banned. Over 20 million housing units have lead-based paint hazards, exposing 3.6 million children under the age of six to a health risk (Federal Healthy Homes Work Group 2013). A recent study in Rochester, New York found that over one third of the children in high-risk neighborhoods had elevated levels of lead in their blood (Korfmacher et al. 2012).

Children in poverty are exposed not only to a range of health-damaging chemical toxins, but also to stress levels so high that researchers now refer to the "toxic stress" of poverty. Exposure to toxic stress (including through an overstressed mother) leads to increased levels of stress hormones (like cortisol and adrenaline) and can cause disruptions in the "developing architecture" of the brain— for instance in the size and neural architecture of various areas of the brain—that result in "functional differences in learning, memory, and aspects of executive functioning" (Shonkoff et al. 2012: e236). Even before these kids are born, exposure *in utero* to toxic chemicals and to maternal stress has been shown to have an adverse impact on their health (Shonkoff et al. 2012) and can produce long-term neurodevelopmental damage (Lupien et al. 2009). Researchers conclude that fetuses and infants are more susceptible than adults on account of their physiologic immaturity (American Lung Association 2001: 359), their critical and sensitive windows of development, their body-surface to body-mass ratio, their consumption of more food and drink per unit of body weight, their higher respiratory rate, and their proximity to the ground.

Once children from poor neighborhoods enter the school system, they are more likely than children from well-off neighborhoods to be exposed to violence at school; and the schools they attend receive less funding (taxbase support) than do schools in well-off neighborhoods. Spending less on schools in poorer neighborhoods means that these schools often have deferred maintenance, lower quality teachers, and fewer support programs and resources than better funded schools. Many of these characteristics could have an impact on the child's physical, mental, and cognitive health, as they all present "health and safety risks" (Miller et al. 2011: S51). For instance, schools in low-income districts are less likely to have daily recess or to participate in the President's Challenge Physical Activity and Fitness Award Program, which results in a lower average number of minutes of combined physical education and recess (Parsad et al. 2006: 15–20).

One program, the National School Lunch Program (NSLP), is set up to mitigate the physical health challenges of poor children by providing free or reduced-cost lunches for economically eligible students. Yet this program includes unhealthy offerings, because it serves not only the dietary needs of the students but also the needs of the Department of Agriculture—namely it supports farmers who have surplus commodities. Changes have been made to make the NSLP more nutritious, but weaknesses in the commodity program still exist, including an "insufficient incentive built into the overall system for the promotion of good nutrition; [and] its current limited ability to incorporate the provision of fresh and/or local produce" (Parker 2008: 45).

In addition, the food industry pressures schools about the available food choices. When nutrition-minded people wanted less beef served in the NSLP, the National Cattlemen's Beef Association was not happy and made its objections clear (Levine 2008: 180). And non-NSLP food options became less healthy when fast-food chains were allowed into the school lunchroom in the mid-1990s. Young children are now exposed to Pizza Hut, Taco Bell, Subway, McDonald's, and other fast-food establishments (Levine 2008: 182). Although all children in the school have the lunch option of fast food, poor children are much less likely than their more advantaged peers to go home to a healthy dinner with fresh vegetables and a fresh salad, since nutritious food is expensive. For them, a less nutritious fast-food lunch is not offset by a healthy dinner. Furthermore, it has been shown that schools of higher-SES students have healthier food options than schools in poor neighborhoods (Delva et al. 2007).

Children are affected by exposure to unhealthy conditions not only during childhood: when they grow into adults they have significant health issues resulting from these early toxic experiences—the damage is already done. The American Academy of Pediatrics notes that the toxic stress during one's early childhood results in "a wide range of physical and mental illnesses later in adult life" (Shonkoff et al. 2012: e237), including diseases as diverse as cardiovascular disease, liver cancer, depression, and obstructive pulmonary disease. Research in the relatively new field of epigenetics, which studies the impact of the environment on one's genes, suggests very troubling long-term consequences (Gudsnuk and Champagne 2012). Through the mechanisms of these genetic impacts, poverty perpetuates itself, since the children are stunted in their ability to excel at school, disadvantaged in the job market, more ill or prone to illness, and more likely to become unemployed (Abramsky 2013: 111).

Conclusion

Poor economic health is devastating for physical and mental health. The connection was made very concisely by the head of the National Cancer Institute, who, in referring to the numerous forms of cancer that are more prevalent among the poor, declared that poverty is a *carcinogen* (American Cancer Society 2011). Yet poverty has remained a daily reality for millions of Americans—a reality that, as this chapter has argued, makes people vulnerable to a myriad of other unhealthy conditions of life. Examining poverty recalls a central idea of this book. While some people would observe a poor person engaged in unhealthy behaviors (eating cheap fast food, not exercising regularly, or living in an overcrowded and unsanitary home) and would blame the person, an approach that resorts to the social determinants of health and looks upstream sees a different reality—one that understands that the choices people make are to a large extent imposed by the conditions of their lives, which are in turn determined by the political and economic world they live in. To tell a poor person to eat healthier foods, for example, makes little sense when that person lives in a food desert, cannot afford to travel to a full-service large grocery store, and can get more calories for less money by buying unhealthy processed food and food from fast-food restaurants. To tell a poor person to exercise more when that person lives in a crime-ridden neighborhood with no street lighting, with broken sidewalks, and with diesel-spewing buses rushing by makes little sense either. We need to shift from the lens of individual responsibility to one that seeks reasonable structural changes. I will take my analysis upstream in future chapters and begin to understand not only the causes of various conditions of life, but also the people who design and implement these structures, thus helping or hindering our ability to avoid risk and access good health.

4

Environmental Health

In 1948 in Donora, Pennsylvania, a blanket of cold air trapped gases from the furnaces and ovens of the steel mills and the soft coal burned to heat homes. The result was a heavy smog that killed about twenty people and left thousands of others ill (Davis 2002: 29). Four years later in London, England, cold air once again trapped the smoke from burning coal, and with an even more horrific effect: 2,800 people choked to death because of air pollution (Davis 2002: 44). These events were dramatic because the cause was visible to all residents and the health impact was immediate. Although visible pollution with swift consequences can still happen on this scale—New Delhi's thick smog of November 2016 has been compared to the Great Smog of London in 1952—environmental health today also means pollution that is less visible to the naked eye, less immediate in its impact, much harder to document, but no less catastrophic in its long-term impact. This chapter explores toxic chemicals such as the "dirty dozen," which include dichloro-diphenyl-trichloroethane (DDT), polychlorinated biphenyls (PCBs), and dioxins; heavy metals such as arsenic, chromium, lead, and mercury; and, to a lesser extent, radioactive materials and fossil fuels and their impact not just on air pollution, but on soil and water pollution as well. While specific chapters on water, occupational health, and transportation elaborate on this discussion, I will document here the extent of the problem and its effects on health, particularly that of vulnerable people: children, people in poverty, people of color. I will also explore why the problem persists and what can be done about it.

Environmental Pollution and Health

The extent of pollution is astounding. "Industry has defecated its toxic detritus all over the countryside" (Epstein 1985: 41), with annual releases of 2.8 billion kilograms (about 3 million tons) of toxic chemicals into the US environment (Pimentel et al. 2007: 654). Environmental degradation caused by "air particulates, military toxics, oilfield wastes, abandoned industrial facilities, incinerators, refineries, and vehicle traffic" (Brown 2008: 85) is everywhere. There is "no safe place" (Brown and Mikkelsen 1997); the daily updates on environmentalhealth.org are testimony to this. Troubling is the fact that we have long known or suspected that these metals and chemicals have serious health consequences. Pioneer environmentalist Rachel Carson told us so in 1962:

> The central problem of our age has therefore become the contamination of man's total environment with such substances of incredible potential for harm—substances that accumulate in the tissues of plants and animals and even penetrate the germ cells to shatter or alter the very material of heredity upon which the shape of the future depends. (Carson 1962: 8)

Sixty years later we have more synthetic chemicals than Carson could have imagined: a thirty-fold increase since 1930, with a total estimated to come close to 80,000, most of which have not been tested for carcinogenicity (Huff 2011). We seem to be on a "treadmill of toxics," with an "ever increasing demand and supply of toxic materials as a major aspect of industrial capitalism" (Adeola 2012: 16–17). Particularly concerning are the persistent organic pollutants (POPs), the dirty dozen being the worst—which, as their name indicates, do not go away and in fact can bioaccumulate over time. In addition, there are petrochemicals (chemicals with a petroleum or hydrocarbon basis, such as benzene and naphthalene), which are toxic. The petrochemical industry in general is a source of many inorganic and organic pollutants and heavy metals. The US government, especially the Department of Defense and the Department of Energy, is also a major environmental polluter (see the box "The Government as Polluter").

The Government as Polluter

Although this chapter focuses on the contribution of corporations to environmental health problems, it is important to remember that the federal government is the largest polluter, having contaminated nearly 60,000 sites (Kasten 2000). In the United States the government discharges "almost 2.5 million tons of toxic and radioactive waste annually without reporting it. The Government Accounting Office estimates that 95 percent of US government toxic pollution is exempt from the government's own reporting procedures" (Simon 2000: 640).

The military is a major contributor; much of its waste production began with weapons development during World War II. The country was trying to produce nuclear and other weapons in record time. Although the use of these weapons had a horrific impact on the populations of other nations, particularly in Japan, where approximately 200,000 people were killed in Hiroshima and Nagasaki, the production of the weapons also had—and continues to have—serious health effects within the United States and in places where the weapons were tested. The government wanted to ignore the health effects, as it was "more concerned with winning World War II and the Cold War than in addressing safety and public health concerns" (Michaels 2008a: 214). In fact the government coined the term "national sacrifice zones ... to refer to areas severely contaminated by radioactive hazards in the course of nuclear weapons manufacturing" (Adeola 2012: 9).

One substance needed for nuclear weapons was uranium, and the government secretly enlisted the help of the Navajo Nation by deceiving Najavo people into believing that they were not working in a uranium mine (Pasternak 2011). The men were exposed to high doses of radon, a radioactive gas that results from the natural breakdown of uranium in rock and soil. US Secretary of the Interior Steward Udall said the government knew that the radiation would probably "kill many of these men, but the agency [Atomic Energy Commission] did and said nothing other than to silence its critics and successfully oppose every case in the courtroom" (Michaels 2008a: 220). The health problems did not end when the mining was done. The land is still littered by mounds of toxic waste, which turned the Najavo reservation into one of the largest uranium-contaminated areas in the United States. The Environmental Protection Agency (EPA) estimates that an eight-year cleanup project is needed (Frosch 2014).

The manufacture of weapons engendered health problems. For one, it required producing plutonium, which has a radioactive by-product. Hanford in Washington was a major site, and officials there somehow decided that more than 120 million gallons of liquid waste could just be dumped into the ground (Michaels 2008a: 215). At a uranium production plant in Ohio, nearby residents thought their neighbor was a benign plant producing cattle feed or pet food, and were mightily surprised when they learned that 300,000 pounds of uranium were released through the plant's stacks (Michaels 2008a: 216). Finally, in Tennessee, at a plant where mercury was used to enrich lithium for hydrogen bombs, an estimated 550,000 pounds of the metal were released into the local air and water between 1950 and 1963 (Michaels 2008a: 215).

After the prototype weapons were produced, they needed to be tested. Testing of atomic bombs occurred in several places, near Great Salt Lake (Williams 1991) and in the Pacific Ocean, between Australia and Hawaii. One Pacific atoll houses a structure with an 18-inch cap known as the Runit Dome, under which one can find 111,000 cubic yards of radioactive debris left after twelve years of nuclear tests (Wall 2015). Fears that the radioactive waste will leach into the ground and in the water have now put the small atoll on the map. Closer to home we have Dugway Proving Grounds in Utah, where the military dropped incendiaries on facsimile buildings and exploded gas-filled bombs to estimate how many were needed for a lethal effect on the enemy (Hooks and Smith 2004: 564). We live with the resulting environmental devastation.

Other military bases that have had an environmental impact include a decommissioned Cold War radar station located on St Lawrence Island, Alaska. The island is still home to PCBs due to the incompetent waste disposal when the military left: barrels of chemicals were simply plowed under the land or left exposed to the elements for decades (Johnson 2015). Finally, the environmental health impact on military bases can come from less obvious sources. Men whose pregnant mothers were at the Camp Lejeune, North Carolina base in the 1950s through the 1980s were affected when various industrial solvents and other chemicals leached into the water supply. The chemicals appear to be responsible for breast cancer in men (Ruckart et al. 2015).

The health impact? One estimate is that 40 percent of deaths are due to environmental degradation (Pimentel et al. 2007). Toxins produce cardiovascular disease, hypertension, diabetes, immune deficiency, thyroid disorders, sexual hormone imbalances, reproductive problems, respiratory problems, serious neurological disturbances, and cancer of all types—liver, pancreatic, intestinal, breast, lung, and brain (Robin 2010: 23). Cancer has been a big concern, but recent attention has also included endocrine disrupters, as reports of the feminization of animals, unusually low male-to-female sex ratios at birth (Davis et al. 2007), and other reproductive problems come to light (Colborn et al. 1996). Another relatively new concern is the health impact from the bioaccumulation of toxins in the food chain. While the whole food chain is at risk, humans ingest the greatest concentration of the toxins because they are at the top (less so vegans and vegetarians). Furthermore, the mental burden of living with such risks can cause grave generalized stress and emotional ill health from fears of contracting particular diseases (Edelstein 1988; Cutchin et al. 2008).

The myriad health impacts from the toxic pollution of our land, soil, and air affect us all, but clearly some groups are more vulnerable than others. Children are particularly at risk: their young growing bodies, even *in utero*, are susceptible to a variety of toxins because they are eating and drinking more, pound for pound, than adults, and their bodies are in a transitional developmental state. DDT exposure *in utero* has been linked to breast cancer (Cohn et al. 2015); childhood exposures to a variety of neurotoxicants (such as lead, arsenic, and magnesium) have been linked to neurodevelopmental disabilities (Grandjean and Landrigan 2014); prenatal exposure to PBA (a chemical found in many everyday items, from food can linings to bike helmets) appears to be connected to breast cancer, prostate cancer, neurological problems, and immunological changes (Breast Cancer Fund 2013); and childhood exposure to air pollution is linked to poor lung functioning later in life (Dockery and Ware 2015). Stated in a more general way, researchers believe that critical periods of development, especially between conception and the first few years of life, "determine to a large degree how we die in later years" (Bezruchka 2015: 206). Chapter 3 noted the "toxic stress" that comes from multiple physical and emotional assaults on young children and its life-long impact.

A second vulnerable group is that of residents of low-income neighborhoods, particularly if a large percentage of them are people of color. Historically, such neighborhoods have a disproportionate exposure to toxic air, water, and soil from surrounding industrial plants and from toxic waste dumps. The fact that we don't share the burden of trash and pollution equally is referred to as environmental racism or environmental injustice (see chapter 3). This inequality is well illustrated in Waterfront South, a depressed area of Camden, New Jersey where there are "two federal Superfund sites, thirteen other known contaminated sites, four junkyards, a petroleum coke transfer station, a scrap metal recycling plant, numerous auto body shops, a paint company, a chemical company, three food processing plants, and other heavy industrial use sites" (Cole and Farrell 2006: 266). It is hard to imagine growing up in a neighborhood with so much pollution.

Fortunately, activists in many affected communities have been instrumental in making such injustice known and forcing some action. A protest in Warren County, North Carolina, for example, is credited with putting environmental racism on the map (Bullard and Johnson 2000). There the illegal dumping of PCB-laced oil on the road led to a government decision to move the waste to a purpose-built dump in a community that was 84 percent African American. The residents were not happy, so they engaged in mass actions that included lying down in front of dump trucks. Over 500 protesters were arrested. The end result was national press coverage and research that documented the relationship between waste and race, most notably in the *Toxic Wastes and Race Report* (Bullard and Johnson 2000). The press coverage and the report then stimulated residents in other communities to ask similar questions. The environmental justice movement came alive. In Pensacola, Florida the toxic dump site from a chemical fertilizer plant and from a wood treatment plant grew to be sixty feet high and came to be known as "Mt Dioxin." Residents fought hard for a reasonable settlement, holding out until there was an agreement to relocate all residents (Bullard and Johnson 2000). Environmental justice issues are manifest not just in the siting of industries and toxic waste dumps, but also in the cleanup process.

Environmental Cleanup Injustice

While the health impact of the siting of industrial plants and waste dumps has been the focus of the environmental injustice movement, as early as the 1990s researchers have also noted the injustice associated with cleaning up toxic sites. A *National Law Journal* article noted that it took longer for abandoned hazardous waste sites in minority areas than for sites in white areas to be placed on the national priority action list; that the EPA was more likely to merely "contain" the waste in minority areas than to eliminate it or rid it of toxins, while in white areas elimination was more likely than containment; and that the average fine for mishandling hazardous waste was $335,566 in white areas yet only $55,318 in minority areas (Lavelle and Coyle 1992).

In 1994 President Clinton signed Executive Order 12898, which required the EPA and other federal agencies to implement environmental justice policies. While this was a promising idea, it appears that not much has changed. For a community to receive significant resources for cleanup it needs to be on the Superfund list, but researchers found (a) that inclusion on the Superfund list was not very likely for sites located in areas with high minority and poor populations and (b) "that the chance of listing for several marginalized and poor populations actually worsens for sites discovered since the executive order" (O'Neil 2007: 1091). The author of the study concludes that, "despite legislation to ensure environmental justice, equity in Superfund listing appears to be worsening" (O'Neil 2007: 1092).

It seems that environmental cleanup justice is not aided enough by the twenty-two-year existence of a civil rights office within the EPA. The office has never made a formal finding of a Title VI violation (Title VI prohibits racial discrimination exercised by those who received federal monies): the office has received nearly 300 Title VI complaints but has rejected or dismissed nearly 90 percent and delayed most of the others. One North Carolina community has had its complaint in the EPA pipeline for eight years and is still waiting. The office seems "more ceremonial than meaningful" (Lombardi et al. 2015), although a relatively new EPA blog at https://blog.epa.gov/blog/tag/mustafa-ali does look promising.

The siting of polluting industry and toxic dumps in poor neighborhoods is analogous to the migration of dirty industries to the less developed countries (Simon 2000: 638)—which was actually encouraged by the World Bank, as an internal World Bank memo documents—and to the exportation of electronic waste ("E-waste") from countries like the United States and European Union members to poor areas mainly in China, India, Pakistan, Ghana, and Nigeria. The toxic waste from discarded electronics exposes both the worker disassembling a unit and the local environment to chemicals that produce serious health problems (LaDou and Lovegrove 2008).

The harm to health that comes from pollutants is horrific enough, but the fact that many companies know that they were harming the environment and people's health makes the situation even more disturbing. In this chapter I will present several cases in which corporations knew the health consequences of their polluting activities but did virtually nothing—except delay the possibility of reasonable oversight and solutions. For instance, Exxon knew in 1977 that using fossil fuels was a major cause of climate change. Its senior scientist reported to Exxon's management committee that "there is general scientific agreement that the most likely manner in which mankind is influencing the global climate is through carbon dioxide release from the burning of fossil fuels" (Hall 2015: n.p.). The impact of climate change on health, which I cover only briefly in this book, is significant. A 2015 article in the *Lancet* said that climate change was "the biggest global health threat of the 21st century" (Costello et al. 2009, quoted in Watts et al. 2015: 1862), noting that "the direct effects of climate change include increased heat stress, floods, drought, and increased frequency of intense storms, with the indirect [effects] threatening population health through adverse changes in air pollution, the spread of disease vectors, food insecurity and under-nutrition, displacement, and mental ill health" (Watts et al. 2015: 1861). Despite having their own senior scientist report that climate change was real, Exxon's leaders denied their significant carbon footprint for twenty-seven years and funded the Global Climate Coalition, think tanks, and researchers who embraced climate denial (Goldenberg 2015). Similarly, the automobile industry worked hard to deny climate change. It has been dismissive not only of the pollution from vehicles, but also of its larger impact on global warming. In fact, "in 1989, major car firms were also founding members of the Global Climate Coalition, a group of powerful United States businesses opposing environmental regulations, which achieved its aim of pulling the US out of the Kyoto treaty" (Woodcock and Aldred 2008: 1745). The industry worked hard to minimize our knowledge of the role of man-made pollution in climate change. Its leaders, like Exxon's, were aware of the scientific evidence but chose to lead a campaign to deny it (Revkin 2009).

While industrial-triggered climate change is an important backdrop to the discussion, our major focus in this chapter is chemical and heavy-metal pollution, and in particular the hazardous and toxic waste from various production processes. Also notable and deserving of mention is pollution from items used in households (Davis and Webster 2002). Household-cleaning chemicals (such as oven cleaners, drain cleaners, tub and tile cleaners) are ubiquitous and often used in a cavalier manner, which does not respect the potency of the chemicals: they can cause serious respiratory, eye, or skin damage (Altman et al. 2011). Cosmetics pose other risks, also little known to the consumer since some things are not listed on the package on the grounds that they are not technically "ingredients." Studies have found phthalates (a family of chemicals linked to birth defects) in the majority of beauty products tested (Brown 2007: 223). Since the labels on lawn and garden pesticides and herbicides require an 11th-grade reading skill to decipher, many people use these toxic products without necessary protection (Lynch and Stretesky 2001).

So, if we step back and look upstream for the causes of environmental pollution from chemicals and heavy metals, we find that it is the production of stuff in order to build our society (e.g., houses, cars, highways, airplanes, and industrial buildings), to generate energy (e.g., heating and cooling, cooking, running industry, and transporting people and products), and to manufacture commercial goods (e.g., clothes, TVs, smart phones, food) that can create toxic waste. That waste is generated (a) as a by-product of the production process, (b) when the item is used, or (c) when it is discarded. It is not just capitalist countries that have harmed the environment in the process of doing these things, but with industrial capitalism we have seen unprecedented rates of resource utilization and waste release (Baer and Singer 2009).

Pollution from the Production of Stuff

Consider four examples of pollution generated through the production of stuff. Many production processes either have a toxic waste by-product or a toxic end product, and some of these products can pollute the waste stream of the onsite production line. One example is the Hooker Chemical and Plastics Corporation, which operated in upstate New York in the 1960s and 1970s and used a local, human-built but never finished canal as a chemical waste dump. After ten years the company covered the dump with dirt and sold the land to the City Board of Education for one dollar. An elementary school was built and home building began on this property. Years later a local resident, Lois Gibbs, grew concerned about the high rates of birth defects and miscarriages in the community and began asking questions. The history of Hooker was revealed and Gibbs' community organizing led to results: 950 families were evacuated and the EPA declared Love Canal a Superfund site (EPA 2012).

A second example (made famous through the film *A Civil Action*, starring John Travolta) comes from Woburn, Massachusetts, where residents sensed a high rate of childhood leukemia in the 1970s and targeted the combined toxic waste-dumping activities of W. R. Grace and Beatrice Foods as likely sources (Brown and Mikkelsen 1997). A court suit led to a settlement and then to a belated EPA cleanup effort.

The third example is that of Ciba, a major chemical company that purchased property in Toms River, New Jersey in 1949 in order to produce vat dyes. The production process of vat dyes uses chemicals that are (almost all of them) explosive, poisonous, or both; and it generates an astonishing amount of nasty waste: 4 million pounds of dye each year produced 18 million pounds of hazardous waste (Fagin 2013: 24–5). Some waste was buried on site (sometimes it was contained, but not always) while other waste was burned at night, which made it invisible to the community (Fagin 2013: 104). More on Toms River later in this chapter.

Finally, in Anniston, Alabama, residents faced Monsanto Chemical, a company that for four decades (1940s through the 1970s) produced PCBs, which were outlawed in 1979, and used them as an industrial coolant. There the problem wasn't a waste by-product but the leakage of the end product, PCBs. The chemical ended up in the water and in the soil and caused elevated levels of thyroid gland damage, skin disorders, liver cancer, and diabetes (Israel 2012). An early company memo from 1935 admitted to knowing that PCBs were not safe, albeit cautiously, by saying that PCBs "cannot be considered non-toxic" (quoted in Grunwald 2002: 4). Monsanto-sponsored studies found additional troubling evidence: fish stocked in nearby creeks died in 3.5 minutes (Grunwald 2002).

Production plants can also have an effect on health due to explosions, faulty design, or weather-caused damage, all of which release toxic chemicals. The 1976 explosion in Sevesco, Italy, which released dioxin, the 1979 partial nuclear meltdown at Three-Mile Island, Pennsylvania, the 1984 deadly gas and chemical leak in Bhopal, India, and the 2005 refinery explosion in Texas City, Texas come to mind—along with the nuclear disaster in Chernobyl, Ukraine in 1986, the British Petroleum Deepwater Horizon oil spill in the Gulf of Mexico in 2010, the nuclear power disaster in Fukushima, Japan in 2011, and the explosion at the chemical warehouse in Tianjin, China in 2015. Abandoned sites are not without problems, as the concern with "brownfields" in many cities makes apparent. A brownfield is a former industrial or commercial site blighted by real or perceived environmental contamination. And, as the Gold King mine cleanup disaster in Colorado in 2015 illustrates, abandoned mines are far from safe. Over time, water collects in the mine tunnels and combines with mine waste that contains many heavy metals such as cadmium and copper. The toxic mix leaches into the nearby rivers. At the Gold King mine, the EPA was trying to reduce leakage when it accidently released a huge plume of yellow, toxic water into the nearby river.

The problem of pollution from producing stuff is of growing concern, as our consumer-driven society pushes for more and more products and as other countries with improving standards of living begin to demand similar goods. Between 1960 and 2006 the consumption expenditures per person almost tripled, which means more extraction of resources (50 percent more than thirty years ago) and more waste (Assadourian 2010: 4). This increase in consumption did not occur naturally but was the consequence of various institutional drivers. Most importantly, business interests—a strong upstream actor—have found myriad ways to coax more consumption out of people by liberalizing credit, by manufacturing products with short lives ("planned obsolescence"), and by marketing new styles, prompting us to change the color of perfectly functioning kitchen appliances on a regular basis. Advertisements constantly bombard us with enticements to buy things we don't need and to replace items that are not broken. The sophisticated advertising pushes products that are "based on customers' fears, insecurities, addictions, and primitive and precognitive urges" (Freudenberg 2014: 68). Concerning the effectiveness of advertising, one study reports that an extra hour of TV watching is associated with a person's spending $208 a year more (Assadourian 2010: 13). Corporations are not lone actors pushing consumption; rather we have seen the emergence of a "corporate consumption complex," a "web of organizations that include the global corporations that produce the goods of the modern consumer economy, the retail conglomerates that sell their products, and the trade associations that represent them in the political arena" (Freudenberg 2014: 95). The consumerism resulting from this powerful web forms a "cultural pattern that leads people to find meaning, contentment, and acceptance primarily through the consumption of goods and services" (Assadourian 2010: 8). Because of the compounded pollution that accompanies increased—and in many instances unregulated—manufacturing, this addiction to consumption is ruining not only our mental health, but our physical health as well, not to mention the health of the environment.

This excessive shopping spree we are on requires a production infrastructure that uses more resources than are sustainable. In America the earth's resources are used at a rate that can sustain only 1.4 billion people; yet Americans live on a planet with 7 billion people (Assadourian 2010: 6). The shopping spree produces increasingly toxic waste, and more of it than people and the environment can handle. We have a system that has pushed "consumption at the expense of human health" (Freudenberg 2014: vii). It is clear that something needs to be done. So I ask: Why is it that so little is done to stop this unsustainable use of resources, the production of so much toxic pollution, and the resulting health problems for the population?

Here I explore three important reasons: we have limited knowledge of chemicals and their environmental health impact; corporate actions amount to deceit and denial of the health hazards of toxins (Markowitz and Rosner 2003a); and governments so far have not regulated toxic substances adequately.

Persistence of Environmental Health Problems: Our Limited Knowledge

The public's general knowledge of the health impact of exposure to environmental chemicals is surprisingly limited. Although Rachel Carson warned us about the potential danger as long ago as in 1962, it was not until 2001 that we began to learn systematically about the health impact of environmental toxins on the population. That year the Centers for Disease Control (CDC) released its first report on the toxic chemicals in our bodies, and three years later the government launched the National Children's Study to monitor children longitudinally (Brown 2008: 97–8). Interested parties, such as the school of public health at various universities, might seem like ideal sources of information about environmental health impacts on the population, but they are staffed by "soft-money" academics—which means that their continued employment is dependent on getting grants. This dependence makes the researchers less likely to take chances on innovative projects that would look upstream to find the sources of health problems in the community (Brown 2008: 93). The EPA is another obvious interested party (which, as a federal regulatory agency, we will discuss later in this chapter), but has contributed little to our knowledge because under the 1976 Toxic Substances Control Act (TSCA) it has limited powers. While the Food and Drug Administration (FDA) requires a pharmaceutical company to provide safety data before a new drug is placed on the market, the TSCA does not have a parallel requirement. Rather the manufacturer of a new industrial chemical needs only to "notify" the EPA. The burden is then on the EPA to document potential risk within 90 days; and then it can require industry testing. There is a "presumption of innocence" in this process, and the burden of proof on the EPA is so high that in its lifetime the TSCA has asked for the industry testing of only about 200 chemicals (Denison 2009) and has regulated only five chemicals: asbestos, dioxin, hexavalent chromium, PCBs, and halogenated chlorofluoroalkanes. "The TSCA is so ineffective that it took a separate act of Congress to amend the TSCA so that the US Environmental Protection Agency (EPA) could regulate asbestos" (Paulson 2011: 983–4). Furthermore, in the case of a site with health problems, the EPA often limits its chemical testing to the "target compound" list for Superfund sites, which may mean that it finds few or none of the toxic chemicals that are nevertheless present at that site (Fagin 2013: 392). This limitation, again, restricts our knowledge.

Much of our knowledge about environmental health begins with community reports of possible problems, such as those about Love Canal and Woburn. The first stage of data collection often consists of disease and death reports gathered by local residents as they realize that many of their neighbors seem to be suffering from similar, usually rare, health problems. In some instances, researchers or public officials decide to explore a citizen claim of environmental toxic exposure, and the task becomes one of learning whether the rate of the problem is unusually high; that is, whether there is a disease "cluster." The initial examination is often an incidence study in which the rate of the disease for the neighborhood in question is examined against an expected rate, on the basis of knowledge of its occurrence in other places, often using the relevant state registry of the specific disease. Unfortunately state registries are typically a bit out of date and incomplete (Fagin 2013: 291), which renders the conclusion ambiguous. But even a relatively firm finding that the area in question has a higher rate of disease than expected is far from being statistically compelling (the residential area has been selected because the rate seems high and the number of people with a disease is small). This makes it hard to argue that the occurrence of the disease isn't just a random event. Furthermore, a high rate does not provide any evidence about the particular toxic source of the health problem.

To go beyond the incidence study is to attempt an analysis of the relationship between the suspected toxin and the disease. At first glance this research task of linking a cause to an effect does not seem more complicated than usual, but it is. Although most people are aware that correlation does not prove causation and that correlational studies struggle with the necessarily ambiguous nature of any research conclusions, the difficulties of environmental health research are more basic. One difficulty is making sure that the affected population is included. Over time, people move in and out of a neighborhood, so a study of all current residents excludes some who were exposed for a long time but left during the past decade or two and includes some who just arrived and had little exposure. A second difficulty is measuring the independent variable, exposure to the toxin. In a simple situation with a known potential source of the problem, the researcher might take into account the proximity of a resident's home to the alleged toxic source and the amount of time the person spends at home—a stay-at-home parent gets more exposure than a parent who goes to work every day outside the community, for example. Gathering proximity data and time-in-the-home data is tedious but not impossible, as a study in China recently showed (Yu et al. 2006), but gathering exposure data can be far more complicated.

Toms River provides an excellent example of such complexities. The community residents were potentially exposed to both toxic air and toxic water. Here let us just consider water. To estimate the exposure of individual households and people to toxic water, the researchers developed a computer model that took into account the location of the source of the toxic water (both the onsite leaky landfill and places on the river where the company had released toxic waste), features of the local aquafer, and knowledge of where each of the twenty-three public wells drew their water from and which wells supplied which households with water. The water distribution (source to well to household) varied over the two-decade-long study period and was further complicated by seasonal fluctuations in draws from different wells (more people in town in the summer drew more water). The computer model thus developed was incredibly complex. It included "all sixteen thousand pipe segments, incorporating variables as obscure as the size of each storage tank and the composition of each pipe" and produced 420 models, one for each month of the study period (Fagin 2013: 387). Information on how much tap water (versus bottled water) was consumed in each home was also collected (Fagin 2013: 397). The result? After a herculean data-collection and computer-modeling project, the plaintiffs ended up with a "powerful but *circumstantial* case" (Fagin 2013: 400, italics

are mine). Fortunately the residents were able to get a damage settlement; but the whole process clearly demonstrates that the task of
trying to link cause and effect in environmental cases can be time-
consuming, prohibitively expensive, and ultimately ambiguous. The
study lasted for five years and cost the government $10 million (Fagin
2013: 345). Concerned with the ambiguity of the data produced
and the cost of such a cluster study of disease, the CDC sponsored
a conference in 1989 in which many of the assembled researchers
agreed that residential cluster studies were futile. As a result, many
states decided not to do such studies any more (Fagin 2013: 283–4).
Whatever information could have been gleaned had they been done
was obviously lost. Good studies of the health impact of chemicals
are few in number also because manufacturers have resisted finding
out the information and reporting to the public the known connections between chemicals and health.

I turn now to consider corporate strategies that have limited our
knowledge of the environmental impact of chemicals and heavy
metals on people's health.

Persistence of Environmental Health Problems: Corporate Strategies that Harm Our Health

Environmental discussions are contentious because a claim of environmental impact challenges the status quo of business operations.
Forcing the discussion upstream means that "agribusiness, the
chemical industry, auto production, energy companies, garbage disposal firms, and many other large sectors of the economy are faced
with challenges to their largely unfettered activities" (Brown 2002:
8). When companies have caused damage through the release of toxic
chemicals into the air, soil, and water and then are exposed, they face
"economic stakes" and "political ramifications" that can be huge
(Brown 2002: 8). This prospect forces them to devise strategies that
limit and distort the information about any possible harm to health.
In many instances, companies have been deceitful about their products and systematically denied they are doing harm (Markowitz and
Rosner 2003a).

As we'll see below, the basic strategies used to deceive the public
and to deny the possibility of health harm from chemicals tend to
follow the playbook of the tobacco companies discussed in chapter 2.
Companies design research in ways that produce conclusions of no
harm and find ways to have them published in seemingly respectable

journals; they denigrate the scientists who say the chemicals are harmful; they aggressively engage in "product defense" by using public relations firms, think tanks, and front groups that argue "no harm"; and they influence the government in myriad ways.

The publication of research studies that declare little or no harm from toxic chemicals

The success of the tobacco industry in its decades-long denial of harm taught other manufacturers that "debating science is much easier and more effective than debating the policy" (Michaels 2008a: xi). The task came to be one of making it appear that the company was interested in finding a scientific answer to an important health question—therefore the company itself would engage in research studies or be willing to reanalyze data. In fact companies became very good at producing poorly designed studies that showed "no harm" for a chemical, at reanalyzing the data in ways that made effects disappear through clever statistics, and at finding ways to make their "evidence" prevail in public discussions.

A good example of a research studies designed by a chemical manufacturer and showing "no harm" is Monsanto's studies of dioxin, a by-product of some of the company's industrial processes. Monsanto chose as study participants people who worked in the chemical plants, not residents who lived around the plant or in the disposal area and might be affected. This was a logical decision, as it is much easier to define chemical exposure levels for workers than it would be to do it for residents, and worker studies using sound methodology would provide important information on health problems that could occur in the context of environmental exposure. Sound research design requires the appropriate inclusion of people in the sample, as well as a reliable classification of those exposed or not exposed. Close examination of the Monsanto-sponsored research studies shows anything but that. In one study twenty-four cases of cancer were excluded for no clear reason; in another study four workers who died of cancer were moved from the exposed group to the unexposed (Robin 2010: 51). While the study reported no harm from dioxin, had it been conducted properly, it "would have produced a diametrically opposed conclusion, namely, that dioxin is a powerful carcinogen" (Robin 2010: 50). The Monsanto studies were so poorly designed that the US National Research Council concluded that they were "plagued with errors of classification ... and hence [were] biased toward a finding of no effect" (quoted in

Robin 2010: 50). Monsanto is not alone in sponsoring such studies. A wide variety of chemical manufacturers have enlisted consulting firms such as ChemRisk, the Weinberg Group, and Exponent, Inc. and asked them to conduct studies that claim that specific chemicals are not risky. In consequence there have been reports that concluded that atrazine (a pesticide) is not a prostate cancer risk; that asbestos is less dangerous than was previously thought; and that risks from perchlorate (a rocket fuel component) are minimal (Michaels 2008a: 46–9). Properly conducted studies find the opposite. Chapter 7 will present other examples of research designs that minimize the chances of associating chemicals with potential harm.

Sometimes new studies are not undertaken, but researchers reanalyze existing data and make methodological decisions that turn statistically significant results into insignificant ones (e.g., redefining variables, including or excluding specific cases, limiting the period between likely exposure and the measurement of the dependent variable). In courtroom settings, chemical manufacturers producing dioxin and Agent Orange successfully used such reanalysis to generate conclusions of "no harm"—until "plaintiffs proved these studies were manipulated" (Lynch and Stretesky 2001: 159). An advisory panel for the International Agency for Research on Cancer (a branch of the WHO) examined a study that demonstrated that carbon black should be classified as a carcinogen. An industry group quickly reanalyzed the data and disputed the finding (Michaels 2008a: 55).

Publishing research with design flaws can be difficult, so a companion tactic of the corporations has been to establish and control journals with impressive names, where their studies are easily accepted and published. For instance, *Regulatory Toxicology and Pharmacology* is the official journal of the International Society for Regulatory Toxicology and Pharmacology. Although the name is impressive-sounding, the society is an association "dominated by scientists who work for industry trade groups and consulting firms" (Michaels 2008a: 53). The journal published an article paid for by Pacific Gas and Electric (PG&E, of *Erin Brockovich* fame) that claimed that, "contrary to fifty years of epidemiologic studies, chromium was 'only weakly carcinogenic for the lungs'" (Michaels 2008a: 54). They could come to that conclusion by combining studies of workers and residents and by examining lung cancer, a disease that would not show up in "excess" among residents because the residents did not breathe the chromium but instead drank it in the contaminated water. Since the number of residents overwhelmed the number of workers in the combined sample, no excess lung cancer was found.

The denigration of scientists

Companies that feel threatened by researchers whose work suggests serious effects of chemicals on health have developed various methods to undermine these researchers' scientific credibility. Chapter 7 reports on the attempts pursued by Monsanto, Union Carbide, Dow, and other companies to undermine the credibility of Markowitz and Rosner, a team of academic researchers who have exposed the health problems associated with silicosis and lead, among other toxins. Another example of a researcher under attack is Herbert Needleman, a psychiatrist and toxicologist at Harvard University who studied lead in the blood of children and its relationship with reduced cognitive functioning. As Davis (2002) documents, an industry trade group, the International Lead Zinc Research Organization, hired dozens of scientists to discredit his work. Ultimately only minor statistical errors were found, but Hill+Knowlton, a public relations firm, was then enlisted to spread the word that design inadequacies were major. "For the better part of two decades, [Needleman] endured a living hell at great personal and financial cost" (Davis 2002: 129). Another example of the denigration of scientists is Tyrone Hayes, who studied an herbicide, atrazine, found that it feminizes frogs, and then connected his findings on frogs to research on atrazine's effect on people. The manufacturer, Syngenta, was not happy. Company documents show that the public relations team at Syngenta was intent on discrediting Hayes. Written in those company documents is a list of four goals regarding Hayes; the first goal was (in so many words) "discredit Hayes." One action toward achieving this was to purchase his name as a search word on the internet, so that, for years, if you searched for his work, the first hit was "Tyrone Hayes Not Credible" (Aviv 2014).

A similar attack on a researcher occurred with the publication of a climate change report by the Intergovernmental Panel on Climate Change (IPCC), the world's leading authority on climate issues. Ben Santer, the author of a chapter on greenhouse gases, was savagely attacked in the media by members of a conservative think tank, the George C. Marshall Institute. For a time, if one googled "Santer IPCC," one would not get the IPCC report but sites that repeated the accusations that his research report was deceptive (Oreskes and Conway 2010: 2–4). Other researchers attacked include Mary Amdur, Lester Lave and Eugene Seskin, Douglas Dockery, Jack Spengler, and Richard Wilson (Brown 2007: 105; Markowitz and Rosner 2013a).

Product defense

In addition to slanting the research, paying for studies with dubious research designs, and attacking researchers, corporations also defend their products by employing public relations firms that know how to develop, package, and present their case to the public and to politicians. Hill+Knowlton is a long-standing and perennially involved public relations company that has orchestrated campaigns to "manufacture doubt" about the harmful effects of chemicals. After its success with the model used in tobacco campaigns, the company became involved in campaigns on asbestos, vinyl chloride, lead, beryllium, dioxin, and fluorocarbons (Michaels 2008a: 18, 36–7, 39, 42, 132–3). It advocated for the sponsoring company in civil court, in the court of public opinion, and in the regulatory arena before government agencies responsible for protecting the environment; and it was successful at reducing the public perception of harm and delaying regulations.

Another way of defending products is through think tanks and front groups. The names of these groups make them sound environmentally responsible. There is, for instance, the Citizens' Alliance for Responsible Energy, which advocates for fossil fuels and is funded (among others) by New Mexico oil and gas producers. And there is the Citizens for Recycling First, set up by the American Coal Ash Association to promote the idea that coal waste is safe (www. sourcewatch.org). These groups make claims about health issues. For instance, the Council on Water Quality receives funding from the aerospace company Lockheed Martin, for whom perchlorate, an additive in rocket fuel, is crucial, and the Council claims that research finds that low levels of perchlorate are harmless—this despite a finding by the National Academy of Sciences of thyroid damage at a low exposure levels (Michaels 2008a: 56). The Annapolis Center for Science-Based Policy is heavily funded by ExxonMobil and concludes in one report: "No one knows whether controlling [airborne particles] will actually yield net benefits to public health" (quoted in Michaels 2008a: 57).

All of these corporate tactics are well documented in the case of climate change. Despite the fact that 97 percent of actively publishing climate scientists agree that human activities have been a cause of global warming (climate.nasa.gov), fossil fuel companies have worked hard for decades to call research into doubt, spread misinformation, and support legislators, front groups, and think tanks that will help them in their climate change denial campaign. The interested reader should examine two publications: Oreskes and Conway's (2010) book *Merchants of Doubt: How a Handful of Scientists Obscured the Truth on Issues from Tobacco Smoke to Global Warming* (together with the documentary *Merchants of Death*); and the Union of Concerned Scientists' "*The Climate Deception Dossiers*" (UCS 2015).

Most of these strategies are somewhat defensive actions enlisted when there is a likely public concern in a particular situation or with a particular chemical. Corporations have also been powerful enough to influence government decision making about environmental health policies and agency mandates, which in many cases is a more proactive tactic of corporations.

Persistence of Environmental Health Problems: The Government

Lobbying is a long-standing tradition in the United States, one that allows any interest group to attempt to influence the government through direct appeal and through campaign financing. There are some rules, but both lobbying and campaign financing are legal and open to all. The obvious downside is that big economic players have the ability to provide serious money, which can drown the voices of citizen groups. In 2014 alone, oil and gas industries, concerned particularly about proposed regulations to reduce greenhouse gases, contributed over 30 million dollars to members of the House and Senate and spent 144 million dollars on lobbying (Center for Responsive Politics n.d.). The fossil fuel industry has a long history of contributions at strategic times: a peak in its contributions came when Congress was considering a "cap-and-trade" bill related to climate change and the American Coalition for Clean Coal Electricity (ACCCE), a coal-producer advocacy group, "invested massively in the 2008 presidential election" (Collomb 2014: 3). Other industries similarly decide that campaign contributions can help them with potential environmental health issues.

Following the 1984 Union Carbide gas leak incident in Bhopal, India, the United States drafted the Emergency Planning and Community Right-to-Know Act of 1986. Among other things, the Act requires certain industries to make their toxic chemical releases public. Chemical and petroleum industries made significant contributions to "legislators deemed influential" in the discussion. Although unsuccessful as the Act did narrowly pass, the industries did exercise "considerable influence on relevant legislators" (Cho et al. 2008: 451 and 463). After the legislation passed, the industry made continued attempts to limit the number of chemicals that were subject to the Act (Fung and O'Rourke 2000: 119). Of note, too, is the finding that firms with higher levels of toxic emissions are more likely than other firms to make contributions to senators and members of the House (Cho et al. 2006). A relatively new concern is the enormous power of industry to define the broader public discussion of controversial issues, including those that directly affect our health. A 2010 Supreme Court ruling, often referred to as "Citizens United," permits corporations to spend "unlimited amounts on political advocacy advertising during election campaigns" (Wiist 2011: 1172).

Industry has been powerful enough to push legislation that makes it difficult for federal agencies to establish and enforce regulations, or even to distribute information to the public. A prime example of such legislation is the Data Quality Act (DQA), which requires federal agencies to develop guidelines to ensure the quality of the information used in establishing regulations and to set up procedures whereby affected persons can challenge the agency. In a rational world these requirements would sound good; but behind them stood the corporations, because such requirements could be used to "stall and, they hope, to stop agencies' attempts to actually issue regulations that protect the environment and public health" (Michaels 2008a: 179). Thus corporations can challenge regulations that are based on solid, peer-reviewed studies by claiming that the assessment was based on faulty computer models, bad data, or inadequate research design. This is precisely what they did in an attempt to stop the dissemination of information on climate change, which had been well vetted—it was based on models that the National Academy of Sciences characterized as "well-regarded" (quoted in Michaels 2008a: 181). Similarly, the DQA gave industry the ability to question a pamphlet written to help auto mechanics to work safely around the asbestos found in brakes. This questioning, allowed by virtue of the DQA delayed the distribution of the pamphlet by three years (Michaels 2008a: 181). This type of stalling tactic is once again reminiscent of tobacco industry's tactics.

Industry influence has not stopped at the US borders; it has also affected international agreements on health. US industry actors have lobbied foreign governments before the formal US delegation met with the international partner. Such strategies have contributed to ozone depletion, global warming, and toxic waste trade. Industry-backed groups can also participate as observers at international negotiations. Thus the Global Climate Coalition, a business advocacy group, attended talks on climate change, and the global recycling industry worked hard to weaken the Basel Convention, which is an attempt to stop the exportation of hazardous waste (Clapp 2001: 4). Industry pressure has meant that the United States has signed but not ratified various international agreements that would make our environment healthier, including the Basel Convention and the Stockholm Convention on Persistent Organic Pollutants.

In addition to applying pressure on the political process through lobbying, financing campaigns, and influencing legislation, industries have strong relationships with the government through "revolving doors" and other mechanisms. When EPA administrators leave the EPA, they take with them considerable knowledge about regulatory rules and loopholes and leave behind long-standing colleagues. When they join a firm regulated by their former agency, they are in a powerful position to get a good deal in any dispute. In 2000, one author counted "20 high-ranking former EPA administrators that have left the agency and become millionaire waste-industry executives, giving rise to charges of a revolving door between the EPA and the hazardous waste management industry" (Simon 2000: 641). Some industries achieve influence behind the scenes; thus the industry had a secret meeting with the government to suggest revisions in some pending EPA regulations (Simon 2000: 641). Many cozy industry–government relationships come from the government's appointing industry-connected individuals to positions of power. The government might even appoint an agency administrator who holds views totally incompatible with the agency's mandate. This is what happened when Dr. John Graham—a man who had gone on record for saying that the costs of regulations outweighed their benefits—was appointed to lead the Office of Management and Budget (OMB) (Michaels 2008a: 179).

Enlightened government activity depends on various advisory boards designed to give agencies good, unbiased expertise on relevant scientific findings. The membership of advisory boards, however, has been anything but unbiased. For instance, in 2002 the administration replaced 15 of the 18 members of the advisory committee to the director of the National Center for Environmental Health (NCEH) "for the most part with representatives of regulated industries, product defense specialists (including ChemRisk's Dr. Dennis Paustenbach), and organizations ideologically opposed to federal regulation" (Michaels 2008a: 193). That same year the US Health and Human Services Secretary Tommy Thompson "personally rejected new members of the advisory panel, the first time a secretary had ever done so. At the same time, Thompson filled the panel with people who had consulted for and testified for the lead paint industry" (Brown 2008: 104). Further examples are discussed in the Union of Concerned Scientists' "Scientific Integrity in Policy Making" report (UCS 2004).

Some argue that, even without such direct influence from economic actors, the government might still be timid about legislating against polluters and supporting research and initiatives that look upstream. Politicians want uncontroversial, inexpensive, and short timeframe interventions, as they do have their own political lives to consider (Scott-Samuel and Smith 2015). Many governments have a "rhetorical commitment" to finding root causes of disease and to reducing health inequities, but when they actually set priorities for programs they look downstream, toward individual factors like genes and "the molecularization of environmental health" (Shostak 2013). Lead paint is a good example of the changed perspective. Because of the work of various doctors, public health researchers, and social reformers, the problem of lead paint came to be understood as the product of a commercial enterprise that turned a blind eye to the health hazards of lead. Coupled with poverty and absentee landlords, peeling lead paint created a serious health hazard, especially for poor children. That knowledge made lead poisoning a preventable disease because people understood the social and economic context of the cause and addressed it. They asked the right question, looked upstream, and saw what action was needed to reduce exposure. These days the research question is very different. Researchers turn to the genetic level to find variants of genes associated with high lead levels and seek to understand gene–environment interactions (Shostak 2013: 2–5). Proponents of this type of approach argue that there is logic in going to the molecular level. By the 1990s molecular genetics had reached the apex of biomedical research (Shostak 2013: 44), and the existing environmental research seemed by comparison to depend on "weak" epidemiological evidence, clearly falling "behind the leading edge" of research; and this affected the status and prestige of funding agencies (Shostak 2013: 45). The researchers involved felt they had to change direction; and they went decidedly downstream.

Improving Environmental Health

I have thus far documented the increased toxicity of our environment, which suggests a terrible health trajectory. Since the time of Rachel Carson, however, many positive things have happened by way of improving our environment, mitigating the damage and enabling us to envision a healthier future. To date, "we have banned some dangerous chemicals and reduced our reliance on others, found rapid and creative ways to substitute more benign materials for dangerous ones such as chlorofluorocarbons. We have enlarged the number of environmental organizations and moved them in the direction of human health concerns" (Brown 2002: 10). And this improvement has benefitted greatly from the work of average people, who have achieved many things, "including the buyout of contaminated areas, economic settlements from polluting companies ... participation in decision making about siting of hazardous facilities, membership on peer review panels for environmental health research, and a host of other actions" (Brown 2007: xii).

Reducing the toxins in our environment is obviously critical and both state-level and federal-level initiatives have shown results. At the state level, Massachusetts passed the Massachusetts Toxics Use Reduction Act (TURA), which led to the reduction of the state's toxic emissions by two thirds in ten years. Surprisingly TURA did not highlight health effects that could have stalled action, as that would have probably appeared to point the finger at particular industries. Instead the goal was to reduce toxins for the sake of making the reductions (Mayer et al. 2002: 580). At the federal level, many parties on all sides of the environmental discussion have credited the Toxics Release Inventory (TRI, part of the Community Right to Know legislation following Bhopal) with success in reducing toxins (Fung and O'Rourke 2000). The regulations require large manufacturing firms to make annual reports to EPA on any of the 651 toxic chemicals they have released. Despite little checking on the accuracy of the reports and the failure of perhaps a third of the firms to submit reports, the consensus is that the TRI is successful and has reduced emissions. It has given environmental activists and journalists information that was critical to the identification of the most egregious polluters and has spurred direct action. Bad media from reports on TRI information, for example, have led to a decline in stock prices (Fung and O'Rourke 2000: 120–1). Corporations are listening.

The future looks bright also because there are many proposals that could improve our environmental health: moving toward the "least toxic alternative"; designing a society with environmental impacts front and center; moving away from fossil fuels to renewable energy; making access to environmental information easier, more accurate, and more complete; moving away from our culture of consumption; and enticing corporations to change their practices. Let us explore each briefly.

The least toxic alternative

We have long accepted "brown chemistry" with its petrochemical basis, toxic products, and toxic waste. The alternative is "green chemistry" with a basis in carbohydrate or "oleic (oily/fatty) feedstock" (Woodhouse 2003: 178). We have begun to acknowledge such a possibility with an EPA program, the "Presidential Green Chemistry Challenge Award," which has been won by several corporations that previously had terrible environmental records: Monsanto worked out a way to manufacture a less toxic RoundUp; the makers of Advil and Motrin reduced waste in the production of products from 60 percent to about 1 percent; and Dow Chemical now has a new green technology, which eliminates about 3.5 million pounds of chlorofluorocarbon agents each year (Woodhouse 2003: 180–1). There is even hope for the agricultural industry. Cuba, forced to alter its agricultural system because of embargoes in the 1990s, changed from agrochemicals to organic production, depending on "predatory insects and microbial antagonists." The result? Not the demise of their agricultural system, but solid evidence that green chemistry can work—and savings of 15.6 million dollars a year for Cuba (Lynch and Stretesky 2001: 160).

Societal design

There are many ways our cities could be designed to be less polluting. The Commission on Health and Climate Change Report suggests that healthy cities with energy-efficient buildings, lots of green space, and easy access to low-cost active transportation could have an impact on climate change and related health outcomes (Watts et al. 2015). Passive solar designs, recycled materials, and the reclaiming of products that are normally landfilled are also possibilities. Xerox requires all manufacturers who supply parts for its copiers to have zero waste (Lynch and Stretesky 2001: 475). The work of John Ochsendorf, an architectural historian and structural engineer at the

MIT, suggests that we need to build with the local climate in mind rather than air-conditioning ourselves needlessly and that we should build to last rather than build for an average forty-five-year building life, which is now typical (Sollinger 2015).

Changes in our consumption culture

As discussed, our consumption culture pushes for more stuff, and more stuff is producing untold waste, much of it toxic. Our cultural orientation needs to be revamped. We cannot continue with a "cultural pattern that leads people to find meaning, contentment, and acceptance primarily through the consumption of goods and services" (Assadourian 2010: 8).

Renewable energy

The move away from fossil fuels toward renewable energy is important for decreasing general air pollution and for slowing climate change. This move involves phasing out coal (Watts et al. 2015) and subsidizing renewable energy as much as we have subsidized fossil fuels. Many corporations are on board with this idea; such corporations include Google and IKEA, which has invested two billion dollars in wind and solar energy. In August 2015, 365 businesses and investors, including General Mills, Mars Inc., Nestle, Staples, Unilever, and VF Corporation, signed a petition to support Obama's Clean Power Plan (Ceres 2015). The EPA has a 100 percent Green Power Users list that features Microsoft, Intel, and Apple (EPA 2015b).

Better information for the democratic process

We need to have access to good information on environmental issues because information is critical to a democratic society. At present we have toxic releases, some of them from the government, that are not reported and "deceit and denial" about lots of chemicals. One success in democratizing the conversation is the incorporation of a wider range of voices on review panels designed to discuss environmental policy. Activists in the Breast Cancer Movement opened this door when they were able to convince the US Department of Defense, which has been responsible for the vast majority of hazardous contamination in the United States, to have activists on review panels (Brown 2007: 51). Another idea is to "open up" sealed settlements. In a sealed settlement a legal suit is resolved out of court and the parties accept terms they agree not to disclose. This means that the public doesn't learn that chemical x was the suspected cause, or how much the plaintiffs received to keep the suit out of court (an indication of damage done). The "open up" proposal is this: "If harm has been caused by a hazard that was the subject of previously sealed documents, a jury could use that earlier secrecy agreement as good cause for assessing punitive damages in this later case" (Michaels 2008a: 236). Such a change is important because, while litigation avoidance plays a central role in corporate behavior, lawsuits have been critical in changing harmful corporate environmental practices (Michaels 2008a: 234). Increasing the possibility of more significant court litigation and opening up sealed settlements could be a factor in changing corporate behavior and having a healthier upstream community.

Changed corporate practices

More corporate change is needed, and this chapter contains many examples of impressive changes to date. One expert on corporate behavior suggests, in an optimistic manner, that one needs to change only the practices of a few hundred corporations to prevent millions of premature deaths and tens of millions of avoidable illnesses and injuries (Freudenberg 2014: 36). One consequential change would be to no longer agree to pay for a corporation's "externalities" associated with environmental pollution. We have allowed corporations to manufacture things, make a profit, and then leave society at large (and sometimes local communities) with the costs of cleaning up the resulting mess. People pay to have their household trash removed; businesses should pay for their trash, too.

Conclusion

The proliferation of toxic chemicals and heavy metals in our air, soil, and water has had profound effects on public health, as evidenced by the success of many lawsuits, the need for Superfund sites, and major governmental remedial actions such as the purchase of the homes in Love Canal and the relocation of all residents near "Mt. Dioxin." Public health is at risk from the proliferation of toxic chemicals, which seem to "have far more rights than people" (quoted in Brown 2007: 59). Although people in poverty and people in minority communities have suffered the most, all of us are affected: poor people, rich people, and people yet to be born, including the descendants of people in the top-earning 1 percent. No one can get away. There is no safe place.

While many environmental cases have received a hearing in the court of public opinion, remedies were obviously too late to stem the considerable health harm. In addition, the evidence for the link between cause and effect is often circumstantial. Environmental health situations have proved frustrating, since trying to chase down the cause of a disease with a long latency period faces impossible odds, disappointing both the affected citizens and the people who want solid information. Furthermore, with chemicals already in commerce, the burden of proof on the EPA is so high that, since the passage of the 1976 Toxic Substances Control Act, no more than five substances have been banned or severely restricted. If we look at how we have allowed new industrial chemicals to enter our commerce, we could conclude that the process does not place our health high enough among our priorities. We have not asked the chemical companies to perform a mandatory pre-market testing or post-market follow-up of their products, as we ask pharmaceutical companies that seek an OK from the FDA. The onus for industrial chemicals falls instead on the EPA. Chemicals enjoy a "presumption of innocence."

Some people argue that our standards of proof are wrong. We can't insist on the strong proof that one obtains from a "gold standard design" by using a randomized control study with consenting people. An alternative standard would respect the strong suspicion of harm in particular situations, would not allow untested industrial chemicals into commerce, would prioritize public health, and would exercise caution. These are central tenets of the precautionary principle as enunciated at the Wingspread Conference of 1998: "Where an activity raises threats of harm to the environment or human health, precautionary measures should be taken even if some cause and effect relationships are not fully established scientifically. In this context the proponent of an activity, rather than the public bears the burden of proof" (https://www.gdrc.org/u-gov/precaution-3.html). Stated simply: "it is better to be safe than sorry." Critics suggest that such precaution will delay the introduction of useful, non-harmful chemicals; but the evidence to date does not support that. The number of "false positives," instances in which claims of potential harm have, with further research, been shown to be groundless, are few and far between (Hansen and Tickner 2013). Others see the precautionary principle as a radical change in how we look at environmental hazards; but this charge neglects the evidence too. There is implicit reference to caution in the Food, Drug, and Cosmetics Act of 1938, the Food Additives Amendment of 1958, and the Occupational Safety and Health Act of 1970 (Brown 2007: 208). A precautionary approach is getting increasing traction internationally (Hansen and Tickner 2013) as well as in American research and environmental actions (Brown 2007).

When we analyze environmental degradation, we need to be willing to look upstream for the cause of the pollution and to keep looking as we find a solution. The economic and political power of various polluting industries has largely caused the environmental health problems we have, and corporations have to be part of the solutions, as this chapter's section "Improving Environmental Health" suggests. The social determinants of health cannot be just rhetoric.

5

Water and Health

Devon R. Goss and Kathryn Strother Ratcliff

Water is life sustaining. We need water to hydrate every cell, tissue, and organ in our body, to carry nutrients around it, to remove waste products from it, and to help lubricate our joints. We need water for basic sanitation functions like washing, for food preparation, and for the growth of healthy foods like fruit and vegetables. Water is needed for raising livestock and the crops they consume. Clean water supports various freshwater and saltwater food sources. Water also affects human health in more peripheral quality-of-life ways. For example, having clean and safe waterways allows individuals to experience health-improving recreation and exercise activities such as swimming, sailing, rowing, and fishing. Americans make nearly two billion trips each year to enjoy a water vacation at the country's beaches, lakes, and rivers (Andreen 2004: 553). Imagine your life without a sufficient supply of clean water—but, alarmingly, that scenario is a reality for some and an increasing threat for all of us.

What happens when the available water isn't clean? Unsanitary water can have horrific and large-scale health consequences. An early classic public health example from the mid-nineteenth century is the Broad Street pump in London, the common water supply for the local community. The well water was polluted through the practice of throwing "night soil"—human excrement—out of windows (or storing it in the basement for later pickup by night-soil collectors). Unbeknownst at the time, the feces of an infected person were a potent transmitter of cholera, an often fatal intestinal disease; so this waste disposal practice had the potential of creating a major health problem in the area, as night soil leached into the ground water. In the case of the Broad Street pump in 1854, the infestation caused a cholera epidemic stopped only by the clever detective work of John

Snow, a local physician who collected data that revealed that cholera cases clustered around the infected pump. Before Snow's revelation that water was the origin of the transmission, no one had given a thought to the quality of drinking water and to the invisible microorganisms that might lurk undetected.

Even today, unsanitary water accounts for an alarming number of deaths from diarrheal illnesses across the globe. The Centers for Disease Control (CDC) reports that diarrhea is the second leading cause of death in children under five, killing about 801,000 young children each year (CDC 2015a). It is also the leading cause of malnutrition in these children (WHO 2013). Next, lack of access to clean water is conducive to poor hygiene, which results in blindness in 6 million people worldwide (*PLoS Medicine* Editorial 2009). Dirty water kills more people than wars and other forms of violence (Pflanz 2010). In the United States, unsanitary water is also a problem, as nearly 20 million people get sick each year from water contaminated by parasites, bacteria, or viruses (Duhigg 2009a). The risks, of course, are not limited to virulent organic contaminants. For instance, runoff from heavy rains can put contaminants (herbicides, pesticides, and manure) from industrialized agriculture (huge farms) and concentrated animal feeding operations (CAFOs) into a nearby stream, estuary, or local aquifer. The contaminants include waterborne pathogens from manure such as Escherichia coli, which damages the lining of the small intestine and causes bloody diarrhea, and toxic chemicals from various pesticides that can cause cancer, neurodegenerative diseases (like Alzheimer's), diabetes, and reproductive and respiratory problems (Hernández et al. 2013; Mostafalou and Abdollahi 2013). Our extraction and processing of energy sources also pollutes waterways. Coal mining extraction and processing has contaminated surface waterways and ground water with a variety of heavy metals and chemicals such as arsenic, cadmium, lead, and sulfur compounds that produce cardiovascular disease, respiratory problems, kidney problems, and various rashes and diarrhea (Holzman 2011; Esch and Hendryx 2011; Simonton and King 2013). In addition, various industries have released toxic chemicals into our waterways—for example, General Electric has released PCBs into the Hudson and Housatonic Rivers—increasing the incidence of liver damage, reproductive damage, and cancer largely through eating fish from contaminated waters (ATSDR 2014). Other industries have released toxins such as arsenic into the water, which causes skin legions and bladder and skin cancer (Barry and Hughes 2008; Schwarzenbach et al. 2010), and mercury, which affects the brain and development (EPA 2014a). I will explore these "upstream" causes of poor health in this chapter.

Since water is a crucial element in maintaining human health and life, both the General Assembly of the United Nations and the World Health Organization (WHO) discuss water as a critical human right, essential to the realization of all rights, including the right to food, life, health, and dignity (WHO 2003). Because water is necessary to life itself and has been recognized by international organizations as an essential human right, any threat to access to good, quality water in adequate amounts is incredibly troubling and health threatening. Yet at this point in time most countries are not taking sufficient steps to ensure the long-term access to safe water for all. Instead we are allowing our water ecosystem to become seriously fouled.

To understand societal neglect of our water ecosystem and its implications for health, this chapter will explore first the concern with safe water accessibility and water insecurity, which threatens the survival of many communities around the globe. We will learn that scarcity is not just a natural phenomenon but one that can be exacerbated by social factors. Then, by literally looking up the stream, we will focus on the drivers of poor water conditions and causes of water pollution, which in turn results in poor health outcomes, sometimes not detectable for years. This will be followed by an outline of the efforts to improve water quality in the United States through regulation and legislation. The final section of this chapter will examine the growing commercialization of water, including the explosion in the consumption of bottled water, to illustrate again how a healthy water supply must begin with affordable access.

Water Insecurity: Problems with Basic Access to Safe Water

Water seems to be everywhere, but in fact water is scarce for our purposes. Although it covers 70 percent of the earth, only 1 percent of it is drinkable—by which I mean easily accessible fresh water; the rest is salinated ocean water or fresh water trapped under polar icecaps (Barlow and Clarke 2002; UN World Water Report 2004). Access to drinking water has been an issue in every human society: "water wars" date back 5,000 years (Gleick 2015). Worldwide 1.2 billion people lack adequate access to clean water and estimates predict that by 2025 this number will increase to 2.6 billion (*PLoS Medicine* Editorial 2009). Even though the United States is one of the most water-rich nations on the planet and has been able to utilize proportionally more water than other countries, this country experiences water scarcity on a regular basis. Witness, for example, the 2015 drought in California that threatened crops and led communities to ban residents from washing cars and watering lawns—among other activities that were once taken for granted. Other signs, too, indicate that the scarcity is not a new issue: ongoing disputes in Oregon around limiting the amount of river flow needed by local native tribes for fishing in order to preserve that water for farming (Barlow and Clarke 2002: 65); perpetual water wars in the southwest, as California, Colorado, Nevada, Arizona, Wyoming, Utah, New Mexico and Mexico try to claim shared water resources (such as the Colorado River) for their own populations; the predicted depletion of the Ogallala aquifer in the Midwest (Barlow and Clarke 2002: 15); and the fact that several large American cities like Las Vegas and Los Angeles have been built in deserts and require 200-mile-long pipelines to a water source.

Shortages also occur in particular areas, for instance in "colonias"— low-income, largely Latino/a communities located mostly along the border with Mexico, but also in urban areas such as Greater Houston. In many colonias the residents cannot afford hookups to the water system, or else they find the quality of the water unacceptable and unhealthy (Bernstein 2005; Jepson 2014). Overall, low-income Latino/a populations in Texas are three times more likely to be infected by waterborne illnesses than other populations (Evans and Kantrowitz 2002). More generally, the poorest and most marginalized communities are the most likely to lack access to clean and safe water (UN 2011). An unfortunate recent example is the water crisis in Flint, Michigan starting in 2014, when the Flint River became the source of drinking water and the resulting corrosion of pipes caused massive lead exposure, particularly harmful to children in poor families and in families of color. In smaller water systems, communities with higher proportions of Latinos/as and with renters (as opposed to home owners) receive drinking water with higher levels of nitrate (an increase of 0.44 mg $NO3/L$ was registered), which suggests inequality in the distribution of drinking water (Balazs et al. 2011). Nitrates are especially dangerous for children, leading to shortness of breath, decreases in cognitive functioning, and even death (Overmann 2015). Among the general American population, only 0.6 percent lack access to safe water or sanitation; however, 13 percent of Native American households do not have access to safe drinking water or basic sanitation. It is clear that access to water affects minorities disproportionately (UN 2011).

Across the world, 1.2 billion people live in areas where there is a threat to water availability (Kumar 2013), and the growth of megacities (in excess of 10 million people) will continue to strain nearby water supplies and the infrastructure needed to provide water. Many countries regularly suffer serious water shortages that are partly due to the topography itself; this natural factor makes daily life difficult. In parts of water-stressed Ethiopia, for example, reaching the shallow pools where one can collect water requires women to walk miles from their family homes, encountering a spectrum of dangers to their health as they do so. On top of that, the need for water doubles every twenty years, far ahead of the rate of human population growth—in fact it surpasses this rate more than twice (Barlow and Clarke 2002: 7). This increase in demand comes from the rise of water-hungry industries in an intensely globalized world. As other countries become industrialized in order to produce consumer goods long familiar to Americans, their water usage escalates. Export-oriented agribusiness, free trade zones producing goods for the global consumer elite, and general water waste put a serious strain on the water supply (Barlow and Clarke 2002: 7–8).

Water Scarcity in Other Countries

Although water has been an abundant resource in most locales in the United States, water scarcity seriously threatens many countries across the world. This phenomenon can occur for a number of reasons—droughts, overpopulation, pollution, or inadequate water infrastructure—and disproportionately affects women and girls, as they are typically in charge of cooking, cleaning, and farming for households. Health concerns of long-distance fetching include dangerous caloric expenditure for those who are malnourished, exposure to bacteria and diseases that may congregate around the water site (Sorenson et al. 2011), and chronic back and neck strain from carrying heavy loads of water over many miles (Crow and Sultana 2002). In some water-stressed countries, such as Kenya and Mozambique, collecting water significantly reduces the amount of time women and girls are able to spend at school (an indirect but significant corollary to health). Having women in rural areas participate in planning and implementing water systems can help reduce the costs of water scarcity and its health consequences for women. For example, women in Keur Moussa, Senegal reduced by half the amount of time they spend collecting water by taking active leadership roles in erosion control projects in their villages, helping stabilize soils, and allowing groundwater to collect in places it hadn't before (Dankelman et al. 2008).

A very different reason for water scarcity is the use of local water by multinational corporations. Mexico, for instance, is home to the second largest bottler of Coca-Cola. The bottling process requires more litres of water than the litres of Coke produced and has prompted Coca-Cola to make sure it has sufficient water resources at its disposal. President Vicente Fox of Mexico (who had been a manager of Coca-Cola operations) made generous concessions to the company, allowing it unprecedented access to the public water supply. The bottling company has paid a trivial amount (less than $40,000) to Mexico while running a plant with $40 million in profits. Locals are concerned that the amount extracted from the aquifer will jeopardize their access to water (Wooters 2008). In Plachimada, India, Coke faced opposition from residents to its bottling plant; the reason was not only water depletion, but also water pollution and the distribution of toxic waste sludge as fertilizer (Blanding 2011: 238–41).

The main cause of water insecurity in the United States is pollution. Recently the US Environmental Protection Agency (EPA) reported that more than half of the country's rivers and streams were in poor condition for aquatic life, due to excessive nitrogen, bacteria, and mercury levels (EPA 2013c). Additionally, nearly a quarter (22 percent) of our lakes were found to be in poor biological condition (EPA 2010). The pollution of waterways means unhealthy aquatic life, which in turn affects human health when individuals eat fish and other marine products like oysters, clams, crabs, and lobsters. More than four fifths (84 percent) of fish in American waters contain levels of mercury unsafe for human consumption, so the government now recommends that individuals limit the amount of fish consumed in order to avoid mercury poisoning (Biodiversity Research Institute 2013). This is ironic, since nutritionists recommend fish as a low-calorie food rich in health-promoting omega 3 fatty acids. Mercury acts on humans as a neurotoxin, interfering with the brain and development, and this makes it especially dangerous for pregnant women and small children (Bose-O'Reilly et al. 2010). Most benefits of eating fish are outstripped by these negative consequences for health.

Who Pollutes the Water in the United States?

Pollution in US water systems is caused by multiple sources, including manufacturing plants and the making of some heavily promoted products such as prescription drugs; but most pollution comes now from industrial agriculture and from energy sources such as drilling and transporting oil, mining coal and converting it to electricity, and hydraulic fracturing. In each case, water pollution is caused by powerful economic actors who do not factor long-term human health into their corporate decision-making. Once again, upstream actors—the industries that have made modern life possible—have a significant impact on human health.

Pollution from industrial agriculture

Agriculture places the heaviest demand on the water supply, using about 65 percent of all the water utilized by humans (USDA 2013), so it should not be surprising that considerable water pollution can also be traced to agriculture. Sediment—soil that has washed off fields into water supplies like nearby streams, estuaries, and other bodies of water—is the most prevalent source of agricultural water pollution (EPA 2014b). Food, like water, is essential to our survival, but how we cultivate our crops to meet large-scale demands should minimize any negative impact on both the quality of our food (see chapter 8) and on the quality of our water—a free-flowing natural resource. At this point in time, both are threatened.

Two aspects of industrial agriculture contribute most to the pollution of water: the manure produced in CAFOs and the use of increasing amounts of pesticides, herbicides, and fertilizers on large industrial farms. CAFOs have grown enormously over the last several decades. The United States had over 600,000 hog farms in the early 1980s; by 2011 the number was down to 70,000. However, don't be fooled by the huge decline in the sheer number of hog farms: what we are seeing here is a significant shift from small, manageable farms to tremendous agribusinesses. These produce a concentration of the industry wherein fewer farms are actually hosting ever larger total numbers of animals. Hog farms with more than 50,000 hogs have grown rapidly; those with fewer than 2,000 have lost ground steadily (Meyer 2012).

Huge numbers of animals correspondingly produce amounts of manure too copious to be distributed on local lands as fertilizer, as was the practice on the small family farm. At CAFOs the manure is often held in lagoons, but the lagoons may fail, or the liquefied manure might be allowed to run into streams and groundwater, emitting toxic gases (Barlow and Clarke 2002; see chapter 8 for a discussion of manure lagoons that fail). Lagoon failure was the problem in New River, North Carolina, where a large hog farm with an 8-acre, 12-foot-deep lagoon released 25 million gallons of hog feces and urine into the local estuary, promoting the growth of dinoflagellates, which in turn caused a major fish kill (Barker 1998). Human health impacts from leakage or lagoon failure come from various contaminants; these include over one hundred pathogenic organisms that can be found in manure, such as Salmonella, E. Coli, viruses, bacteria, and parasites, all of which can have acute negative effects on health— they can even cause death (Ebner 2007; Hribar and Schultz 2010). Of growing concern is a second type of contaminant, antibiotics and other veterinary pharmaceuticals from animal feed. Overexposure to these drugs can reduce their effectiveness in treating human illness, among other negative consequences. A third type of concern is over macronutrients like nitrogen from animal feed. When combined with oxygen, nitrogen produces nitrates that have been linked to blue-baby syndrome, respiratory diseases, hypothyroidism, birth defects, and general poor health (Burkholder et al. 2007; Hribar and Schultz 2010; EPA 2015a).

Another health impact of CAFOs is the creation of dead zones, areas of water uninhabitable to life, caused by the excess nitrogen and phosphorus from the huge amount of manure that is carried by runoff to nearby waterways. For instance, chicken farms on the Delmarva Peninsula in Maryland generate 1.1 billion pounds of chicken manure every year and are largely responsible for the dead zone that plagues the Chesapeake Bay (Rumpler 2010). The relation to human health is indirect, but dead zones mean fewer fish for human consumption and the overall degradation of our ecosystem, which has long-term effects on human health. The planet is an interconnected system. Death and disease anywhere along the food chain is not a healthy sign for humans.

In addition to the rise of CAFOs, we have witnessed the growth of large crop farms that produce our wheat, corn, and other vegetables and fruits and caused the decline of smaller family farms. This trend has led to a nutrient-deprived monoculture in the grocery produce aisle. In order to gain mass appeal, ship fresh food further, and increase the shelf life of these singular crops, industrial farms are using ever-increasing amounts of pesticides and herbicides (as will be noted in chapter 8), and these are in turn polluting our waterways. One billion pounds of industrial weed and bug killers are used in the United States every year and often run off into the water supply, contaminating the drinking water and endangering wildlife. Pesticides also pose a threat to private wells, which are not regulated by municipal water guidelines. More than half of the wells in the United States are contaminated with pesticides and nitrates (Barlow and Clarke 2002). General human health concerns with pesticides include cancer, neurodegenerative diseases (like Alzheimer's), diabetes, reproductive and respiratory problems, and chronic kidney disease (Hernández et al. 2013; Mostafalou and Abdollahi 2013). One widely used pesticide is atrazine (see chapter 7). When atrazine is sprayed on crops, it can wash into water supplies and has become one of the most common contaminants of drinking water in the United States (Duhigg 2009c). This contamination is particularly troubling, because even small amounts of atrazine present in drinking water have been linked to birth defects, low weight at birth, and preterm delivery (Villanueva et al. 2005).

The herbicide Roundup is discussed in chapter 8. It is spread increasingly and liberally in the field, thanks to the popularity of "Roundup Ready" crops (crops that are not affected by this herbicide). While it won't harm genetically modified plants, Roundup is harmful for human health. Its active ingredient, glyphosate, has dangerous properties when consumed in excess. The EPA states that glyphosate has the potential to cause breathing problems and lung damage when present in drinking water over the suggested threshold for human safety (EPA n.d.). But the story does not stop there. Roundup is not a pure glyphosate but a mixture of chemicals: it contains "adjuvants" that enhance the effectiveness of the glyphosate, and research shows that this cocktail is up to 125 times more toxic than glyphosate alone (Mesnage et al. 2014: 7). This finding runs counter to the public relations statements of the manufacturers, who have made Roundup sound like a safe herbicide. "This inconsistency between scientific fact and industrial claim may be attributed to huge economic interests, which have been found to falsify health risk assessments and delay health policy decisions" (Mesnage et al. 2014: 7).

Fertilizers are also culprits in water pollution. Large-scale corn production requires extensive additions of nitrogen to the soil, nearly half of which are not absorbed by the plants and instead join the runoff from the fields. It is estimated that agricultural sources are responsible for more than 70 percent of the nitrogen and phosphorus delivered to the Gulf of Mexico, where dead zones are a serious problem (Heffernan et al. 2010).

While some of the runoff travels great distances to cause harm, the quality of water in communities proximate to industrial farms is at even greater risk. According to demographic studies, racial minorities are more likely than white individuals to live near large factory farms, which increases their potential for being exposed to unsanitary drinking water conditions (Wing and Wolf 2000; Wilson et al. 2002). Living near a CAFO has more serious health consequences than downstream exposure to contaminated water, since the nearby residents are exposed not only to concentrated water pollution but also to low air quality, with reported health problems such as irritation to throat, eyes, and nose, a general decline in the quality of life, and mental health disorders. Clearly the siting of CAFOs near low-income communities with minority residents presents yet another example of an environmental equity issue that contributes to health disparities (Wilson et al. 2002).

Pollution from the energy industry

Water pollution can also be traced to the extraction and transportation of energy, including of oil, coal, and natural gas. Environmental damage from the Santa Barbara Oil drilling rig spill in 1969, the nearby underground pipe line spill in 2015, the Exxon Valdez oil transport disaster in Alaska in 1989, and the British Petroleum Deepwater Horizon drilling disaster off New Orleans in 2010 all made international headlines (see chapters 4 and 6 for further discussion). Less well known is the impact of waste products from oil drilling on human health. How communities work with industry to handle waste can reveal its effect on public health.

In oil-friendly Louisiana, for example, drilling waste was declared to be non-toxic, which allowed oil companies to dump waste at little cost. The lack of regulation for drilling waste in Louisiana led to mass exposure to hydrogen sulfide, which can cause headaches, nausea, and eye and mucous membrane irritation. A court suit against Exxon ended up in a settlement sealed from the public, so the evidence about specific health harms in that case will never be known. While this outcome limits justice for the people harmed, it was hardly a surprise, given the fact that Exxon was following Louisiana laws, which were passed by legislators who had cozy relations with the energy industry (Roberts and Toffolon-Weiss 2001). Next door in Alabama, on the other hand, the drilling waste has been more appropriately labeled as toxic, and a considerable charge is levied for dumping, so the government can adequately dispose of the waste.

Oil and those who profit from its extraction are not the only culprits. Coal is a major source of energy in the United States and worldwide and has serious health consequences for our water supply when it is mined, cleaned, burned, and converted into energy. Coal is first extracted, a process that puts miners at risk, then coal companies typically wash impurities from the mined coal. What is left over is sludge or slurry, a black liquid with dissolved minerals and chemicals. This waste is often injected back into mines or pooled in vast lagoons for disposal. The waste can then seep into the water table and reach residents. The amount of sludge is staggering. In one eight-mile radius in West Virginia, 1.9 billion gallons were injected in a five-year period. Elevated levels of heavy metals such as selenium, beryllium, and arsenic have been found in the drinking water in coal mining areas (Epstein et al. 2011: 82). The health consequences of these heavy metals include skin lesions, hair loss, and nerve damage (Fawell and Nieuwenhuijsen 2003), intestinal lesions (EPA 2013b), problems with the circulatory system, and possibly cancer (EPA 2013a). Other health impacts are congenital birth anomalies, which occur at a higher rate in mountaintop mining communities (Ahern et al. 2011), and coronary heart disease and heart attack morbidity, which have spiked in Appalachian coal mining areas (Hendryx and Zullig 2009). In 2014, Elk River in West Virginia suffered a toxic spill from a storage tank at a plant that produces chemicals used in the separation and cleaning of coal. The spill was upstream from the municipal water intake for Charleston, West Virginia, which meant that 300,000 residents lost access to potable water (Virginia Tech 2014). In this case, an entire city was suddenly without water to drink or wash, and returning to "normal" took weeks—if not months—of remediation and trepidation on the part of local citizens.

It doesn't take a dramatic accident for coal to be a major threat to our water supply. Coal-fired power plants are implicated as the largest source of toxic water pollution in the United States: they dump lead, mercury, and other heavy metals into watersheds on a regular basis (Duhigg 2009b). The Environmental Integrity Project found that nearly 70 percent of the coal-fired power plants surveyed were violating the Clean Water Act (CWA) by polluting public waters with arsenic, mercury, selenium, and other metals (Duggan et al. 2013). These pollutants are absorbed by aquatic animals and humans, through food and water consumption and water-based recreational activities, and have been found to be dangerous to human health, even at small levels (ATSDR 2011). The health horrors of coal ash, waste from the conversion of coal into electricity, have made front-page news. In 2008, 5.4 million cubic yards of coal ash flooded the community of Harriman, Tennessee and required more than a billion dollars for cleanup. More recently, in 2014, a North Carolina plant operated by Duke Energy, one of the largest electricity companies in the United States, leaked and caused a 70-mile gray sludge coating of the Dan River. Duke Energy has fourteen plants in North Carolina and over the decades has accumulated 100 million tons of coal ash stored in unlined earthen ponds near rivers and other bodies of water. Early warnings of problems began in 1986, but the company elected merely to monitor the coal ash and not to be proactive in developing dry, lined landfills away from waterways. The state did not demand any action because Duke is a powerful political player that spends millions on political contributions and maintains "a very close relationship with the state regulators" (Stahl 2014). North Carolina's failure to act led to US government involvement and ultimately a $102 million fine against Duke Energy.

Natural gas is widely cited by lobbyists as a cleaner alternative to coal. However, it was Pacific Gas and Electric's casual handling of toxic waste from a natural gas compressor station in Hinkley, California that led to the hexavalent chromium water pollution controversy exposed by local resident-turned-activist Erin Brockovich in the mid-1990s. More recently, environmental activists were among the first to draw attention to the risks associated with the relatively new but hotly debated process of hydraulic fracturing (or "fracking"), which involves capturing natural gas from shale. In some areas, fracturing presents a serious threat to the local water supply because the process uses so much water. In a period of less than two years, hydraulic fracturing used 65.8 billion gallons of water, an amount equivalent to what 2.5 million Americans use in a year. Many of the fracturing sites are in areas that are not water-rich. In fact "nearly half (47 percent) of the wells were developed in water basins with high or extremely high water stress" (Freyman and Salmon 2013).

In terms of direct consequences for health, fracking involves using high-pressure water injections with additives, many of which are carcinogenic or mutagenic, to increase fissures in the rock and to release natural gas used for energy to power homes and cars (Howarth et al. 2011; Soraghan 2011). Although gas companies claim that fracturing is one of the cleanest ways to produce energy, the practice carries the potential for waterways to be contaminated with both natural gas elements and the chemicals used in the process (Schmidt

2011). Groundwater around fracking sites has been found to be contaminated with methane, benzene, and hydrocarbons, which can cause reproductive problems, neurotoxicity, premature birth, not to mention explosions (McDermott-Levy et al. 2013; Casey et al. 2015; Kassotis et al. 2015). Recently the drinking water of residents near active hydraulic fracturing sites was found to contain methane levels seventeen times higher than those of the water of residents who lived in areas without drilling (Osborn et al. 2011).

Although few studies exist that examine the health impacts of ingesting methane, many residents who live close to natural gas fracturing sites complain of myriad health issues, including asthma, muscle pain, and nosebleeds (Schmidt 2011). The EPA began to investigate the potential for fracking pollution in Dimock, Pennsylvania, where Cabot Oil and Gas Corporation operated, but terminated the study before coming to a conclusion. Dimock residents protested the EPA decision, arguing that the findings to date had suggested that fracturing was linked to dangerous methane levels in water (Drajem 2013). The discontinuation of the study, however, coincided with the timing of the Obama administration's push for natural gas drilling (Banerjee 2013), suggesting that science was not the only determinant of policy. Politics was clearly a force in the approval of what is known as the "Halliburton Loophole" (after the powerful energy corporation that would benefit most), which exempts the process of fracturing from the pollution regulations set out by the CWA, making it difficult for the government to regulate any potential pollution (Soraghan 2011).

Pharmaceuticals and Water Pollution

In any single month, about half of Americans (48.7 percent, according to the CDC) take at least one prescription drug. That's a lot of drugs, which unfortunately don't stay in the individual effecting a cure, but find their way into our lakes, rivers, and drinking water as they exit our bodies, are discarded in our toilets, are released during manufacture, or otherwise enter the waste stream. Once there, as biologically active substances, they have the potential of affecting the ecosystem, the well-being of marine life, and the health of people. The impact on the ecosystem is understudied, though the work of Emma Rosi-Marshall has begun to document serious effects. Another group of researchers has studied the extent of pollutants in Lake Michigan. They began with the working assumption that Lake Michigan was so big that drugs entering it would be diluted to the point of being undetectable. They were wrong. They found evidence of thirty-two pharmaceuticals and personal care products, fourteen of which were at concentrations that indicated medium or high ecological risk (Blair et al. 2013). Municipal wastewater treatment facilities are usually not designed to deal with complex pharmaceuticals (Verlicchi et al. 2010), hence drugs can enter our drinking water; and they do so undetected, since the EPA is not checking on any pharmaceuticals in our drinking water. Making drugs from "green chemistry" does offer some hope (Scudellari 2015).

Pollution from other industries

Fossil fuels and large-scale agribusiness are not the only industrial threats to potable water. Other upstream sources contribute significantly. The growth of plastics and other chemical compounds used in manufacturing has been linked to water pollution and illness. High on the list of hazardous contaminants are polychlorinated biphenyls (PCBs), organic compounds classified as "persistent organic pollutants," which were once used widely to make plastics as well as industrial lubricants and coolants, among other things. The EPA now considers PCBs to be a probable human carcinogen and prohibits industrial discharges (ATSDR 2014). The primary health hazard from PCBs in water comes from eating fish. Research testing blood samples shows elevated PCB readings for residents near PCB-contaminated rivers (Fitzgerald et al. 2007) and serious health effects for children who were exposed in utero. For example, pregnant women who consumed a moderate amount of fish from PCB-contaminated waters were found to have children with more deficits in intelligence, object recognition, and motor functioning than children not exposed to PCBs in utero (Darvill et al. 2000; Schantz et al. 2003). Even small amounts of exposure to PCBs have been shown to cause irritation to the skin and eyes (Ross 2004). Other research on exposure to PCBs in the soil and air indicates that it exacerbates diabetes (Silverstone et al. 2012) and a myriad of cardiovascular, gastrointestinal, and neurological problems (ATSDR 2014), causing additional concerns around water-borne PCBs.

Monsanto manufactured PCBs in Alabama for three decades, ending in the 1970s. As noted in chapter 4, dumping and leakage of the product into the water and soil around the plant caused health problems for residents, such as skin disorders, liver cancer, and diabetes (Israel 2012). Monsanto knew as early as 1937 that PCBs were a serious health hazard (Robin 2010: 16), but denied the hazard.

Monsanto sold PCBs to major manufacturers, including General Electric (GE), which used them to insulate equipment from over-heating in its Fort Edward and Hudson Falls capacitor plants along the Hudson River in New York and in its Pittsfield plant on the Housatonic River, which flows from Massachusetts through Connecticut to the Long Island Sound. As early as the 1970s, GE engineers noted that PCBs contain "known or suspected carcino-gens"; "have been of environmental concern since the 1960s"; and are a "matter of growing concern as to their effect on some species of wildlife" (quoted from internal GE memos in Lyons 2014). Reminiscent of the tobacco industry's decades of blatant denial regarding the health risks of cigarettes, CEO John F. Welch Jr. spoke at a 1998 GE shareholder meeting, saying "PCBs do not pose health risks" (Welch and Daly 1998: 24), despite clear company knowledge that they do.

GE went further in following the "tobacco playbook" when it hired former government employees like Ann R. Klee, who had worked with the EPA and had insider information on the various processes of government oversight of environmental issues. During a 2012 depo-sition regarding the Hudson River, Klee, as GE's vice president of Corporate Environmental Programs, said that there are "no adverse health effects associated with PCBs," an opinion in conflict with that of her former employer, the EPA (quoted in Lyons 2014). In addition, GE knew some basic methodological tricks to make PCB research results come out favorably: one GE study followed people for only five years (the latency period for serious problems is longer) and included workers such as secretaries, who were not exposed much to PCBs and whose inclusion would weaken the relationship found. Finally, GE designed a multimillion-dollar public relations campaign to control the media discourse. The campaign aired ideas to "create" a "climate" favorable to the company, "lead with GE science," and "establish intelligence networks at regulatory agencies" (http://web.timesun-ion.com/ge_dredging/graphics/1993_memo_of_capacitors_found_in_ river.pdf). GE has spent millions on lobbying, political campaign contributions, and corporate front groups (such as the Citizens for a Sound Economy) and has successfully worked to weaken health and environmental standards (Donohoe and Robinson 2010).

An enduring difficulty with many long-latency health issues, but particularly with those that come from water and other environ-mental exposures, is that the issue is often found decades after the harmful deeds have been done. Thus one finds in today's news media coverage of a water-borne health problem that has its source in practices done decades ago. As this chapter was being written, two health- and water-related situations became news long after the pollution occurred. One involves DuPpont, which has been dumping the chemical C8 into the Ohio River since the late 1950s and is suspected of causing kidney cancer and other health problems (Welsh-Huggins 2015); the other involves Mallinckrodt US LLC, responsible for dumping tons of mercury into Maine's Penobscot River since the late 1960s (Maine Supreme Judicial Court 2014). These discoveries set important precedents; but, for those affected, they come too late.

Clean Water Legislation

Water is clearly vital to human health, and in many ways the government has recognized this basic principle. The general regulation to improve waterways and drinking water in the United States is the CWA, which became law in 1972, during the Nixon presidency, bearing hopes that it would help protect waterways from pollution and restore those already contaminated. At the time the CWA was passed, the country's waterways were in crisis. Two thirds of the lakes, rivers, and coastal waters in the United States were designated as unsafe for human recreational use (Milazzo 2006). Additionally, 87 percent of swordfish samples contained dangerous levels of mercury, which rendered them unfit for human consumption (Adler et al. 1993: 5). Although Nixon vetoed the Act due to the expense of cleaning up the nation's water, he was ultimately supportive of the overall mission of the Act, which became law when Congress overturned his veto. Despite protests and objections to the bill from corporations and small business owners, the CWA had a surprising amount of bipartisan support (Milazzo 2006).

The CWA did indeed improve the quality of the nation's waterways by decreasing industrial pollution and by stemming the loss of wetlands (Andreen 2013). One of the best examples of success is the cleanup of the Cuyahoga River in Cleveland, Ohio. The river caught on fire in 1969, when sparks ignited oil-soaked debris that polluted the waters from industrial waste. After the passage of the CWA the river underwent a serious cleanup effort, and now is home to more than forty types of fish (Maag 2009). Yet reports on the overall success of the CWA are mixed. While the EPA said that 93 percent of major industrial facilities and 87 percent of major municipal facilities were in compliance with clean water standards in 1990 (Glicksman and Batzel 2010), a 2003 EPA survey "found that the rate of significant noncompliance with the CWA among 6,600 major facilities—those with the largest discharges—was approximately 25 percent" (Rechtschaffen 2004: 3). Then, in 2005, over 600 major facilities reported that they violated their permitted discharge limits about every other month (Glicksman and Batzel 2010). The high and continuing noncompliance figures are due in part to failure at the state level, which is sometimes attributed to the existence of close ties between industry and government—as in the cases of Duke Energy and the North Carolina government, or Exxon and the Louisiana government. Noncompliance also stems from a lack of resources for combatting anti-regulatory forces at both the state and the federal level; from the failure of the federal EPA to do more because of the loyalties of regional EPA administrators to their states; and from the threat of political backlash in case the federal government intervenes against corporate interests (Rechtschaffen 2004).

Despite these failures, the CWA is actually more successful in mitigating industrial and municipal pollution than in regulating wastewater from agribusiness. This is because the CWA only enables the EPA to regulate contaminants that move through pipes, that is, "point sources," as opposed to chemicals that may be sprayed or spread in the course of agricultural processes and result in the contamination of groundwater from runoff or seepage, that is, "non-point sources" (Brown and Foemke 2012). Thus the CWA has no authority over the environmental damage from CAFOs and large industrial crop farming, since all this is non-point-source pollution. This lack of oversight has meant that agriculture is "responsible for up to three-quarters of the pollution in the waters with the poorest quality" (Glicksman and Batzel 2010).

A proposal by the EPA to expand its scope so as to include standing waters such as ponds, wetlands, and ditches met defeat in the fall of 2015, when the US Court of Appeals for the Sixth Circuit issued a nationwide stay against the adoption of a wider definition (Adler 2015). The opposition and the successful political pressure that defeated the new rule came from "many of the same polluters discharging millions of pounds of toxics into our waterways" (Fields 2015: 9). These industries have joined together to form the "Waters Advocacy Coalition," a front group that lobbies against the "vigorous enforcement of the Clean Water Act by the EPA" (Fields 2015: 13). US Representative James Oberstar (D-Minn), whose House Committee was responsible for many water quality issues, concluded in 2009: "Without oversight and enforcement, companies will use our lakes and rivers as dumping grounds—and that's exactly what is apparently going on" (Duhigg 2009a: 4).

The Commodification of Water

Despite the relatively plentiful supply of water in the United States and despite the UN discussion of access to water as a basic human right, access to water as a public good is being threatened by commodification. Commodification refers to the buying and selling of an item in the normal process of capitalism—a commercial exchange with rules largely set by for-profit companies and with little input from the democratic process. The commercialization of water ends up profiting only a handful of individuals while simultaneously limiting poor people's access to a crucial resource. Since health requires access to water, the trajectory of increasing commodification is concerning. In defense of the bottled-water industry, Peter Brabeck, the CEO of Nestlé, responded to the idea that water should be a human right by saying: "That's an extreme solution. And the other view says that water is a foodstuff like any other, and like any other foodstuff it should have a market value" (https://www.youtube.com/watch?v=TPY64EJcsG4). An alternative to Brabeck's philosophy is that water is more like air than like food. It's a naturally occurring resource. There is no cost to produce water (or air), as there is cost for farmers and food companies to produce food; there is only a cost to move the water from a source to the public via reservoirs and pipelines, and sometimes to clean it. That cost is typically small, making the price of water to people quite reasonable; and the small cost is far from being "an extreme solution," if determined by a public process that is not profit-minded.

Despite the human rights argument, turning water into a commodity is a reality (Bayliss 2014). The World Bank and the International Monetary Fund encourage the privatization of water (Prud'homme 2011: 267); some municipalities have turned to private companies to provide residents with water; and, in US states where landownership gives people unlimited rights to the ground water below the land, landowners are seeking multimillion dollar bids for access to "their" water. Thus T. Boone Pickens, a billionaire Texas business financier, envisions the Ogallala aquifer beneath his property as "surplus water," an asset in need of a market (Prud'homme 2011: 262). Texas has a "rule of capture" law (unofficially known as "pump or perish") that allows unlimited pumping of groundwater, even if it drains all water from an adjacent property. If a billionaire can win access to water and other, less powerful people can lose it, that's a serious public health problem.

The commodification of Water: Privatization

Because of the difficulty that municipalities in the United States have in funding their water systems, there has been a recent push to privatize municipal water. This has generated new concerns about water access. The privatization of water involves transferring some of the assets or operations from public water systems to the private sphere. This transfer can occur at any stage of the system, from water treatment and testing to the operations of the entire system (Gleick et al. 2002). Privatization is most often driven by technical concerns, for instance problems with an infrastructure in need of repairs, and by financial considerations, as privatization can be a way to help municipalities balance their budgets.

While the majority of Americans receive their water from public water systems, around 73 million Americans obtain water services from privately owned water systems or from water systems run under a public–private partnership. Private drinking water is a 4.3-billion-dollar business annually (National Association of Water Companies 2011). Atlanta became the largest municipality to privatize its water system: it did so in 1998, when United Water, a subsidiary of the French company Suez, was put in control of the city's water system in a twenty-year, 428-million-dollar contract (Jehl 2003). However, budgetary and transparency issues, as well as failure to abide by the terms of the contract, eventually led to the dissolution of the agreement between Atlanta and United Water in 2003, and the city water system is now back in public hands.

In 2002, in Stockton, California, Mayor Gary Podesto awarded a $600-million contract to a Colorado-based corporation, OMI, and to a London-based corporation, Thames Water. The contract included full control over the city's water and sewage systems for twenty years. Concerned citizens protested and the contract was eventually annulled in 2006, when a judge ruled that the corporation had violated California environmental laws and ordered the municipality of Stockton to resume control over the water system. Other communities that have fought water privatization successfully are Nashville, Tennessee; Birmingham, Alabama; Pekin, Illinois; Huber Heights, Ohio; and Orange County, California (Barlow and Clarke 2002).

Most observers of the privatization of public water systems worry that this phenomenon would make a public good upon which our health depends so expensive that poor people would no longer afford it. For example, the privatization of water systems in Buenos Aires, Argentina and in Manila, Philippines resulted in substantial increases in water rates for citizens, although the water systems operate more efficiently under privatization. The higher rates mean even more strife and hardship for those already living in poverty (Estache and Trujillo 2003; Wu and Malaluan 2008). In some areas the cost of privatized water is so high that people resort to drinking contaminated water (Jaffee and Newman 2013).

The privatization of water systems also jeopardizes the public's ability to exercise oversight of water systems; its power to resolve disputes and renegotiate contracts is compromised at a time when the quality of water may not be protected (Gleick et al. 2002). Communities of citizens in other countries have seen their public water supply dry up and leave people with no recourse.

The privatization of water has led to dramatic conflicts around the world (Prud'homme 2011: 276). In Cochabamba, Bolivia in 1999, the local government signed a long-term lucrative contract with Aguas del Tunari, a consortium company controlled mostly by US interests, in order to privatize the water system (Finnegan 2002). The privatization of Cochabamba's water system was strongly encouraged and facilitated by international organizations like the World Bank and the International Monetary Fund, without regard for how these changes would affect the price of water for citizens (Barlow and Clarke 2002). After Aguas del Tunari took over the city's water system, water rates for the citizens increased by nearly 35 percent (Barlow and Clarke 2002). The people of Cochabamba protested the privatization of their water system by taking to the streets in the hundreds of thousands. After a week they succeeded in having President Hugo Banzer denounce the governmental contract with Aguas del Tunari.

In the United States the bottled-water industry was minimal until well into the 1970s, but afterwards its growth has been explosive and transformed an elite niche product into a nearly ubiquitous consumer object (Jaffee and Newman 2013). While Americans drank a mere 1.6 gallons of bottled water in 1976, by 2014 average drinking had increased to 34 gallons per year (International Bottled Water Association 2014). The success of the bottled-water industry came primarily from a media campaign that played on consumers' fears about the safety of tap water. The convenience and fashionableness of bottled water played a role too. This success is really impressive: the industry sold individuals a commodity that was already freely available (Gleick 2011). The largest bottled-water retailer in America is the Swiss corporation Nestlé, which has been the center of protests from local residents in several states—most notably in Michigan and Maine, where this corporation has pumped spring water. Spring water is an official Food and Drug Administration (FDA) designation, which means that the water is pumped directly from a spring or from a borehole that has a hydrological connection to a surface spring. Such a coveted designation has placed considerable pressure on springs, a particularly fragile and vulnerable water resource (Hall 2009: 22). In addition, the pumping can affect surrounding ground water, and thus the local supply of water. Without the citizens' knowledge, Nestlé began to purchase and bottle millions of gallons of water annually from the town springs in Fryeburg, Maine, in order to use them in one of its popular labels, Poland Springs. At times, Fryeburg's citizens were forced to go without tap water, yet Nestlé was still able to collect water for its bottling plant (Royte 2008).

Health risks associated with bottled water stem not only from decreased access to water in some locations, as in Maine, or from a slippery slope argument that corporations can reasonably set a market value on access. Environmental and individual health damage also results from manufacturing the bottles, from transporting the water and the bottles, and from disposing of the bottles. Manufacturing so many bottles, most of which are designed for individual one-time consumption, requires tens of millions of barrels of oil per year (Hall 2009), which come accompanied by all the health risks that oil extraction, transport, and use involve. And then even the water that has been stored in those bottles can put its consumers' health in jeopardy. For a long time Bisphenol A (BPA) was used in making the plastic bottles and could leach into the water that was to be consumed. According to the National Institute of Health (NIH), "some animal studies report effects in fetuses and newborns exposed to BPA," and exposure is well known and widespread in the general public (https://www.niehs.nih.gov/health/topics/agents/sya-bpa). Storage conditions, which are not regulated, can have further implications for health. The longer water is stored in plastic bottles (in homes or on grocery-store shelves), the higher its concentration of harmful bacteria colonies, especially when the temperature of the storage area varies substantially (Raj 2005). In contrast, storing tap water at varied temperatures causes only a minimal bacterial growth.

The impact of commodified bottled water extends to the transportation of water from a source to a bottling plant and then to retail outlets, with all the pollution that comes from trucks, boats and planes and the fuel they burn. One of the most egregious examples of transportation waste is that of Fiji bottled water, the second most imported brand of bottled water in the United States. The water is pumped from an aquifer in the Fijian rainforest and then shipped to the United States, traveling more than 5,000 miles and generating 190 tons of carbon dioxide in the process (Royte 2008) before it arrives in American grocery stores. Ironically, the Republic of Fiji itself experiences water deprivation, as this island country in Melanesia lacks the proper infrastructure to deliver clean and plentiful drinking water to its own population. Thus in 2007 half of Fijians didn't have access to clean water, while relatively affluent consumers around the world could drink bottled natural artesian water from Fiji (Royte 2008).

Combined, the energy used to pump, process, transport, and chill bottled water consumes more than 50 million barrels of oil annually (Arnold and Larsen 2006). The environmental footprint of bottled water is noticeably more damaging than that of tap water—one litre of bottled mineral water generates 600 times more carbon dioxide than one litre of tap water (Fry 2008). After use, of course, all these bottles need to be disposed. Although bottled water is usually produced in recyclable plastic bottles, the recycling rate for these bottles is very low (around 13 percent), which means that the majority of bottled-water containers end up in a landfill, strewn around the landscape, or swirling around our oceans. In 2005 alone, 2 million tons of plastic bottles used for bottled water ended up in landfills (Olso, with Poling and Solomon 1999; also visit http://www.nrdc.org/water/drinking/bw/bwinx.asp). The Great Pacific Garbage Patch is the largest of several swirling oceanic gyres filled with mainly plastic refuse—a stunning visual reminder of the amount of garbage that human beings produce and that ends up in the water.

Great Pacific Garbage Patch

The Great Pacific Garbage Patch is an area of garbage, especially plastic, that has collected in the middle of the Pacific Ocean; it takes up roughly the same amount of space as the state of Texas. The garbage patch is located in the North Pacific subtropical gyre, which creates a clockwise rotation of water currents, trapping the garbage inside the gyre and adding to the mass of the garbage patch. The plastic that is collected in the middle of the ocean is dangerous to the seabirds, fish, and turtles who ingest it. Citizens have used the Great Pacific Garbage Patch as a rallying cry for the elimination of plastic, including the ban on plastic shopping bags. The fact that Midway Island, 2,000 miles from the nearest continent, is littered with plastic garbage is astounding (https://vimeo.com/25563376).

Although tap water is generally as safe as, or safer than, bottled water, there are still issues with the country's municipal water systems. Unincorporated communities are not covered by these systems and instead draw their water through groundwater wells. These communities are often populated by racial minorities or by poorer individuals who have few options if their groundwater is contaminated (Ranganathan and Balazs 2015). In order to keep the need for bottled water at bay, it is essential for public water systems to be updated so that tap water is consistently safe and pure. Two years after the CWA was enacted in 1972, the Safe Drinking Water Act became law. In contrast to the CWA, which governs the nation's streams, lakes, and other waterways, the Safe Drinking Water Act has the sole function to assure the safety of drinking water (Knotts 1999). Before its enactment, 30 percent of the nation's drinking water samples contained chemicals in excess of the Public Health Service limits (Adler et al. 1993: 5). Despite this important legislation, however, since 2004 62 million Americans have been exposed to municipal-provided drinking water that did not meet government health guidelines (Duhigg 2009d).

The reasons for this exposure to chemicals in public drinking water systems are twofold. First, the Safe Drinking Water Act has been slow to update the contaminants that the Act regulates. Although there are 60,000 chemicals that are used within the United States, the Safe Drinking Water Act only regulates ninety-one contaminants, the most recent update to the list having occurred in 2000 (Duhigg 2009d). Second, the public water systems' crumbling infrastructure also makes providing citizens with clean and safe drinking water difficult. In Canada, water system infrastructure problems are particularly prominent in First Nation territories and have been blamed for the introduction of contaminants into local water supplies that caused health problems such as chronic skin disorders (Mascarenhas 2007).

Although the need to update the infrastructure of US water systems is well acknowledged, finding the funds in order to make the improvements is difficult (Royte 2008). According to the American Water Works Association, the nation's drinking water systems will need as much as a 1-trillion-dollar investment in updating and upgrading its infrastructure (American Water Works Association 2010), and the process will require considerable political will and commitment. Some observers recommend a compromise whereby some aspects of building infrastructure and cleaning the water could be in the hands of private corporations, as long as oversight of the process would guarantee reasonable, affordable access for the public (Gleick 2015). Even the Cato Institute, a libertarian stronghold, is cautious: "Many privatizations have been troublesome. Proper supervision has been missing. Regulatory bodies charged with enforcing contracts have been nonexistent, incompetent or too weak" (Prud'homme 2011: 277).

Conclusion

Water is a clear example of the global interconnectivity of life and of our shared future. Water can be captured in the short run by a particular country or locale, but in the end it belongs to the Earth's reservoir, evaporating and returning according to the hydrologic cycle that governs it. Because humans need water to live, any decrease in access to safe water is a serious threat to human health and life. Looking upstream and identifying the social determinants that threaten a clean water supply is critical to protecting this essential resource and preserving our health.

Although the United States is one of the most water-rich countries on the planet, water-based injustice still occurs within this country. While the most marginalized members of society are often at greater risk of experiencing a shortage of clean water, we have seen in this chapter that water scarcity and pollution affects everyone. To examine why these phenomena are present among us and affecting our health, I have looked upstream, searching for connections to power and the political economy, and noted a variety of large agricultural, energy extraction, and manufacturing practices that have endangered our health.

Compounding the threat of pollution are the issues of scarcity and access. The fact that the Colorado River stopped flowing into the Gulf of California for fifty years and is now only restored to 1 percent of its historic flow suggests a serious problem of demand exceeding supply (Postel 2014). Access is becoming an even bigger issue, due to the commodification of water and its potential to render the purchase of sufficient amounts too pricey for many Americans.

There is nothing more central to our health than clean water; and this chapter has demonstrated that looking just at the condition of our water is not enough. We need to understand the powerful political and economic factors affecting those conditions. Corporate power—such as that behind coal-to-energy operations like Duke Energy, oil-drilling waste producers in Louisiana, hog farms in New River, North Carolina, fracking industries like Halliburton, and bottlers like Nestlé—needs to hear loud and clear that, when it comes to clean water, disregard for a public good produces disastrous consequences for the health of all humans. Part of the message will come from clean water legislation that is strong and consistently enforced. The huge EPA fine ($102 million) recently levied against Duke Energy could be an important first step in sending this message in a way that cannot be ignored.

It is in everyone's interest and for the sake of future generations to make sure that this ever-returning resource becomes and remains clean and able to sustain our health. A threat to the health of small water creatures is an early warning that human health might be at stake. Once again, the wisdom of the precautionary principle seems evident. When there are many credible indications that toxins abound in our water, then waiting for absolute proof is not smart. To go back to the Broad Street Pump example mentioned at the beginning of this chapter, two observers noted: "If the government officials in London had demanded absolute certainty, no preventive measures would have been taken for another thirty years until the cholera bacterium (*Vibrio cholera*) was identified" (Michaels and Monforton 2005: S45). The cholera epidemic deaths that would have resulted from inaction are unimaginable.

6
Automobiles and Health

The automobile, America's ubiquitous symbol of homegrown inge-nuity and personal freedom, has served to shape the urban landscape and define modern society in the twentieth century. Although other forms of moving people from place to place are important, I focus here on the automobile because it has come to dominate the personal transportation options available in many parts of the world and clearly demonstrates the role of the social determinants of health (SDoH) and their widespread consequences for health. While cars may appeal to an individual's thirst for adventure and autonomy, our collec-tive dependence on the automobile has seriously polluted the air we breathe, as well as the ground and the water around us; has killed and injured many people; and has altered the built environment in unhealthy ways. Each of these issues merits detailed investigation and raises specific questions. What are the health risks associated with our fossil fuel-driven economy and how might our automotive infra-structure compound these risks? How have economic actors, politi-cal choices, and power dynamics contributed to the development of this dependence on cars for personal transportation, or to the closely related dependence on diesel buses and on trucks, not trains, for cargo shipments? Finally, what efforts have been made to alleviate this general "automobile effect" on health, and what remains to be done?

Health Impacts of the Automobile, Trucks, and Buses: Pollution, Crashes, and Global Warming

A major health impact of our use of automobiles comes from the pollution produced by the gasoline-powered internal combustion engine. Early on, this pollution was made especially toxic through the unnecessary introduction of leaded gasoline. The use of leaded gasoline was phased out in the 1970s; but today, even without lead, exhaust from gas-powered road vehicles is still a major contributor to principal air pollutants, accounting for 77 percent of the carbon monoxide, 28 percent of the small particulate matter, 47 percent of the volatile organic compounds, and 56 percent of the nitrogen oxides (Ewing and Kreutzer 2006).

Leaded Gasoline

Gasoline or petrol does not naturally come with lead and when lead is added to gasoline, the combination is much more danger-ous for health than gasoline alone. Lead is an additive, a known poison, and a very potent neurotoxin. The story of how we ended up using leaded gasoline for about fifty years goes back to the 1920s. Automobile manufacturers ran into "knocking" problems when cars using high-octane gasoline accelerated. Then General Motors (GM) began experimenting with additives and found that tetraethyl lead (TEL) effectively stopped the knocking. Despite some existing non-toxic solutions to the knocking problem, adding TEL to gasoline became the preferred solution due to the vested interest of GM, holder of an early patent on TEL. GM contracted with DuPont (with whom it had an interlocking directorate rela-tionship) and formed the Ethyl Gasoline Corporation, dedicated to producing and marketing the TEL (Hollaender and Storrer 2014).

The direct health effects of vehicle emissions come from gases, such as carbon monoxide and nitrogen oxides, and also from tiny solids—small particulate matter—and include asthma, diminished lung function, chronic obstructive pulmonary disease, cancer, cardi-opulmonary problems, cerebrovascular problems, premature aging of lung tissues, and cardiovascular mortality (Bullard 2005; Boothe and Shendell 2008; Boehmer et al. 2013; American Lung Association 2013). The tiny solids ("ultrafine" particulate matter) are of increas-ing concern, as research shows that these ultrafine particles can not only get deep into the lungs but also migrate into the vascular system, where they cause increased blood pressure and increase the risk of cardiovascular disease (Chung et al. 2015; Corlin 2015). Particularly vulnerable are children, elderly people, and those with pre-existing conditions such as asthma, cardiovascular disease, and diabetes (American Lung Association 2013). Recent work has suggested that prenatal exposure to transportation pollution can have serious effects on fetuses: a pregnant woman's exposure to traffic-related air pollution is related to the incidence of autism in the baby (Roberts et al. 2013), low birth weight, and infant mortality (American Lung Association 2013). Prenatal exposure to airborne hydrocarbons is associated with cancer risk in newborns (Ewing and Kreutzer 2006).

In contrast to many other sources of air pollution, vehicles are mobile sources that release exhaust at the ground level, where people are living, walking, and biking (Kinney et al. 2000). Thirty-five million people live within 300 feet of a major road, which exposes them to traffic-related air pollution at the place of their residence (APHA 2010). In urban areas, pedestrians and bikers are in constant contact with exhaust fumes. Although transportation is not the only source of urban air pollution, vehicle emissions are the main reason why many air quality districts in the United States are not in compliance with the 1970 Clean Air Act's National Ambient Air Quality Standards (Bullard 2005). Moreover, the demographics of exposure to polluted air reveal a significant bias: while 57 percent of whites live in a county that does not meet at least one of the Environmental Protection Agency (EPA)'s ambient air quality standards, the percentage rises to 65 for African Americans and to 80 for Latinos/as (Bullard 2005). Why this is so becomes clear when we discuss the building of interstate highways and busy arterials through urban areas.

Clean Air Act

Since automobiles and other road vehicles contribute so much to our air pollution problem, regulatory remedies mainly designed to protect our health have been vital. In the United States the primary legislation is the Clean Air Act of 1970 (APHA 2010: 3), which has been periodically amended (in 1977 and 1990). The Act has been hotly contested, since it requires changes in vehicles. Leading up to the 1990 amendments, industry money that sought to influence the debate was considerable: the members of the House Energy and Commerce Committee received an average of $15,000 each, up to a total of $612,000; GM paid lawyers and lobbyists $1.8 million to fight clean air legislation; political action committees (PACs) of GM, Chrysler, and Ford gave nearly 2 million to congressional candidates; and other industry PACs invested $23 million in fighting clean air legislation (Luger 2000: 160). The environmental forces and public opinion have been strong enough to prevent the industry from prevailing as much as it would have liked, but industry forces were still successful in delaying and weakening many aspects of the amendments. Current assessments by the EPA and other organizations continue to report that cleaner gas and more stringent vehicle standards are needed. Air pollution, a large part of which comes from vehicles, continues to remain deadly for many people and health altering for others.

Diesel-powered trucks and buses, whose development followed the success of the automobile, present particular health risks since diesel exhaust emits fifteen times more small particles per mile than gas engines do (Gentner et al. 2012) and, as noted, these small particles penetrate deeply into the respiratory system, causing a lot of health damage. Urban dwellers in poorer areas of the city complain that, apart from having to contend with mobile sources of diesel from the trucks and buses that move up and down their streets, they are likely to have bus depots in their neighborhoods. In Harlem, New York City, for example, residents protested that they had excessive exposure to diesel because the principal truck route for the delivery of goods in and out of Manhattan passes through their neighborhood. They also had an amazingly high number of bus depots—eight—and correspondingly eight bus routes (Kinney et al. 2000), all contributing to an unfair burden of diesel air pollution in their community.

In addition to the quality of the air, vehicles create a health hazard from the noise they generate. This health impact ranges from annoyance to increased risk for stroke, myocardial infarction, and serious sleep disturbance (Nega et al. 2013). A recent study in London found evidence of increased risk of cardiovascular mortality and morbidity even at moderate levels of road noise (Halonen et al. 2015). For some people the noise is constant, as the traffic flows 24/7. Others contend with the noise of vehicles stopping, starting, gearing down, and accelerating. Like air quality, noise levels are associated with class and ethnicity (Nega et al. 2013).

As local news outlets demonstrate regularly, traffic accidents are another realm in which automobiles have an obvious and major negative influence on health. The numbers are staggering. All in all, over 3 million people have died in auto accidents in the United States (three times the number of combat deaths suffered in all the country's wars since 1776). Presently over 32,000 Americans die in car accidents each year (NHTSA 2012), this being the leading cause of death for people aged five to thirty-four (CDC 2013), and over 2.3 million are injured in motor vehicle crashes (NHTSA 2012). Pedestrians are at risk too: each year about 4,700 pedestrians are killed and more than 65,000 injured (NHTSA 2012).

Finally, the health effects of cars extend to the long-term consequences of phenomena such as global warming. These are strongly related to the considerable use of fossil fuels in our automobile-dependent society, which has caused the release of huge quantities of carbon dioxide, a greenhouse gas that contributes to global warming. The long-term health outcomes of global warming include threats to our food supply, heat-related deaths, loss of residential areas, proliferation of water-borne and insect-borne diseases such that places become more favorable to the mating and survival of vectors of disease, and exacerbation of air pollution with its attendant effects on health (Levy and Patz 2015). Although it is important to list these impacts, a full coverage of the connection between automobiles and global warming is beyond the scope of this book.

To summarize, the effects of our dependence on automobiles on health are mediated by the effects of automobiles on conditions of living—effects such as air pollution, accidents, and global warming. Another major and complex category of impacts is mediated by changes in our built environment that are designed to accommodate an extraordinarily high usage of cars. The need for highways and parking lots is a leading causal factor in this category of impacts on health. I turn now to all these effects, and I do it by way of moving upstream, that is, by examining the relevant SDoH—the political and economic forces that produced our car culture and set us up for this entire array of ill effects.

The Dependence on Cars and the Health Impact of the Built Environment

For many people, the love affair with the car presented itself as a natural evolution from the days of the horse and buggy. Less messy on the street and much faster, the car was a good idea in many ways. It offered comfort, convenience, privacy, and independence. We certainly celebrate our current horsepower by noting how quickly our cars accelerate from zero to sixty, something the old horsepower could not do. The move to the automobile, however, was not a "natural evolution," as we will see. The question is: Why are we so dependent on such an unhealthy form of transportation? Here again looking upstream to understand the very idea of SDoH is instructive. America's dependence on the automobile comes from a century of corporate and governmental actions that destroyed a viable electric transportation system and then privileged gas-powered vehicles. Many authors talk about the "conspiracy" of powerful economic and political players to put the United States on the way to its automobile, oil, and gas dependence (Snell 1974; Kwitny 1981). Although a complex network of actors was instrumental in building the American car culture, GM played a starring role; hence, given my limited space here, I will concentrate primarily on GM's specific influence on automotive history. And history it is, as it takes us back 100 years. But it is a history that set the stage for the privileging of automobiles in our common space—for the modern tendency to design the urban landscape so as to accommodate moving and parked cars. Our built environment is very different from what it would have been if GM had not been so powerful.

If we were to look at public transportation in the early 1900s, we would find many urban communities with viable, quiet, pollution-free electric passenger trains. In Los Angeles, about 3,000 such trains transported people throughout a fifty-six-city area. GM wanted to sell cars, and this popular light-rail public transportation system competed with its business plan. Efficiently and with an astounding lack of transparency, GM destroyed the competition by purchasing and then dismantling the electric train lines and selling off the rights of way. In the period of about twenty years, "over 100 electric trolley systems in more than forty-five cities had been dismantled, and 90 percent of the trolley network was gone" (Luger 2000: 13). The era of American dependence on cars had begun. A similar tactic was used to de-electrify cargo trains and create dependence on trucks for long-distance hauling.

Trains

Interested in more than cars and buses for the transportation of people, GM also set its sights on transporting freight. Just as electrified trains in the city had meant competition for the growing automobile industry, electric long-distance trains were strong competitors to the development of a freight-hauling truck industry. So, beginning in 1930, GM entered the train locomotive business and successfully dieselized the American railroad industry. The country went from a 7:1 ratio of electric to diesel locomotives in 1935 to a 100:1 ratio of diesel to electric locomotives in 1970.

Additionally, GM was interested in an *in*efficient train system, so that its trucks would be selected for transporting freight. Revenues were 25 to 35 times greater with car and truck sales than with trains. While the suppression of electric and steam alternatives to diesel was playing out in America, nearly every other industrialized nation in the world was doing the opposite, namely electrifying its trains (Snell 1974).

The demise of American railroads has meant that freight is still primarily shipped by truck. In 2011 "trucks moved 9.2 billion tons of freight, or about 67 percent of all freight tonnage transported domestically" (US Department of Commerce n.d.), even though railroads are considerably cheaper when you count in the unhealthy costs associated with truck emissions, noise, fatalities and injuries. These "external costs" for trucks amount to 1.11 cents per ton-mile, a much higher figure than the 0.25 cents per ton-mile for rail (Forkenbrock 2001). Shipping by truck is much less healthy for people and the environment and is even detrimental to the economy. What would it take to change this historical outcome?

Automobiles need roadways, and in 1932 GM was instrumental in forming the National Highway Users Conference (now called the American Highway Users Alliance), a lobbying group that successfully pushed for highway building. Headed by two different presidents of GM until 1956, the National Highway Users Conference consisted of representatives from the Motor Vehicle Manufacturers Association, the American Petroleum Institute, the American Trucking Association, the Rubber Manufacturers Association, and the American Automobile Association who together presented a common front against competing transportation interests (Snell 1974). They lobbied states and local officials to establish highway "trust funds" that mandated spending gasoline tax revenues solely on highway building (Snell 1974: 338; Brown et al. 2009a). Highway building accelerated when GM President Charles Wilson became the US Secretary of Defense in 1953 and elevated highways to an important component of US national security. President Eisenhower was responsive to pleas for highway building, echoing Wilson's stand that highways were a matter of national security. It was Eisenhower's frustrating experience with "slow-moving military transport" during World War II and his belief that people in cities needed a way to be evacuated quickly in the event of a nuclear attack that stimulated his support for the interstate highway system (Rudel 2009: 143). Thus an array of industry connections in powerful positions won Eisenhower's stamp of approval, which led to the Highway Act of 1956.

The interstate system was the biggest public works project in the world, costing 128.9 billion dollars (Hayden 2012: 11). The federal government provided 90 percent of the funding for projects, so the response from states was immediate. Highways sprung up everywhere. Industry lobbying led not only to the passage of the Highway Act, but also to the establishment of the Federal Highway Trust Fund, which earmarked gasoline tax money for roadbuilding, much like similar funds at the state level (Snell 1974). The Trust Fund guaranteed the federal government's long-term commitment to the automobile infrastructure.

With this backing, US roadbuilding would not stop after the initial push for interstate highways in the 1960s and 1970s. Although money for new interstate construction ended in 1996 and new construction began to drop two decades earlier (construction in 1966–76 was half that of the decade before: see Brown et al. 2009b: 174), since the middle of the last century the government has continued to make roadbuilding and improvements in the movement of cars a standard priority (APHA 2010). The mind-set of those who want traffic to move quickly and efficiently has been incorporated into many current road projects. The most "ubiquitous tool" for assessing a transportation project's success is the level of service (LOS) calculation, which examines automobile delay at peak travel times, making "commuter car trips favored over every other potential use of a roadway" (McCann 2013: 14).

Furthermore, transportation money is still allocated primarily for this kind of infrastructure—and not for mass transit, bike lanes, or walking paths. Currently "eighty percent of federal transportation funding goes to building highways and improving road infrastructure" (Robert Wood Johnson Foundation 2012). Thirty states restrict the use of gasoline tax revenues to highway programs; and, as gasoline tax is the largest source of transportation funding, this restriction severely limits the growth of alternative transportation (Bullard 2005). The American Recovery and Reinvestment Act gave the states $27.5 billion as an incentive for road projects and only $6.8 billion for public transit (www.accountablerecovery.org). So, although more money is going now to mass transit, pedestrian paths, and bikeways than before, in the federal transportation bill the dollars "for these modes remain a fraction of what is spent on highways" (APHA 2010: 13).

At the very time when the highways were being built under the push of the National Highway Users Conference and Eisenhower's Highway Act, other historical events, intertwined in mutually supportive ways, conspired to encourage car ownership. A major housing shortage was afoot after World War II; it stemmed from a lack of new building, both during the Depression and throughout the wartime years, and from an increase in the demand for housing, as 12 million vets returned and the baby boom was beginning. As we have seen in chapter 3, increased demand and economic prosperity created a situation in which many middle-class white families could take advantage of mortgages backed by the Federal Housing Administration (FHA); and these encouraged suburban single-family home building while discouraging urban homes with so-called "redlining policies." Middle-class white people moved to the suburbs, bought more cars, and then found that they had easy access to the urban areas through the Interstate Highway System. A residential pattern of thorough suburbanization emerged: currently half (51 percent) of the US population lives in newly built suburban areas (Mather et al. 2011). And in many of these areas car ownership is a requirement.

America is now paved with roads and parking lots designed to accommodate the privilege of traveling by automobile. Thus the built environment of today is profoundly affected by GM's actions in the early years of the twentieth century. Ten percent of arable land in the United States is now used by auto infrastructure and over half of the country's urban space is devoted to cars. Los Angeles, the "car capital of the nation," has eight parking spaces for every car; they are needed because the venues for shops are widely separated and walking between them is made very difficult (Luger 2000: 9). The landscape has been changed dramatically in order to support the automobile as a structural component of human life. And the demand for more and faster roads will continue, as seductive advertisements for cars begin to rival the previous advertisement campaigns for tobacco. Through allusions to dreaming (Honda, Jaguar), adventure (Dodge Ram "grab life by the horns"), and pleasure (BMW and Toyota), these advertisements make cars feel "aspirational" (Freudenberg 2014: 45). Some advocates of automobile transportation even refer to the "freedom to travel" as a "fundamental human right" (Douglas et al. 2011: 162), comparable with the right to free speech.

As a result, Americans travel overwhelmingly in private vehicles: four fifths (84 percent) of urban trips in the United States are by car. In Austria, Italy, Sweden, and Switzerland, on the other hand, less than two fifths of urban trips are by car. Private vehicles account for an amazing 91 percent of all person-miles traveled in the United States (Frank and Engelke 2001: 28, 29). Correspondingly, Americans are less likely to walk, cycle, or use public transportation than are people in most other countries.

The United States is decidedly the leader, but other countries are beginning to catch up; this inglorious reliance—or rather dependency—on the car is spreading fast. Data from the United Kingdom show a thirty-year period of increase in trips by car (from 429 to 613 trips a year), a decrease in trips by foot (from 325 to 224 trips a year) and a decrease in bike trips (from 30 to 19 trips a year). The study of changes in the use of cars, vans, and taxis in the United Kingdom over a period of fifty years reveals an increase from 50 billion to 700 billion kilometers (Douglas et al. 2011: 163–4). Car ownership is increasing dramatically in China, compounding the health problems caused there by air pollution (Freudenberg 2014: 47).

Building highways and roads and using cars not only exposes drivers, passengers, and residents to major health-damaging factors but changes the character of an area in the long term, making it less pleasant and less safe for walking and cycling. A vicious cycle of unhealthiness begins (APHA 2010). Residents have no choice but to drive; and, with more drivers, more roads are needed. More roads make cycling and walking less attractive, so people cycle and walk less. Even if a trip is short, they use the car. In fact three quarters of short trips (2 miles or less) in America are made by car (Robert Wood Johnson Foundation 2012). Many neighborhoods spiral downward, becoming pedestrian-unfriendly and less healthy. In this way the built environment reduces the amount of residents' physical activity and directly contributes to negative health outcomes such as obesity, premature mortality, and social isolation; by the same stroke it denies people the social interaction that promotes their health (Freudenberg 2014: 35). Given America's obesity epidemic, this barrier to sufficient levels of activity is troubling.

The Automobile, the Highways, and the Destruction of the Urban Environment

People's dependence on automobiles has altered the urban landscape even beyond the paving of car-dependent suburbs and rural communities. Despite the long-known health hazards of exhaust and noise, highways and other major roads have been disproportionately made to pass through poor neighborhoods, with little attention to their possible health impacts. A recurrent problem has been the construction of highways that bisect neighborhoods or create obstacles for the flow of pedestrians and local traffic within the neighborhood.

Apart from adding to air pollution for urban residents, the siting of highways in the vicinity of residential areas has also brought about the destruction of neighborhoods, a major quality-of-life concern. People can no longer easily socialize with friends living on the other side of a divided neighborhood, and access to local stores may be seriously limited. The landscape is seemingly designed for healthy forty-year-old males driving cars and produces children, older people, and disabled people who are housebound to some degree (Freund and Martin 2007: 232). Besides, a neighborhood can literally be cut off from its city base, as happened to a South Brooklyn neighborhood when three highways transformed it into "an impoverished peninsula," from which "you can see Manhattan but you can't get there" (Kasinitz, quoted in Kay 1997: 381). These are unhealthy changes in the life of residents. What is more, because cars are expensive and the public transport infrastructure is far from ideal, many poor people in urban areas lack the means to get to a well-stocked grocery store, to a doctor, or to a job. In such communities not having a car means a lot more than being unable to afford a preferred mode of transportation. Lack of access to transportation has both direct and indirect consequences for health—which I discussed in chapter 3. These and other disparities are referred to as transportation racism, a pattern in the distribution of advantages and disadvantages that discriminates against poor people and people of color. The construction of highways through urban areas, discussed next, is another example of transportation racism.

One classic example from New York City is instructive. It involves Robert Moses, a public works developer from 1920 to 1964. His plans for new roads in New York City showed no concern for the impact of a huge cement structure on people as the roadways ripped through the physical and social fabric of neighborhoods. For instance, Moses had the Gowanus Parkway built in Brooklyn in 1941. He designed it to be an elevated structure on Third Avenue, which was the heart of the Sunset Park neighborhood, "a tree-lined street with movie theaters, restaurants, small shops, few cars, and a narrow subway line" (Freilla 2004: 77). Despite pleas from the residents to move the expressway over one block, to a street that had been the dividing line between residential areas and the industrial shore, with its factories and warehouses, Moses built the Gowanus on Third Avenue. Doing so displaced more than 100 stores and 1,300 families and led to divestment in the neighborhood. Vacant lots and abandoned buildings increased. Trucks that were not permitted on the Gowanus Parkway were diverted to the street below, transforming "the sounds of Third Avenue from friendly chatter to a cacophony of rumbling tractor-trailers, blasting truck horns and screeching brakes" (Freilla 2004: 77). The predominantly poor immigrants who lived in the area lost their neighborhood and their quality of life.

The neighborhood destruction caused by interstate and other road building has not been evenly distributed. Social class and ethnicity are disturbing factors in deciding who suffers from the health impacts of the transportation industry. The building of Interstate 40 in Nashville, Tennessee provides a glaring example, as plans there were "redrawn to route the highway through the flourishing Jefferson Street corridor, home to roughly 80 percent of Nashville's African American-owned businesses" (Benfield et al. 1999: 122). In Syracuse, New York, Interstate 81 was built through the 15th Ward, the center of the city's black population; in New Orleans, the Claiborne Expressway was built over the main thoroughfare in a black neighborhood (Vock 2014); and in St. Paul, Minnesota, Interstate 94 tore through the low-income black neighborhood of Rondo (Bernstein and Solomon 2012). In Portland, Oregon, Interstate-205 ended up going through less well-off neighborhoods because citizens from five relatively affluent ones cited property value and neighborhood destruction as reasons why the interstate should not come through their communities. They successfully petitioned the Portland City Council and the freeway was rerouted around the protesting neighborhoods and made to pass through others (for instance Lent), which lacked the resources and hence the power to oppose the building of a freeway (Fackler 2009).

Highways and major arterial thoroughfares through urban areas are the main channels through which people are exposed to damaging amounts of air pollutants from automobiles, trucks, and buses. Proximity to exhaust, caused by either living close to the roadways or having to walk near them, makes poor people and people of color disproportionately vulnerable to health hazards. Fortunately urban planners and others have recognized this problem along with others, which stem from high-speed traffic in dense pedestrian areas, and new visions of urban space have emerged. As aging freeways are in need of rehabilitation, such visions can be implemented. In many towns the chosen path is not just to renew the existing infrastructure but to remove that eyesore and build out-of-sight tunnels in its place (e.g., the Big Dig in Boston). Unfortunately reclaiming from the interstate the space above the ground cannot rebuild the neighborhoods that were destroyed many decades ago. But paying attention to transportation racism led to the opening of Offices of Civil Rights in federal agencies, including the Federal Transit Administration and the Federal Highway Administration. Recognizing the problems of transportation racism generated in building the interstate system, these offices work to prevent similar patterns from arising in current road and other transportation construction. For instance, in Oakland, California several non-profit organizations successfully sued the Bay Area Rapid Transit (BART), arguing that it violated the civil rights of local residents when it planned to build a connector through mostly African American Oakland neighborhoods and to provide no stops within the area (Bernstein and Solomon 2012).

The Politics of Automobile Health and Safety

Clearly politics and power have played a role in the siting of infrastructure. In many cases, powerful industrial actors got the upper hand in determining the transportation fate of citizens and the health and safety risks that accompany that fate. Dependency on gasoline-powered cars means just as much dependency on the fossil fuel industry. Leaded or not, gasoline causes health problems even before it reaches a car's tank. First it needs to be drilled and transported, and both these activities can have huge environmental health-related impacts. The *Exxon Valdez* shipping disaster of 1989 affected Alaska, and the British Petroleum (BP) drilling disaster of 2010 affected the Gulf Coast area by spreading huge amounts of crude oil into fragile coastline environments, destroying marine food supplies, and compromising the quality of life of thousands of residents. Other spills in the United States since 2010 have included the Yellowstone River oil spill, Arthur Kill storage tank spill in New Jersey, Magnolia refinery spill in Arkansas, Mayflower oil spill in Arkansas, Cushing storage terminal spill in Oklahoma, and the North Dakota pipeline spill—all causing health problems for the nearby residents. The increase in the transportation of crude oil by rail is troubling (from 9,500 carloads in 2008 to 234,000 in 2012; Burton and Stretesky 2014: 84). In Canada a particularly deadly tank car train derailment in Lac Megantic, Quebec in 2013 killed forty-seven people. The impact is obviously felt in many countries where oil is drilled. A full discussion of the global repercussions of our societies' dependence on oil should include the impact on war.

Just as some powerful economic interests in American society have promoted the automobile over other modes of transportation, other similar interests have opposed constructive discussions about making the actual vehicles less hazardous to health. For example, the damage to human health and to the environment could have been a lot smaller had we turned to electrically powered vehicles (fully electric or hybrid) before the turn of the twenty-first century. Surprisingly, electric cars are not a new phenomenon. Invented in the 1890s, they represented nearly 40 percent of American autos by 1900 (Sierra Club 2013). Like light rail, whose demise we witnessed, they lost their important role as GM and the National Highway Users Conference members pushed for gas-powered vehicles. In America electric cars became a rare novelty in the twentieth century, but in 1976 the possibility of government-supported research on electric cars emerged. It was short-lived as then President Ford vetoed the Electric and Hybrid Vehicle Research, Development and Demonstration Act of 1976 (Peters and Wooley 1976). Electric cars made a brief comeback in California fifteen years later, when the legislature passed a zero-emissions mandate. The new legislation asked car companies to manufacture and lease or sell an increasing number of zero-emissions cars. The car industry, however, lobbied successfully for a concession, stating that companies had only to produce enough cars to meet demand. Corporate logic considered electric cars as unprofitable, in part because little money could be made on maintenance or replacement parts, in contrast to the potential profits from the internal-combustion engine. Thus history repeated itself: GM decided to sabotage the legislation by manufacturing a car that few people would like. The company met its obligations under the mandate but did so by designing and leasing a car intended for failure. Called "the EV1," GM's first electric car was advertised without any of the hyperpromotion panache typical of automobile ads and relied on a battery with limited range. Having produced a dud, GM kept demand down, which released it from the electric car business. In 2004, when the EV1's leases expired, GM bought the cars back and sent them to a crushing facility.

Although the power of the automobile industry and the complicity of various government agencies and unit heads delayed the research on and production of the electric car, the promise lives on. A recent documentary titled *Revenge of the Electric Car* (2011, dir. Chris Paine) features Bob Lutz, a Vice President of GM who had been vehemently dismissive of electric cars. In one scene he quotes from a flood of emails he received when the public learned of his negative attitude:

"You are a rotten SOB"; "You sold out to the oil companies"; "You've killed my grandchildren. I hope you rot in hell." He then claims that these emails changed his mind about the electric car and put him behind the Chevy Volt, an electric hybrid. Tesla and Nissan are currently producing viable all-electric cars, and charging stations are starting to appear in communities that are likely to support this option. In the decades ahead, automobiles powered by more environmentally friendly energy sources may outnumber fully gas-powered vehicles, but earlier support for electric and hybrid alternatives from the government and the automobile companies would have accelerated this healthy transition.

Other economic and political struggles have been over proposals to make standard automobiles less of a threat to the health of those who use them. In fact, for a long time, the government took a silent backseat to automobile safety and allowed the automobile industry to socially construct a belief that the driver, rather than the actual design of vehicles, was the problem that caused widespread death and destruction on the highways. The industry argued that human carelessness was the reason for "accidents" and that driver-oriented accident prevention programs were the answer. The government agreed, and for a long time "federal policy had twin goals: punish the careless driver, and instill good driving habits in the general population" (MacLennan 1988: 237).

But more careful analysis exposed the folly of blaming the driver for all car-related injuries and deaths. An article in a 1955 issue of the *Journal of the American Medical Association* estimated that three quarters of vehicle occupant fatalities could be prevented through proper motor vehicle design (Hemenway 2001: 383). Finally, in 1966, Congress passed the Highway Safety Act and the National Traffic and Motor Vehicle Safety Act, which led to some solid safety initiatives. No longer was the driver the main focus of improved safety; the vehicle became the target. The 1966 Act was a "radical departure from the government's respectful hands-off approach to the automobile industry" (MacLennan 1988: 240). The "industry's hostility to regulation intensified" (MacLennan 1988: 243) in the 1970s, when requirements for safety equipment in cars became more stringent. Even today, despite better oversight of safety features in cars, the power of the automobile lobby still enables horrific problems to persist. For example, the industry touted the popular Sport Utility Vehicle (SUV) towards the end of the twentieth century, lobbying for fewer penalties and restrictions even when its bosses realized that this top-heavy, oversized vehicle was not safe.

Sport Utility Vehicles (SUVs)

American roadways are now filled with SUVs. There was a tenfold increase in the number of new vehicles sold between 1982 and 2000, from about 1.78 percent to 17 percent (Bradsher 2002: xvi). Healthwise, the impact has been anything but benign. The occupancy death rate for SUVs is about 6 percent greater than the rate per million miles of passenger car travel. These increased deaths are largely the result of SUV rollovers and SUVs hitting passenger cars (rather than cars hitting cars). In addition, the inefficiency of gas-guzzling SUVs contributes to air pollution and thereby to even more negative effects on health (Bradsher 2002: xvii). Automobile companies promoted SUVs even though they knew that these vehicles were more dangerous, because they were also more profitable (Freudenberg 2014: 45).

How SUVs came to be such a dominant vehicle is basically a story of short-sighted government regulation about emissions and fuel efficiency, combined with the ability of the automobile manufacturers to take advantage of loopholes: all these allowed the making of a very profitable type of car, which was more hazardous to our health than standard passenger vehicles.

America became seriously concerned with fuel economy and emissions standards in the 1970s. In their discussions, regulators decided to distinguish between two types of vehicles: passenger vehicles and commercial vehicles used in small businesses. The latter were typically light trucks, pickups, and vans and amounted to a small percentage (less than 20 percent) of all vehicles sold at that time. These light trucks were treated favorably in the emissions discussions with American Motors and its Jeep (Bradsher 2002: 23–5). The more general sensitivity of Washington, DC to the light-truck category came (a) from a general concern that small businesses—the major owners of light trucks—needed special treatment to survive and (b) from the idea that the main target of new emissions standards had to be passenger vehicles, because those were the dominant road vehicles.

After emissions standards, attention turned to fuel efficiency (the regulations became known as the Corporate Average Fuel Economy (CAFE) program). By the time of serious CAFE discussions, American Motors was joined by other manufacturers, who produced vehicles like the Chevrolet Blazer and the Ford Bronco; and those, too, could fit the category of light trucks. When the Transportation Department debated the categorization of vehicles, they agreed to include Jeeps and other utility vehicles into the category of "automobiles which are not passenger automobiles" (Bradsher 2002: 27). The special treatment of SUVs on emission and fuel economy has been profitable for the industry, but it put more SUVs on the road, along with all the attendant health implications.

In 1978, in an attempt to encourage manufacturers to produce fuel-efficient vehicles, the government imposed a tax on "gas-guzzlers": it was a not insignificant tax, which could add nearly $8,000 to the cost of fancy sports cars. Again, arguments suggesting that vehicles in the light-truck category should not be subject to the tax won the day. Station wagons were subject to the tax, but not SUVs. Instead SUV manufacturers now had the green light to produce vehicles with fewer regulations and greater profitability. "If you could save 30 percent off the cost by not meeting the safety standards, it could make a project a whole lot more attractive," said William Chapin, the former Jeep executive (quoted in Bradsher 2002: 49).

Various attempts to raise the CAFE standards through the years have been met with opposition from "tightly knit coalitions of trade associations, lobbyists, and congressional supporters" (Schmidt 2002: A467). For instance, a House vote in 2001 to raise light-truck standards was defeated 269 to 160. Congressional supporters included representatives from Michigan, Missouri, and Texas—all of them states with significant SUV manufacturing plants. Other supporters included the United Automobile Workers (UAW), once they learned that both Chrysler and GM would close plants if the fuel standards were raised (Bradsher 2002: 391–5).

An early lone voice from the automobile industry, the Ford Motor Company, acknowledged that, while the company was dependent on SUVs for much of its profit, it did realize that they cause serious safety and environmental problems (Bradsher 2002). It was not until 2010 that serious discussion of improving passenger car and SUV fuel requirements began (http://www.nhtsa.gov/staticfiles/rulemaking/pdf/cafe/2017–2025_CAFE-GHG_Supplemental_NOI07292011.pdf).

Another well-documented example of the enduring power of the automobile industry to affect our health involves the development of the airbag. A debate began in the 1970s and continued until 1991, when regulations mandated airbags. The auto industry declared the airbag "unnecessary, too expensive, and impractical" (Luger 2000: 122) and fought it early on in the White House, where Henry Ford II and the president of Ford, Lee Iacocca, met with Nixon and succeeded in delaying the regulations. The auto industry also went to federal court to win a further reprieve. Early in the Reagan administration, Raymond Peck, the newly appointed head of the National Highway Traffic Safety Administration (NHTSA)—the regulatory agency responsible for the airbag mandate—rescinded the ruling. Consumer groups and insurance companies challenged the rescission and the case ended up in the Supreme Court, which in a ruling in favor of safety criticized the auto industry by saying: "For nearly a decade, the automobile industry has waged the regulatory equivalent of war against the air bag" (Luger 2000: 124). Despite the reprimand, the Supreme Court did not reinstate the airbag mandate but turned the decision back to the NHTSA, indicating that the airbag requirement could be waived if sufficiently many states would mandate seat belt use. The industry felt it had one last chance of defeating the airbag and put its economic muscle behind a campaign to get states to mandate seat belts. In the mid-1980s the industry set aside $15 million annually for the anti-airbag campaign and passionately lobbied state legislators. An Illinois legislator said: "I haven't seen a bill this heavily lobbied in a long time" (Luger 2000: 125–6). Despite the attempt to affect state legislation, the auto industry failed to persuade enough states to pass mandatory seatbelt legislation, so the airbag standard was established, with a compliance date set for 1993. Although its various attempts at influencing the White House, the courts, and the state legislatures were ultimately unsuccessful, the auto industry had been powerful enough to delay the application of a safety standard for more than two decades.

The industry continues to fight health and safety legislation. It makes huge campaign donations, hires former NHTSA employees (including a former head) to help it argue its case before state legislators and Congress, and spends over $100 million a year to influence the government (Luger 2000: 184). This power is all the more significant as the auto industry is central to the economy of so many states and to the national economy. The industry is literally too big to fail, a fact not lost on Democrats or Republicans. The government rescue of the automobile industry in 2008–9 was a clear indication of that centrality.

Despite the delays in automobile health and safety regulations orchestrated by the automobile industry, the government has managed to implement a broad set of features such as safety belts, shatter-resistant windshields, head rests, child booster seats, and airbags. In addition, the federal government pushed for improvements in highway safety, such as improved illumination, guardrails, and better marking of lanes. The results of these safety initiatives have been impressive: motor vehicle-related death rates have decreased (CDC 1999)—a result largely credited to these changes in automobiles and in the highways and not to any changes in driver education or behaviors.

Citizen Activism for Safer and Healthier Forms of Transportation

If even the federal government of the United States has struggled to implement basic safety features in cars, how can ordinary people work to improve the health outcomes of their transportation system? Several grassroots groups have been active over many years, fighting for changes in the dominant approaches to the transportation of people—automobiles and dirty diesel buses—and in the infrastructure required to support our car culture. In the early days of interstate road building, people in various communities had the foresight to realize the folly of building major roadways and bridges in the middle of towns. In Washington, DC, the proposal for the Three Sisters Bridge, a six-lane connector for proposed new highways, triggered a variety of freeway-revolt activists. One set of protestors consisted of a coalition of mostly white residents from a suburb in Maryland and African American residents from DC, who argued against "white highways through black bedrooms" (Mohl 2004: 679). Civil disobedience and lawsuits, one making it to the Supreme Court, helped delay the decision on the bridge, which was ultimately defeated in 1977. Supporting the citizen-led campaign, the nation's first Secretary of Transportation, Alan Boyd, agreed that "there comes a point when the insatiable appetite of cars for additional roads must be denied" (Schrag 2004: 657).

Other cities that experienced early freeway revolts are San Francisco, Miami, and Baltimore. Some of the protests were successful (San Francisco and Baltimore), some not (Miami), depending on the nature of the coalitions that formed, the press response to the protests, and the state of various laws, mandates, and regulations about highway development and housing relocation allowances that were current at the time (Mohl 2004: 697).

More recently, citizens have raised their voice in several trans-portation cases. In Portland in 2007, a new bridge was proposed to replace the aging I-5 and I-205 bridges that cross the Columbia River and provide transportation between Washington and Oregon. The proposed bridge, dubbed the Columbia River Crossing, would have been ten lanes wide and included light rail. Designed to be built where the I-5 highway currently stands, traffic would substantially increase into North Portland (a lower income community). This increased traffic raised significant health concerns among com-munity members; it also presented the potential for harmful noise pollution, which could lead to the development of chronic disease and to deficits in cognitive functioning. Additionally, the upsurge in traffic would likely result in poor air quality, posing risks of asthma, blood disorders, and lung cancer to nearby residents (Cannon and Frederick 2011). Citizen voices for health were loud in Portland, but it is unclear how much difference they made. It was largely budgetary concerns and the inability of legislators from Oregon and Washington to sign off on the project that doomed the bridge. The project was disbanded in the summer of 2013.

Citizens in San Francisco, on the other hand, have a proven grass-roots organization called PODER (People Organizing to Demand Environmental and Economic Rights), which has been instrumental in initiating the study of poor air quality due to transportation and then demanding action in order to improve the unhealthy conditions. Its successful achievements include more hybrid buses and an alter-native truck route intended to keep trucks off residential streets (Wier et al. 2009). A national coalition of grassroots organizations formed the Transportation Equity Network (TEN), which argued that the decision-making process for transportation should be responsive to the needs of transit-dependent and low-income communities. As a result of TEN's work, federal legislation has placed stronger public participation requirements on both regional and state transporta-tion planning organizations (Stolz 2005). Finally, WE ACT (West Harlem Environmental Action) in West Harlem and Alternatives for Community and Environment (ACE) in Boston have rallied around diesel-polluted air and asthma threats. They push for cleaner buses and for a more equitable siting of bus depots (Brown et al. 2003). These varied citizen initiatives have begun to change our built environment.

New urban initiatives have emerged as well. Such is the Surface Transportation Policy Project (http://transact.org), a national group that supports smarter transportation choices, safer communities, improved public health, social equity, and a vibrant economy and has spawned the National Complete Streets Coalition, which promotes the idea that streets are not just for automobiles but need to be made safe for pedestrians of all ages and abilities, for cyclists, and for transit vehicles too. Since 2005, when the Complete Streets movement took off, nearly 500 local jurisdictions and half the states have adopted Complete Street policies (McCann 2013: 2). In Illinois a new law now requires the state's department of transportation to make sure that bicycles and pedestrians can be accommodated on all roads in urbanized areas (LaPlante and McCann 2008).

Conclusion

This chapter has documented the role of powerful economic actors, particularly GM, which had a strong interest in the internal combustion engine, in gasoline (at one time leaded gasoline), in road building, and in profit over safety. Various decisions this company made greatly altered the course of the US transportation system, the amount of fossil fuels used, the amount of air pollution, and the built environment in America. These conditions of life in urban and suburban areas seem now to be taken-for-granted aspects of living in the twenty-first century, but our examination of the history of the automobile in the United States took us upstream, where we could see why these conditions of life developed. That history shows quite clearly that the paving of America did not evolve naturally; GM and corporations with oil and tire interests joined together and pushed for it, aided by political appointments of prominent, GM-connected people and by a variety of government policies. Through the conditions of life they influenced, these SDoH have had untold health consequences at the individual, community, and even global level.

Economic actors are not the only powerful forces that have thwarted health and safety advances in transportation. While at many critical points the government has proved an important regulator, government agencies and employees have encouraged our less than healthy dependence on unsafe cars and discouraged the development of safer alternatives. The government was clearly complicit in delaying many safety features and in augmenting the automobile manufacturers' profit line. Hopeful government policies have appeared, however, that bridge public and private sector interests.

In particular, the government has taken steps to encourage the use of public transportation and to make urban areas more walkable and bikeable. More cities now have bike-sharing programs (New York City has a new strong program) and light-rail systems (e.g., Baltimore and Seattle). In 2015 Seattle began a subsidy program for low-income public transit users. New York City has a successful Transportation Alternatives group, which works with the city council and the mayor to redesign dangerous arterial streets, to reduce pedestrian deaths, and to make obsolete the nickname "Boulevard of Death" or Queens Boulevard. The health benefits of each of these initiatives could be considerable, since "walkable, bikeable, [public] transit-oriented communities" are associated with healthier populations. People get the physical activity they need and maintain a healthier body weight; they also have less exposure to air pollution and lower rates of traffic injuries (Robert Wood Johnson Foundation 2012). Some states have addressed pollution from car use. In 2015 the legislature in Oregon imposed the Clean Fuels Program in order to reduce the carbon intensity of gas and diesel fuel, and in doing so had considerable business support. The California legislature has passed a series of laws that have addressed the topics of clean air, global warming, and safer, less polluting cars. Included in one of these laws is a mandate that 15 percent of all cars sold in the state should run on zero or near-zero emissions. The laws have been controversial and attracted "strong national opposition from both the automobile and energy industries" (Freudenberg 2014: 197), but for the most part have withstood Supreme Court scrutiny.

All of these government initiatives suggest that individuals who decide to take individual actions are not enough. Our interests—economic, political, social, and cultural—as a society have produced a built environment that prioritizes cars and highways. Advertisements, movies, and other media have produced a powerful car culture. People want comfortable cars, fast cars, showy cars. Doing without a car (or minimizing usage of a car) and walking, cycling, or using public transportation instead is both difficult and not sanctioned by cultural values in most of our societies. Changing the powerful car culture requires more than individual action. We will need policy changes that design and revalue a friendlier and healthier built environment and reduce our dependence on the automobile. And change is desperately needed. At stake here is not only the health of neighborhood residents, but also global health. It is, after all, our oil-based economy that has had global impacts like climate change, rising seas, forced migration, and devastating weather patterns, all of which affect human health.

Some would suggest that the original impetus for our car culture was Los Angeles when GM's actions there destroyed an excellent, quiet, nearly pollution-free public transportation system. That legacy makes recent news from Los Angeles all the more striking. Los Angeles Mayor Garcetti was interviewed on his first day on the job in July of 2013 and commented that he felt that LA would have a "second golden age for public transit" with rail lines from downtown to Santa Monica and subways (Young and Hobson 2013). Perhaps the American car capital will lead the way to healthier forms of transportation. If Los Angeles can change, there is indeed hope.

7
Occupational Health

Jobs can be dangerous to a person's health. In the United States, a powerful early example of occupational health risks emerged from the tragedy at the New York City Triangle Shirtwaist Factory, a garment industry sweatshop employing primarily young Jewish and Italian immigrant women. A 1911 fire at the factory led to the deaths of 145 workers who were unable to escape the flames because their employer had locked the exit doors in order to keep track of so many young women. Workers burned to death or died jumping from the building. The enormity of the tragedy generated an awareness of dangerous working conditions and prompted a major investigation of workplace hazards (Stein 1962; also visit http://www.history.com/topics/triangle-shirtwaist-fire). Despite this cautionary tale and efforts to address it, serious occupational health threats continue. In 1991, a fire at the Imperial Products poultry plant in North Carolina—which employed primarily African American women—led to the deaths of twenty-five workers because management, fearing that workers would steal chickens, had locked the doors. How can such tragic workplace events eighty years apart remain so similar? What are the social, political, and economic conditions that perpetuate disregard for the health and safety of workers, particularly ethnic and racial minorities, women, and economically disadvantaged individuals, who are consistently more at risk than others?

The reality that aspects of our working lives can seriously jeopardize our health has been known for a long time. A case of lead poisoning in the fourth century BC, described in a Hippocratic treatise, is generally accepted as the first occupational disease in our records. In the late eighteenth century, chimney sweeps in England developed cancer. Death, injury, and disease statistics from recent years document the persistence of occupational health problems today. In 2008, US occupational injuries caused 5,214 deaths, work-related disease caused 49,000 deaths, and an estimated 4.6 million workers had a non-fatal occupational injury or illness (Levy et al. 2011: 5). In 2007 occupational injuries and diseases were responsible for "an estimated $250 billion in medical expenses and indirect costs, such as lost wages and benefits" (Taylor and Murray 2013: 339). One of the reasons why the impact is so great is that people typically spend about one third of their waking hours in work settings where their bodies are often subjected to wear and tear from physical, mental, and emotional demands and to constant or repeated exposure to toxins and other noxious conditions. This chapter explores reasons why work can be so dangerous to workers' health, why an upstream view of the cause of occupational health problems is so important, why such problems persist, and, finally, what regulations and other actions have improved our occupational health.

Classic Occupational Hazards: Chimney Sweeps, Radium Girls, Mad Hatters, Gauley Bridge, and Yellow Dirt

CHIMNEY SWEEPS   In the 1700s and 1800s, children spent their days as chimney sweeps, often nearly naked, cleaning the soot from household chimney flues; their size made them ideal for the job. These children were in constant contact with grime and ash, and particles of soot lodged beneath their skin. They often developed scrotal tumors. A doctor who treated them rejected the typical explanation that the tumors were caused by the young patients' generally dirty lifestyle or through sexual transmission; instead he uncovered a man-made occupational disease. His revelations ultimately triggered a law in 1875 that forbade the use of children as chimney sweeps (Cullingford 2003).

RADIUM GIRLS   In the 1920s, the Waterbury Clock Company in Connecticut manufactured clocks with luminous glow-in-the-dark dials. Radium, the magic behind the glow, was carcinogenic for workers through inhalation, ingestion, and skin contact. The workers were mainly young girls tasked with painting the numbers on the dials with small paintbrushes. To be more efficient and to complete the dials faster, the girls were encouraged to "lip-point" their paintbrushes by putting them in their mouths, which pulled together and hence sharpened the bristles. But the paint bristles that went into their mouths were laced with carcinogenic radium.

Some young dial painters died within ten years of working at Waterbury Clock; others died later, after suffering for years from crumbling bones and rotted jaws (Owens 2014; The Medical Bag 2014).

MAD HATTERS   When parents read *Alice in Wonderland* to their children, many do not realize that they are providing a lesson in occupational health. The Hatter was patterned after the occupational hazards of mid-nineteenth-century Britain, where hatmakers were exposed to mercury under poorly ventilated conditions as they worked to shape the wool-felt hats. Typical symptoms included tremors, irritability, slurred speech, depression, and other neurological symptoms (CDC 2012).

GAULEY BRIDGE   In the 1930s a power company, a subsidiary of Union Carbide, began construction of a tunnel near Gauley Bridge in West Virginia; the plan was to divert river water to a power plant. The tunnel was a major excavation through a mountain that turned out to be 99 percent pure silicon dioxide, or free silica. Known for centuries to be a serious health hazard, silica exposure was greatly reduced by "wet drilling." Wet drilling slowed down the work, and the time schedule for the project did not allow such a luxury. State law required wet drilling, but investigators found that the "water was turned on only when the mine inspectors appeared and turned off again upon their departure" (Bayer 1988: 168). The conditions for the workers, most of whom were African American, were so horrific that many of them died within months, and in a few years nearly 500 fell victim to silicosis. The occupational disaster received national attention and Gauley Bridge became a symbol of occupational disease hazards.

YELLOW DIRT   During World War II the United States was in urgent need of uranium for the Manhattan Project to produce atomic bombs. The government found a bountiful supply of uranium on the land of the Navajo Nation in northeastern Arizona, secretly funded the mining, and hired Navajo workers. Not knowing that they were mining uranium and not being told that the material was a health hazard, the workers often wore little protection. But the government was fully aware of the potential health problem: in ten to twenty years after significant exposure, the workers would face a high risk of lung cancer (Pasternak 2011).

Occupational Sources of Disease, Injury, and Death

Some industries are more hazardous than others. In terms of the number of fatalities, agriculture (including forestry and fishing), transportation, and construction are the big three, mining replacing construction if the rate of fatalities is the measure (BLS 2015). But health risks occur even in occupations that seem likely to be relatively safe: tech jobs, healthcare positions, even retail and office work. An excellent online resource on occupational health, with video links, is available at www.losh.ucla.edu/resources-2/work-health-equity-module. The sources of disease, injury, and death are many; they can be grouped into (a) physical demands and exposures, (b) adverse psychological or social job stressors, and (c) the organization of the work setting. Physical demands and exposures include heavy lifting, malfunctioning machinery, and debilitating repetitive motions. Poor ergonomics in a workstation, such as high computer screens, has been linked to ruptured spinal disks, and exposure to noise on the job can cause hearing loss, one of the most common occupational injuries in the world (Robert Wood Johnson Foundation 2011b: 3). In industrial work settings in particular, possible noxious exposure to various chemicals and deadly dust (Rosner and Markowitz 2005) is extensive. The listing of chemical hazards alone goes on for pages, as documented by the occupational cancer list of the National Institute of Occupational Safety and Health (NIOSH; visit http://www.cdc.gov/niosh/npg/npgsyn-a.html). Note that these physical exposures are not caused by the workers' behavior but by the employer's decision to leave them in the workplace—an upstream cause.

A second type of occupational health hazard, adverse psychological and social job stressors, has long been overlooked, but recent research has begun to remedy this neglect by examining the health effects of such things as general stress (Bongers et al. 2002), sexual harassment on the job (Krieger et al. 2006), emotional labor (Andrews et al. 2008), and organizational injustice (Greenberg 2010: 210; Okechukwu et al. 2013). Emotional labor is well illustrated by the challenges of being a front-line staff person (e.g., a waiter or an airline attendant) who, frequently confronted by angry people, needs to keep smiling through verbal abuse. "Organizational injustice" refers to people's perceptions of unfairness in organizations. People who feel that they receive inconsistent or insufficient information about their job or that they are criticized unfairly are good examples of such injustice (Kivimaki et al. 2004). A perceived or demonstrated lack of respect for one's job function is also a serious stressor (Baron et al. 2011). Research on adverse psychological and social job stressors provides important documentation about the power of such stressors on health: they can cause high blood pressure, insomnia, coronary heart disease, and other indicators of poor health (Marmot et al. 1997; Schnall et al. 2000; Kuper and Marmot 2003). Again, though very different from physical demands, psychological and social job stressors typically have upstream causes, as they are a result, intentional or not, of the workplace design.

A third factor, the organization of the work setting, also has important health implications. Some people work in job settings in which they have little or no control over their work. Higher ups who determine the working conditions may have no idea of how rules and schedules affect the worker. An excellent example comes from San Francisco, where bus drivers reported unusually high rates of hypertension, back pain, gastrointestinal problems, and respiratory difficulties. A major reason was that the drivers were subjected to rigid computer-designed schedules that required the impossible: getting from Point A to Point B in an amount of time only feasible for a small passenger vehicle driving in off-peak hours. The bus drivers were often late and passengers were often angry. Penalized if they were too late, the drivers responded by giving up rest time, dashing into fast-food stores when they needed to eat, and then going to a bar at the end of the day to relieve the day's tensions. Their health problems were the result of fast pace, stress, and attempts to meet the demands of an unrealistic schedule (Syme 2004; visit http://www.cdc.gov/pcd/ issues/2004/jan/03_0001.htm)—all upstream causes.

Speed alone can be a dangerous element in the organization of the workplace (Kubicek et al. 2014). Imagine a boss who insists on an increased quota of butchered meat in a slaughterhouse. Using knives too quickly is clearly a recipe for disaster. Recent research examined this speed-up phenomenon in a restaurant setting and found that speed of service was implicated in burns, cuts, and workers slipping and falling (Jayaraman et al. 2011). Speed can be an obvious hazard if it discourages safety. Although he may be given plastic goggles, a chemical worker might not wear them if he needs to rush to make a production quota. The goggles may be ill fitting or may fog up and slow him down. Not wearing them is risky behavior, but easily rationalized in order to meet the immediate demands of the job.

A more general and relatively new issue in the organization of the workplace comes from the impact of globalization on work. The outsourcing and the subcontracting of jobs have become more commonplace and make the global workplace less safe, as they create "complex conditions of legal responsibility that can confuse the different employer parties, [and] confound OHS [Occupational Health and Safety] accountability" (Eakin et al. 2010: S30). But there are also less visible threats for the workers in the sending countries whose jobs are endangered by globalization. Such global interconnectivity produces more temporary and insecure jobs, with the result that existing workers become less likely to speak up and to resist job hazards (Silverstein 2008; Baron et al. 2011). The structure of the global economy is a clear upstream cause.

Workers at Particular Risk: Gender, Race or Ethnicity, and Class

Occupational demands and exposures, psychosocial stressors, and work organization have the potential of affecting all workers, especially if they lack the ability to voice their concerns in the context of social and economic power structures. Historically, and continuing today, some people are at greater risk because their gender, class, or race or ethnicity has relegated their employment to more dangerous or less regulated industries or occupations (Friedman-Jimenez 1989; Pellow and Park 2002: 99; Taylor and Murray 2013; Landsbergis et al. 2014). For instance, we have a gendered division of labor: some occupations are nearly all female and some nearly all male. Even when men and women are in the same occupation, tasks assigned within those occupations may be gendered. For example, men and women working in a poultry plant have different jobs, women being more likely to use knives and scissors than men. Similarly, male and female gardeners do different things, women being more likely to plant and weed, men to prune (Ratcliff 2002; Messing 2014). This gendering of occupations and of jobs within occupations means that men and women have different exposures to health hazards. Such differences are reflected in occupational injury statistics. Women are more likely than men to be injured by repetitive motion, inhalation of harmful substances, and assaults and violent acts. They are more likely to be exposed to the emotional stress inherent in clerical, sales, and service jobs where "the customer is always right" (no matter how rude). Women often contend with poorly designed workplaces and tools—such as the height of a work area or the size of a handgrip—that are based on average male measurements. And, quite importantly, women's disproportionate exposure to sexual harassment at the workplace is an enduring problem (Ratcliff 2002).

Healthcare is a huge industry that is predominantly female. More than three fourths of healthcare practitioners and nearly 90 percent of healthcare support workers are women (www.bls.gov/cps/cpsaat11. pdf). Despite the fact that healthcare is an industry focused on health, to work in that industry can be, ironically, a health hazard. Occupational risks for healthcare workers are many and varied: back injuries, needle sticks, an array of chemical hazards from substances that have not been tested for occupational risk (drugs used for cancer treatment, anesthetic waste gases, chemicals for sterilizing and disinfecting), assaults by patients, and infectious diseases lead the list (Charney and Schrimer 2007).

Not surprisingly, the number of occupational health hazards in healthcare settings is disturbingly high. Referred to as an epidemic by some, the rate of non-fatal occupational injuries and illness is double the rate in other private industries and "higher than the rates in construction and manufacturing—two industries that are traditionally thought to be relatively hazardous" (OSHA 2013).

Some healthcare workers are more at risk than others. Home healthcare workers, 95 percent of whom are female, suffer greatly because their work site is invisible and unregulated. The job often requires them to lift or move a large person singlehandedly, without the lifting equipment available in a hospital or nursing home setting. The resulting overexertion and back pain means that the rate of incidence of lost workdays for these workers is twice the rate for general industry workers (Seavey and Marguand 2011: 46). In other contexts, notably among men who lifted heavy objects all day, back pain was taken seriously and safety guidelines were developed. One could calibrate the items they lifted and standardize allowable maximum weights. But this is obviously impossible with patients who come in all different shapes, sizes, and degrees of mobility.

In other occupations women are not predominant but suffer more than men as a result of biological susceptibility. Thus in plastic-manufacturing industries women make up less than a third of the employees, but health damage is more severe for them than for men, because the manufacturing process involves endocrine-disrupting chemicals associated with female breast cancer and other reproductive hazards (DeMatteo et al. 2012).

The disproportionate impact of occupations on the health of people from the lower class and from ethnic minorities is related to the fact that people in these groups tend to get employment in very dangerous occupations, such as agriculture. For example, Hispanics represent only 15.6 percent of all employed people but as many as 50 percent of agricultural workers in the United States (www.bls. gov/cps/cpsaat11.pdf). Farm labor exposes workers to pesticides and herbicides, which can cause various health problems for the digestive, neurological, respiratory, circulatory, dermatological, renal, and reproductive systems (Payán-Rentería et al. 2012). In California, where 90 percent of agricultural workers are Hispanic, researchers studying the herbicide atrazine first found that frogs exposed to the chemical were emasculated and now are finding that agricultural workers are at increased risk of prostate and breast cancer and of begetting children with birth defects (Hayes 2011). There is growing concern that concentrated animal feeding operations (CAFOs) pose more risks to workers than small farms do, as CAFOs have more gaseous and particulate matter emissions such as hydrogen sulfide and endotoxin, which could have health impacts (Mitloehner and Calvo 2008).

One reason why agricultural work continues to be dangerous is that some of the occupational protections afforded by the National Labor Relations Act and by the Fair Labor Standards Act do not cover agricultural workers. This omission is due to the "doctrine of agricultural exceptionalism—a practice that historically emerged from negotiations between Southern politicians seeking to protect agriculture's access to cheap labor (which at the time was predominantly African American) and Franklin D. Roosevelt's administration attempting to promote New Deal social and economic reform" (Flocks 2012: 269). Seasonal and migrant laborers continue to be a significant part of the workforce, and their temporary status and ethnicity render them less protected.

In addition to agriculture, cleaning is also the province of minority workers, particularly minority women. The Bureau of Labor's category of "maids and housekeeping cleaners" is 88.6 percent female and 43.8 percent Hispanic (www.bls.gov/cps/cpsaat11.pdf). These workers clean hospitals, other workplaces, hotels, public toilets, and private homes. In the process they are exposed to many cleaning chemicals that cause respiratory and dermatologic diseases. They face physical demands (e.g., prolonged standing, heavy lifting, and awkward postures) that can cause musculoskeletal disorders and also psychosocial stressors such as lack of respect and low potential for promotion; and these in turn can lead to a host of other chronic health problems (Charles et al. 2009).

The Persistence of Occupational Health Problems

If such conditions plague so many people, why do occupational health problems persist? Some risks are unfortunately inevitable—intrinsic to the job. Workers in mines, structural metal workers on skyscrapers, or loggers endanger their lives and are at greater risk of injuries due to unforeseeable but broadly predictable hazards of weather and working conditions that can't be fully controlled. The perils incurred by fishermen on the high seas have even been romanticized in a reality TV show, *Deadliest Catch*, which depicts fishing as a profession designed only for the most daring. But, while "ice road truckers" in Alaska yield only to the most savage elements, many occupational risks could be prevented and are not. This happens for a variety of reasons. Sometimes no one knows that there is a problem, not even the workers themselves, because the damage does not surface until years or decades later—well beyond the lifespan of adventures on TV, and with far less drama. Asbestosis and silicosis demonstrate a latency period: it is frequently twenty years or more before initial symptoms appear. If the worker develops symptoms after terminating employment at the workplace where the exposure occurred, then making the link to that place of work may be impossible.

Workers' Compensation

A very different reason why we know less about occupational health problems is that we have built a system of compensation for injured workers that has at its core the idea that blame will not be assessed. A type of law commonly known as workers' compensation laws were enacted across Europe and in various states of the United States in the first decades of the twentieth century. These laws established a no-fault system of compensation when a worker was injured or killed. Corporate responsibility for deaths on the job changed dramatically. "Now they were presented as accidental events, for which there was no corporate criminal liability and which merely required compensation" (Rosner 2000: 538). Reimbursement for health claims is often easier for a worker who receives this kind of compensation, but that worker is then denied the possibility of suing the employer. Industry likes these laws because they have been able to pressure state legislatures into limiting the benefits accorded to workers (LaDou 2002: 289).

Another reason why we have limited knowledge of occupational hazards is that the link between a problem and the characteristics of the work setting is often not made; and this, in turn, is because no one ever asked questions to connect the dots and no research was done. We simply don't look upstream when we seek answers. This lack of questioning occurs more often in occupations that seem risk-free. While classically "dirty jobs" like construction, coal mining, or steel manufacturing and smelter work have always anticipated danger and prompted researchers to investigate, nothing of the kind happens in seemingly "clean industries"—healthcare, electronics, secretarial, clerical, and retail work. Visitors tend to come out with the impression that such workplaces are clean, and therefore "safe." But looks can be deceiving.

The high-tech electronics industry—where people manufacture and assemble silicon chips, disk surfaces, disk-drive heads, and circuit board assemblies for computers and produce solid state devices for telecommunication switching and transmission equipment—may provide protective gear, but what is it protecting? In Silicon Valley workers don gloves, facial masks, and special gowns, in an environment designed to keep the tiniest pieces of dust away from the semiconductor chip. Yet these so-called "clean rooms" are neither clean nor safe for workers. Filters trap the dust, but nothing protects the workers' lungs from the toxic fumes that fill the room (Stranahan 2002). In fact there are long-documented problems that have been ignored and are getting worse. For one thing, the electronics industry is constantly changing products and production methods by using new, "state of the art" technology. Unfortunately, the greater speed and power of our favorite electronic devices have been associated with greater toxicity. As smaller components are produced (such as smaller chips), "more solvents are needed to wash away ever smaller 'killer particles' that could jam a circuit. Small and faster may also mean using even more toxic chemicals" (Pellow and Park 2002: 107). A recent study at the Endicott New York IBM plant, for example, found that workers exposed to trichloroethylene and perchlorethylene (chlorinated solvents) had higher than expected rates of non-Hodgkins lymphoma and rectal cancer (Borkowski and Monforton 2014). In South Korea workers in the "clean rooms" of Samsung's semiconductor plants are complaining of life-threatening diseases such as leukemia, lymphoma, and brain cancer after fewer than ten years of work (Grossman 2011).

Other "clean industries" include secretarial, clerical, computer, and retail work, where ergonomic hazards abound. Ergonomic hazards come from an unhealthy fit between the worker and the equipment or movement requirements of the job. Many of these hazards seem invisible. A worker's chair might be the wrong height or might fail to provide the needed support, or a worker may be required to make repetitive motions, stand still for long periods, or stand in an awkward stance. Each instance makes trivial demands on the human body and may appear perfectly safe to an observer, because the cumulative effect over time cannot be perceived in the moment (Messing 2014). These ergonomic hazards can cause a variety of disabling and painful musculoskeletal disorders (e.g., carpal tunnel syndrome, tension neck syndrome, low back pain). Cumulative trauma disorder and repetitive strain injury are now among the most costly occupational hazards (Marras et al. 2009).

Even when connections between the workplace and health are known, that knowledge might not come into play for an individual worker. Many cases of work-related disease and injury are not properly classified by medical professionals as occupational. Lacking training, doctors "have little intrinsic interest in work and workplaces, lack the vocabulary to interview workers, and have scant knowledge of hazards" (Gochfeld 2005: 116); in consequence, upstream questions are not asked. Even among the physicians who work in occupational settings, many "either do not know how to recognize it [occupational disease] or design tests that bear no relevance to exposure" (Draper 2003: 99). Occupational medical specialists are rare (less than 1 percent of physicians), even though occupational injuries and illnesses are among the five leading causes of morbidity and mortality (LaDou 2005). After a brief spike of interest in occupational medicine with the passage of the Occupational Safety and Health Act in 1970, residency programs have decreased. The Institute of Medicine in the United States, along with other bodies, has decried the critical shortage of specialty-trained occupational health professionals (LaDou 2002: 287).

The Persistence of Occupational Health Problems: The Power of Industry

The biggest reason why occupational health problems continue is not underdiagnosis or lack of detection; rather it is a blatant disregard for awareness and prevention. Many companies don't want workers or others to understand health problems because of the upstream analysis that would then occur. They keep workers in the dark by under-informing them about potential health problems and by denying the severity of such risks in favor of a bottom line that, they argue, would be beneficial to all—including to the workers in question, who need their jobs in order to make ends meet. So companies use their power to make their claims of "no harm" prevail; and that power comes from their size, revenues, economic importance to the community, and political connections, as well as from the workers' corresponding lack of power and organization. The case of a company producing DBCP—a pesticide that, when injected into the soil protects fruit from a destructive worm—is an instructive example of how companies claim "no harm." Members of the all-male workforce at one DBCP production plant started talking among themselves about the difficulty of fathering children and realized that almost all of them had been unsuccessful. That discovery led to an investigation into the chemical by studying its effect on animals. The research showed testicular atrophy (shriveling of the testes) in the animals. Despite this finding, a company spokesperson claimed to be "shocked" at the suggestion that the chemical might cause sterility in workers. A neutral observer would probably find it easy to imagine a connection between testicular atrophy and difficulty in producing sperm; but the company persisted in denying that connection (http://www.youtube.com/watch?v=75__L8hX-1o; Bingham and Monforton 2013).

In another case at a Zonolite mine in Libby, Montana, workers hired as sweepers had to clean out the multistory mill where vermiculite was processed. The accumulated dust was overwhelming—more than a foot deep in many places. And the dust contained asbestos, a naturally occurring contaminant in vermiculite. The owners of the mine were fully aware of the dangers of asbestos-laced vermiculite but continued to tell the workers that the dust had "nothing in it that will hurt you" (Schneider and McCumber 2004: 67). Respirators were available but they clogged up within fifteen minutes of use and were virtually impossible to clean, leaving the ill-informed worker little choice but to forego protection in order to get the job done (Schneider and McCumber 2004: 67). In a different case, at production plants for ethyl gas, workers were exposed to tetraethyl lead, an additive for gasoline, which caused neurological symptoms typically manifested in hallucinations and convulsions. These symptoms were so pervasive that the factory became known as "the house of butter-flies." The manufacturer implicitly acknowledged that the company knew about the work hazards when it tried to defend itself by saying that workers were responsible for their own deaths because, "regardless of warnings and provision for their protection, [they] had failed to appreciate the dangers of constant absorption of the fluid by their hands and arms" (Markowitz and Rosner 2003a: 22–3). If the workers were supposed to know the dangers, then management must certainly have known about them.

Blaming the worker for his or her health problems rather than admitting that a manufacturing process might be dangerous has historic continuity. In 1912 the National Association of Manufacturers referred to the "crime of carelessness" (https://www.youtube.com/watch?v=eMsU1HNce-Y), which clearly blames the worker. Labeling a health problem in a way that suggests that it was caused by the worker or was an accident clearly takes attention away from the organization of the work setting and from possible structural conditions that the employer controls, such as exposures to toxins and hazardous working conditions (Quinn 2003). An accident is a random event—something not foreseeable and not conforming to a pattern—and not something for which the employer is responsible. Yet many things that are labeled "accidents" in the work setting are the predictable result of workplace design or of the exposures that occur in it. Such health outcomes need to be discussed as injuries and diseases, not as accidents (Freund and McGuire 1999: 60–1), and seen as upstream decisions about design.

Blaming the worker remains a popular way to account for workplace injuries and illness. Employers have suggested that particular worker characteristics—smoking, diet, lack of exercise, innate moral deficiencies, irresponsibility, and sloth—have created health problems (Quinn 2003; Krieger 2010). Corporate spokespeople said that working with asbestos did not cause asbestosis; it was "defective lungs that took in too many fibers" (Davis 2007: 302). The lead industry said that workers' getting poisoned with lead came from their sloppy and careless behavior (Michaels and Monforton 2005: S41). The lifestyle of miners, which included "housing conditions and hurtful forms of recreation, especially alcohol" (quoted in Smith 1981: 345), has been typically cited as the cause of their health problems. These claims are generally supported by a type of "lifestyle research" that tends to blame the worker, not the work setting. Lifestyle research is supported not only by employers, who had obvious reasons; it became popular among scientists too, who saw in it the possibility of large, yet elegant and "scientific" case-control and prospective studies that could statistically document relationships. One downside for the health of workers is that research done according to this model is time-consuming and usually cannot be completed quickly enough to produce the requisite changes and improve current working conditions (Bohme et al. 2005: 340).

Furthermore, the proliferation of large-scale lifestyle studies has made case reports of health hazards (including reports by clinical doctors), which rely on small samples of workers in a particular industry, seem suspect and unconvincing (Fagin 2013: 206–7). Yet small-sample anecdotal case reporting can bring potential hazards to public awareness and can stimulate further research to document the problem. A good example is the case of a rare form of cancer, angiosarcoma, which was found in four workers in one B. F. Goodrich factory. Although based on a few cases, this concentration of illness was alarming and, fortunately, was treated seriously. More research followed; the aim was to understand the link and mitigate future risk (Michaels and Monforton 2005: S42).

More typical, though, are industries that effectively limit the amount of accurate information available in order to avoid shining a spotlight on a potential problem that would require an upstream solution. Corporations have worked hard to "manufacture doubt" about many occupational hazards (Michaels 2008a). They have done this in myriad ways. In one case, the medical director of Brush Wellman, a manufacturer of beryllium, was able to become joint author of an article in which the argument was made that any apparent carcinogenic effect of beryllium is likely due to confounding variables (LaDou et al. 2007: 412). The claim was made despite the views of the International Agency for Research on Cancer, which found a carcinogenic connection to be likely (LaDou et al. 2007). Corporations and industry-based research groups increasingly fund the relevant science, a move that allows them to control the results. Data on the corporate funding of university research alone show an increase from $264 million in 1980 to $2 billion in 2001 and a history of corporate "manipulation of evidence, data, and analysis" favorable to the industry (Egilman and Bohme 2005: 332).

Sometimes the actual research is done in-house, sometimes in academic settings. Either way, publications often obscure the funding source, leaving any possible conflict of interest hidden from the reader. Thus a well-known UK epidemiologist, Sir Richard Doll, published studies of asbestos and vinyl chloride showing few or no health hazards, while he was being paid to work for the relevant industries as a consultant (Sass et al. 2005; Hardell et al. 2007: 230). Similarly, Hans-Olav Adami of Karolinska Institute in Stockholm and Dmitri Trichopoulos of Harvard, well known for research on public health hazards, were "well-compensated for their efforts on behalf of the pesticide and solvents industries" (Davis 2007: 312), yet they did not make these financial arrangements known when they published their research.

One reason why much of this industry-led research gives little insight into the real occupational health problems is that the study design is often biased toward negative results (i.e., toward finding no link between the suspected toxin and a health problem). The bias results from various subtle and not so subtle methodological design decisions (see Egilman and Billings 2005; for more general comments on biases in occupational health epidemiological studies, see McCulloch 2005). Sample size is one. Although small samples used in anecdotal reports have proven quite useful, as in the case of the rare cancer detected at the Goodrich factory, small samples are often useless in quantitative research because, when numbers are small, it is hard to find a statistically significant difference between the exposed and the unexposed groups. Industry is well aware that a small sample can preclude a finding of difference that signals the existence of a health problem. For example, a chromium industry-sponsored study of four factories found a statistically significant increase in lung cancer risk for workers exposed to hexavalent chromium. This information could have been important, as the government was trying to understand the appropriate levels of exposure for workers. Instead, a publication appeared that analyzed data from only two of the four plants. The shrunken sample had little statistical power and no ability to show a relationship between exposure and disease (Michaels et al. 2006).

Latency in the presentation of illness is another important factor in toxic exposure research. If a chemical hazard doesn't show immediate harmful effects, then the study design must be long enough to cover that latency period. If one wants negative results, one cuts short the follow-up period and misses the likely effect. This is exactly what was done in the hexavalent chromium research, where fewer than half of the workers were followed for the necessary twenty years that covered the latency period for this toxin (Gennaro and Tomatis 2005; Michaels et al. 2006).

Another research challenge is finding an appropriate comparison group. Some studies compare the entire workforce at a plant to the general population. Researchers refer to the problem of a general population comparison group as the "healthy-worker effect," meaning that such data might show no difference in health because workers are generally healthier than the population at large (Gennaro and Tomatis 2005). After all, workers are healthy enough to get work and to continue to work, while many members of the general population are not. A more logical comparison group would be one made up of appropriately "matched" workers at a different type of factory, or of less exposed "matched" workers at the same factory. Manufacturers are likely to favor the population comparison because it makes "their factories seem safer than they really were" (Fagin 2013: 235). Population comparisons not only understate the impact of the work setting as a result of the healthy-worker effect, but also include workers who may have had only minimal exposure to the toxin. Such a study "dilutes" the exposed group and has a "comparison bias" (Parodi et al. 2007). Other researchers have further explored the exposure misclassification and argued that it "probably occurs in all studies" and "the direction of the bias is largely predictable, that is, a bias of relative risks toward the null" (Blair et al. 2007). A further problem of representing the exposed group comes from the exclusion of contract workers from the sample. "This is often the case in studies of US refinery workers, among whom the most heavily exposed workers are often 'contract workers'" (Gennaro and Tomatis 2005).

If independent research (not funded by the industry) is done, industry works hard to keep the health hazards from seeing the light of day in a publication (Pearce 2008), and sometimes even attempts to intimidate the researchers (Richter et al. 2001; Aviv 2014). Markowitz and Rosner have written extensively about this kind of intimidation, which they have encountered as they sought to make the dangers of industrial pollution (to workers and to the environment) known to the public. They wrote at one point that "Monsanto, Dow, Union Carbide, Goodrich, Goodyear, and Uniroyal, among others, sought to undermine our credibility as scholars and the credibility of the information we documented in our book" (Markowitz and Rosner 2013a: 307). Industry also took aim at a well-known asbestos researcher, Irving Selikoff, who received from a law firm, at the behest of the asbestos industry, a letter that was a "veiled threat to sue Selikoff or other scientists who publicly discussed the asbestos hazards revealed by their research" (Bohme et al. 2005: 342). IBM was similarly able to intimidate a major international journal, *Clinics in Occupational and Environmental Medicine*, which ended up withdrawing the acceptance of the "first article showing that those who worked in 'clean rooms' as IBM chip makers had higher rates of several types of cancer" (Davis 2007: 327).

Corporations are also silencing clinicians who find serious occupational health problems. The case of Dr. Kern, a faculty member at Brown University Medical School (LaDou 2002; Gochfeld 2005), illustrates the power of the industry over an academically employed occupational health expert. Dr. Kern was a clinician at the Brown-affiliated Memorial Hospital, where he diagnosed multiple cases of interstitial lung disease that occurred among nylon flockers at a nearby manufacturing firm, Microfibres. Microfibres was not only an industry concerned about Kern's publicizing his results, but also a donor to Memorial Hospital. In fact the owner of Microfibres and two family members served on the hospital board. When Kern refused to back down and presented his results, his "clinic was closed, the teaching program curtailed, and soon thereafter he was discharged from his hospital and university positions" (LaDou 2002: 292). An article in *Academe*, the American Association of University Professors' magazine, talked about the case, formulating a "need to confront excessive commercialism and financial conflicts on campus" (Washburn 2011: 8).

The more typical example of how the industry uses its economic muscle to affect the work of an occupational health professional is that of the "company doctor," a health professional paid directly by the corporation to look after the health of the employees. Such an arrangement has an "inherent potential for conflict of interest" (Gochfeld 2005: 120; see also Draper 2003: 2). Rather than making the workers' health the foremost priority, the healthcare provider is often motivated by "fear of publicity, desire not to alarm workers, the cost of remedial measures, and concern that knowing about a risk may leave them more liable for resulting disease" (Draper 2003: 97; see also Gochfeld 2005: 119). If doctors identify a possible workplace hazard and ask "that resources be spent to address it, managers may treat them as whistleblowers or troublemakers" (Draper 2003: 97). As a result, occupational physicians become "far more skilled at suppressing the complaints of the employees about adverse conditions than they [are] ... at getting the condition corrected" (Imbus 2004: 99). Additional evidence that conflicts are often decided in favor of the company comes from lawsuits brought against industry. In the court setting, few occupational health physicians are willing to testify on behalf of the worker. Many more testify on the side of the defense, the industry (LaDou et al. 2007: 415). Even historians are more likely to testify for industry than for the workers (Rosner and Markowitz 2009: 274).

Occupational Nurses

While the number of occupational health physicians working in and for corporations has declined, the number of occupational health nurses in such settings has increased. A recent estimate suggests that there are twenty occupational health nurses working in industry for every one occupational physician (LaDou 2002: 293). This position of occupational nurse retains the same inherent conflict of interest that doctors practicing within the industry face. In fact one analysis suggests that their lesser power makes the nurses even more vulnerable to the power of industry, and even less likely to represent the workers' interests (Draper et al. 2011). Other occupational health practitioners, such as industrial hygienists, are also "coming under increasing pressure to make themselves relevant to management interests. As a result, their main function has become protecting the health of companies, rather than protecting the health of workers" (Quinn 2003: 426).

The Persistence of Occupational Health Problems: Lack of Worker Power

Corporations are powerful not only because of their economic resources and influence, but also because workers have so little power themselves. Currently, much of this powerlessness stems from an inability to organize and protest the conditions at work, itself due to the fact that union membership is so low. In 2013, less than 12 percent of wage and salary workers were members of unions (http://www.bls.gov/news.release/pdf/union2.pdf). The first characteristic of a non-union job is that it is less likely to provide health insurance for workers. Without insurance, a worker is less likely to go to a doctor, especially with a vague complaint; thus symptoms are not identified. Second, without a workers' union, employers are likely to provide less information about occupational hazards.

Working in a non-union environment presents other problems as well. The chance that employees will engage in unified action to report health and safety issues to management is very low. Understandably, employees may be unwilling to act on their own to redress such issues for fear of losing their jobs, regardless of how unsafe and unhealthy they may be. The plight of women at the Albuquerque, New Mexico plant of Lenkurt—a subsidiary of General Telephone and Electric Corporation (GTE) that specialized in telephone switching and transmission equipment—provides a striking example of the kinds of horrendous health problems that non-union employees will put up with in silence. The workforce was largely female; and these women, exposed to various solvents, acids, plastics, and other toxic chemicals, suffered from an array of health problems that included cancers, frequent miscarriages, excessive menstrual bleeding and hysterectomies, bizarre skin disorders, and odd neurological problems (Fox 1991). Yet they were not only reluctant to complain to their employers, but also hesitant to inform their families of the problems, knowing that the families depended on their incomes. In general, employers are well aware of the greater power they have when a union is not around; and GTE explicitly chose the Albuquerque area because of "the city's weak tradition of organized labor" (Fox 1991: 30).

The corporation's power over the worker also comes from the company's economic contribution to the community at large and to workers individually. The Zonolite mine in Libby, Montana, where sweepers were unwittingly exposed to asbestos, had been one of the most reliable employers in town for many decades (Schneider and McCumber 2004: 66). Sometimes, although serious occupational health hazards are known, even the union is in support of a corporation, because union members are also invested in protecting jobs. Thus in Toms River, New Jersey, the union helped organize protests against environmental groups like Greenpeace, which was raising serious questions about the toxic production process of a local chemical plant. Jobs at the plant in Toms River were declared "the best blue-collar jobs in the county" (Fagin 2013: 199) and the union decided that saving the jobs was its number one priority.

The company (which, over time and through mergers, came to have various names such as Toms River Chemical Company, CIBA, or CIBA-Geigy), contributed significantly to the community in other ways. Company executives were the primary force behind the opening of the first hospital in the county, the restoration of a public golf course with a new swimming pool, and the reopening of a country club "whose sixty-seven acres quickly became the private playground of the town's business and political elite" (Fagin 2013: 42–3). The company manager, aware of the goodwill that existed, was able to say: "If the responsible people of this area want a prosperous community with continuing growth, we must realize there will be changes in our natural surroundings. Very few of us are willing to live like the Indians, in spite of our idyllic dreams" (Fagin 2013: 58). Newspaper coverage even defended the chemical company as a good neighbor and declared it good for the economy (Fagin 2013:

109), and a documentary, partly funded by the company, stressed the trade-off between jobs and pollution (Fagin 2013: 229). This perverse "trade-off" might explain why, in a different company setting, after two workers who had been required to crawl into vats of toxic sludge in a San Francisco chrome plating business died and the plant was closed, another worker said: "I'd go back in a minute if I could" (Fagan and Walker 1997: 1).

The Persistence of Occupational Health Problems: The Government's Role

The main federal agency now in charge of making the workplace safe is the Occupational Safety and Health Administration (OSHA), created in 1970. Other important agencies for worker health are the NIOSH (mentioned earlier), the Department of Labor Mine Safety and Health Administration (MSHA), and the Environmental Protection Agency (EPA). In this chapter I will focus mainly on OSHA, to illustrate the government's role in addressing occupational health. At the time of its creation, labor organizations saw OSHA as merely symbolic, an agency established to placate labor but probably ineffective in implementing any real workplace changes (Calavita 1983). Despite this skepticism, over the years OSHA has recommended and implemented important legislation for worker safety, including "right to know" legislation that requires the labeling of all toxic chemicals used in the workplace. Prior to this legislation, workers had to work next to rusty drums of unlabeled toxic sludge and in environments filled with unknown chemicals. They were afraid to ask what was in the drums or what was in the air, and employers didn't have to tell. These laws have been created to guarantee workers their right to receive information about the health effects of workplace chemicals, to look over records of their own exposure, and to get instruction about the methods they should use to handle chemicals safely. In addition, OSHA publishes an "annual candidates list" of suspected carcinogens, which is a way to inform workers that they should be careful around certain chemicals because, although no definitive studies have been produced, preliminary evidence suggests that the chemicals in question might be harmful.

OSHA has generated worker grassroots activity by encouraging the formation of committees on occupational safety and health (COSH) that train rank-and-file workers in safety and health issues, facilitating coalitions across industries (e.g., asbestos workers) and generally empowering workers. In terms of the impact on health, these OSHA activities are positive: occupational health incidents and death rates have gone down since their inception.

But in many ways OSHA has not been that strong. A big problem is that OSHA is underfunded (Kotelchuck 2000). Among other things, this weakness has led to a shortage of inspectors, which means that there is a lot of room for companies to proceed as they wish and ignore OSHA standards. With lax inspection, employers can be devious and not get caught, as in the case of the coal mining industry. Coal miners are susceptible to black lung disease, which gives them shortness of breath and emphysema. Decades ago coal miners' mobilization led to a federal regulation on mine safety and health that required mines to keep the dust level down in order to prevent black lung disease. Air samples taken from mines were inspected for dust. Not having enough inspectors to make the rounds of mines and collect samples, however, regulators relied on samples sent in by the mines. To skew the results, mine operators would spray Endust (a popular furniture cleaner that repels dust) on the filters before installing them to collect the samples. In one year, 847 mines sent in 4,710 faked samples (Hilts 1991). Such deception is an effective way to cut down on the measured dust and, unfortunately, on the accuracy of the sample. Actual threats to the health of workers remain hidden.

Even when inspectors are present, a lot is typically missed or remains unaddressed. "OSHA inspectors frequently overlook dangerous working conditions, and even when they find serious health and safety violations, inspectors often cannot compel firms to eliminate the hazards discovered" (Kniesner and Leeth 1995: 47). Sometimes inspectors aren't well trained enough for a specific worksite. For example, in February of 2008 a fire broke out in the Imperial Sugar factory in Georgia and caused fourteen deaths and the hospitalization of forty people, eight with critical burns. The potential for this fire was not spotted in time because the inspectors who came did not know to look for the large accumulation of sugar dust on top of electric motors (Murray 2009). On other occasions, hazardous working conditions are not apparent to the inspectors because the regulatory agency might give the onsite manager advance warning of an upcoming inspection, allowing cleanup of toxic materials just before. At one mine, inspectors notified the supervisor in advance, giving them "time to wet the ore down to keep the asbestos dust from being collected in the air samples" (Schneider and McCumber 2004: 263). And, if violations are uncovered, the penalty for non-compliance is minimal. It is simple business sense for a company to favor a small fine over the higher cost of prevention (Egilman and Bohme 2005: 333). Even the CATO Institute, a politically conservative pro-business think tank, recognizes the limits of OSHA's regulatory power:

> OSHA inspectors frequently overlook dangerous working conditions, and even when they find serious health and safety violations, inspectors often cannot compel firms to eliminate the hazards discovered. To encourage timely compliance, administrators often slash assessed penalties, further reducing the already minor economic incentives for firms to observe health and safety standards. Firms realize that it is unlikely that they will be inspected ... and if they are inspected, firms can avoid paying severe fines by simply agreeing to abide by OSHA's regulations in the future. (Quoted from the Cato Institute by Silverstein 2008: 417)

If OSHA could make surprise visits and levy large fines when the workplace endangers the worker, then the workplace would be much safer. Such power levied by a government agency, however, would raise a few political red flags.

One of the reasons why OSHA has not been as supportive of workers' health as it might be is precisely political infighting. Occupational safety and health brings out all the typical business-versus-labor and capitalism-versus-worker arguments. The political environment of OSHA and the economic fortunes of the country have determined whether or not OSHA has been able to enforce regulations and properly inspect workplaces (Gochfeld 2005: 119). Many times business interests win over the workers' health. For instance, OSHA developed a regulation for brown lung, the textile industry equivalent of black lung for miners, but the political winds in Washington, DC quashed OSHA's pamphlet discussing the disease because it contained a photograph deemed inflammatory for the industry (Shor 2014). A second example of business interests prevailing over the workers' health involves ergonomics (fitting the job to the worker). It took ten years for OSHA to develop ergonomic standards, because the industry claimed that ergonomic hazards had not been proven (Kotelchuck 2000). When the ergonomics standard passed, the employers complained that there was too much government regulation. It wasn't long before the standard was rescinded (Ratcliff 2002; Clapp et al. 2006; LaDou et al. 2007: 419).

Another reason why OSHA is not a strong force for occupational health is the agency's dependence on what the industry tells it. Building on a model of the mid-1900s, when standards for exposure in the workplace "were determined by informal agreement between industrial and government experts" (Davis 2007: 385), the lack of good data on many chemicals continues. "Of the more than six hundred different chemical threshold limit values (TLVs) of the ACGIH [American Conference of Government and Industrial Hygienists], one hundred rest solely on the opinion of company experts. Many of these are more than three decades old ... One out of every six workplace standards is based on no studies whatsoever" (Davis 2007: 385). This dependence on industry for data is further illustrated by an example from the electronics industry. After OSHA raised concerns about the industry's illness rate, the Semiconductor Industry Association played a game of semantics, redefining one-time or instantaneous chemical exposures as injuries, which do not have to be reported to the state if they do not result in lost work time—as opposed to illnesses, which must be reported (Pellow and Park 2002: 101). The industry was able to play this game, which clearly benefitted the employers and jeopardized the workers, because the government's definition of reportable conditions was ambiguous. The result was an underreporting of occupational illness in the semiconductor manufacturing industry (Ratcliff 2002).

OSHA would be a better steward of workers' health if its leadership and that of other federal agencies mandated to protect our health represented the worker better. Unfortunately, the heads of these agencies often do not demonstrate a particular allegiance to the worker. In fact top government officials in OSHA as well as in other agencies can sometimes be more accurately described as cases of "the fox guarding the hen house." The potential for conflicts of interest is evident when government officials are appointed to regulatory posts after pursuing careers in the industries they are then expected to regulate. One man who was appointed to head OSHA illustrates this problem all too well. Prior to his appointment, Edwin Foulke had represented the US Chamber of Commerce (an industry group), was opposed to ergonomic standards, and testified that OSHA should develop voluntary compliance programs, which have no provision for a neutral party to check on what is happening and no penalties for violations—a measure that made them nearly useless for improving worker health. Once at OSHA, Foulke applied the industry's familiar "blame the victim" tactic in a talk titled "Adults Do the Darndest Things," blaming occupational health problems on the workers' naivety or stupidity (Skrzycki 2006).

Another example of a "fox guarding the henhouse" came to light in the summer of 2007, when there was a terrible mine disaster at the Crandall Canyon mine in Utah. The federal mine safety administrator, Richard Stickler, had a prior record of not taking care of workers.

When he was an industry executive, his own mine had terrible health and safety statistics, twice as poor as the national average. Then, when he worked in Pennsylvania as director of Deep Mine Safety, an investigation of a Pennsylvania mine disaster led to a grand jury conclusion that the regulatory system was out of date and weak. These are poor credentials for a man who became responsible for the quality of the regulatory system at a federal level (Buckley and Frosch 2007).

A final disquieting example is the US Chemical Safety Board (CSB), an independent federal agency mandated to investigate industrial chemical "accidents." The president of the United States appoints the members, who are then confirmed by the Senate. In May 2014 a CSB board member testified before the House Committee on Oversight and Government Reform, declaring that in discussions at the CSB any disagreement was seen as "disloyalty," producing an environment less than ideal for the careful analysis of complicated health data. "Those whose opinions differed from those of senior leadership or the Chair were marginalized and vilified" (Borkowski and Monforton 2014: 5).

The government's lack of support for workers' health can also be detected in the irrationality of health standards. OSHA and MSHA both establish toxic exposure limits for workers. Yet, oddly, the standards differ. MSHA has an asbestos exposure limit that is twenty times higher than OSHA's limit (Schneider and McCumber 2004: 262). Other irrationalities of federal regulation include differential fines imposed for violations. Corporations became "more concerned about compliance with Environmental Protection Agency (EPA) regulations than with OSHA regulations. Pragmatically, the former often carried high penalties for violations, whereas OSHA penalties were usually less costly and often forgiven upon subsequent compliance" (Gochfeld 2005: 120).

Improving Occupational Health

Despite setbacks and the power of interested parties to deny possible health hazards in the workplace, occupational health has improved over the years. We have come a long way since the nineteenth century, when occupational health pioneer Alice Hamilton was seen as radical because she talked about "man-made" health problems. In many industries awareness of hazards has increased dramatically and rates of disease, injury, and death have decreased (Silverstein 2008).

Two Heroes of Occupational Health

Born in 1869, Alice Hamilton dedicated her life work to marginalized, less powerful people. She earned a medical degree and, before accepting an offer from Harvard to become the first female medical faculty member there, she insisted that her contract allow her to work half-time at Hull House, a Chicago settlement house. Settlement houses, residential institutions in poor areas with social reform-minded social workers who lived among community residents, gave poor people a place where they could come together and work with social workers and others to ameliorate poor living conditions. Hamilton wanted to spend time at Hull House in order to be able to talk to workers and learn directly about their work-related health problems. She visited many work places and was appalled by the conditions the workers endured. She heard stories about painters with lead palsy, steel workers exposed to carbon monoxide, and people working in dusty conditions without protection. She asked employers about the poor health conditions and would sometimes hear that workers did not last long before they returned to the old country. She queried, "To die?" and heard them respond, "Yes, I suppose" (https://www.youtube.com/watch?v=E75pST2QTEM). On the basis of her interviews and observations, she declared that there were *"man-made occupational diseases."* While this sounds obvious now, it wasn't 100 years ago. In fact, declaring such a connection led to her being called a communist. Alice Hamilton wrote numerous articles about occupational health, especially the hazards of lead (Baron and Brown 2009). Her contributions were acknowledged when the National Institute for Occupational Safety and Health named its research facility the Alice Hamilton Laboratory for Occupational Safety and Health.

A more recent hero in occupational health is Dr. Irving Selikoff. His work in this field began in the mid-1960s, when many patients at his lung clinic in New Jersey were workers at the Union Asbestos and Rubber Company factory. Noticing a similarity in his patients' breathing problems, he decided to gather systematic medical histories on nearly 1,000 workers (without the help of the company) and found that they contracted lung cancer at several times the rate that would be expected. The lung tissue of his deceased patients was filled with asbestos fibers. His first publication of the data in 1961 was "derided by industry scientists" (Schneider and McCumber 2004: 104). More research and more publications by Selikoff led to the first major international conference on the dangers of asbestos. Shortly thereafter Selikoff raised issues about the asbestos used in the 1968–72 construction of the World Trade Center buildings. He noted that the asbestos fireproofing was being sprayed on the structures and warned that a "hundred tons of asbestos fibers were 'falling like snow' from steel skeletons of the rising towers ... [and] told union health experts that not one man of the thousands who worked on or near the spraying would be alive in 20 years" (Schneider and McCumber 2004: 333). The resulting protests led to a nationwide banning of the spraying of asbestos. Unfortunately, when the Twin Towers fell on September 11, 2001 asbestos was released. Immediate respiratory health problems of people in the surrounding area were caused by a toxic dust storm of pulverized concrete, fiberglass, metal, and other debris. What are the long-term health consequences for New Yorkers who survived that terrible event? Asbestos has a long latency period, so the final story of the sprayed asbestos fireproofing has yet to unfold.

Improvements have come in part because of federal agencies, which, despite some foot dragging and political push and pull from industry, have made important changes in workplace standards and conditions, changes that improve occupational health. An annual report titled "The Year in US Occupational Health and Safety" (Borkowski and Monforton 2014) highlights such improvements at both federal and state levels (and documents continuing issues). In reports covering three years (2011–14), the authors note specific successes: research on oft-neglected hazards, including those for Latino/a poultry workers; state legislation designed to end the worst abuses of temporary workers in Massachusetts; new rules in Wyoming for oil and gas workers; regulations for the protection of healthcare workers in Washington state from exposure to hazardous medications like anti-cancer drugs; new bills of rights for domestic workers in California and Massachusetts; and safeguards for healthcare workers in Texas and Maryland from on-the-job violence.

At the federal level, encouraging signs include improved input from workers about occupational conditions. For instance, in a 2014 hearing on silica-related lung disease, Santos Almendarez from the Fe y Justicia Worker Center in Houston described the lack of protection from dust when he worked making granite kitchen countertops. His testimony was in Spanish—a first in the history of OSHA rulemaking

(Borkowski and Monforton 2014: 4). Similarly, hearing the voices of worker advocates—such as the National Council of La Raza—about the health dangers of increasing the speed of the line at a poultry-slaughtering facility from 140 to 175 birds a minute led to the withdrawal of that proposal (Borkowski and Monforton 2014: 14).

Grassroots activism has also been an important impetus for change. With support from OSHA, a national farmworker advocacy program, Farmrworker Justice (FJ), was able to train *promotores de salud* (health promoters) and to employ them at "ferneries"—places where decorative ferns are produced—to help workers reduce the health damage from being hunched close to the ground for much of the day (Baron et al. 2011: 18). More significantly, workers and community activists in Silicon Valley have demonstrated the power of coalitions concerned with health. The Santa Clara Center for Occupational Safety and Health (SCCOSH) joined with the Silicon Valley Toxics Coalition (SVTC) to raise occupational and environmental health issues that stemmed from the "clean" electronics industry. The organizers worked hard to include people of color and women. The group faced opposition from the industry, but was able to stimulate research that demonstrated the occupational health issues, including possible reproductive risks for both men and women. One concrete result was a report urging comprehensive health tests for semiconductor industry employees in Santa Clara County (Pellow and Park 2002).

Other coalitions of occupational health groups and environmental justice groups have been effective in changing work and community conditions. In Philadelphia, for instance, PhilPOSH joined with the Environmental Cancer Prevention Center to make strong statements about workplace hazards and public health. The support was strong enough to convince legislators to pass the nation's first citywide "right to know" law (Mayer et al. 2012). Similarly, in New Jersey, a coalition of worker groups and environmentalists noted the existence of unknown hazardous chemicals in workplaces and potential exposures in the community and effectively framed it as a violation of human rights, remedied only by the right to know. The approach was successful and the New Jersey Worker and Community Right to Know Act was the result (Mayer 2009).

Conclusion

Workers face many hazards tied to their employment that can result in bodily injuries, diseases, or even death. While we no longer have employers publicly proclaiming a cavalier disregard for the health of workers, as they did in Alice Hamilton's time, or the horrendous workplace injury and mortality statistics of the last two centuries, occupational health problems persist.

That persistence is not due to lack of information about the hazards. Instead, employers have actively avoided the responsibility of addressing occupationally based threats to the health of their workers. They have steadfastly resisted most suggestions to look upstream. Whether through failure to devote resources to recognizing and implementing remedies for workers' health hazards, through public denial of health risks, through threats to researchers or clinicians who report such risks, or through active efforts to use political influence to limit government responses that could protect workers, the overall impact of employers has been harmful. Most often out of self-interest, employers have argued that remedying occupational health problems would have a disastrous impact on the number of jobs available in a local economy, and perhaps even on the existence of the industry itself.

Such a "your life or your job" argument presents a false dilemma. Our choices simply cannot be to try to live without a job or accept a job that is likely to have serious health implications. Knowingly accepting a shortened life with "laughter denied, picnics never held, words never spoken" (Schneider and McCumber 2004: 358) should not be an option. There has to be a middle ground. That middle ground cannot come from workers alone. Although the workers' mobilization has been instrumental to change, their impact has been limited by the declining influence of unions in many employment sectors and by their lack of resources for gathering the requisite evidence. The ability of workers has also been undercut by job insecurities, often tied to globalization, that cause workers to hold back from pushing for protections that, often stoked by threats from employers, they fear could limit jobs.

The role of government agencies in promoting occupational health and safety would seem to have substantial potential in establishing a middle ground, but the government is limited by corporate and political pressures. While the government needs to rededicate itself to ensuring our "life, liberty, and pursuit of happiness" by promoting public health, it alone can't implement the needed change. Business buy-in is essential.

Convincing businesses to be more responsible and to look upstream for solutions will not be easy, yet employers' acceptance of better working conditions does not necessarily lead to the downward economic trajectory they often predict. In the vinyl chloride industry, new OSHA regulations led industry spokespeople to issue "dire predictions of job loss and plant closures"; but the plants met the new regulations in less than two years, and sales volume grew rapidly (Sass et al. 2005). If reasonable regulations are established and loopholes closed so that the regulations cover all employers in a given industry, an equal playing field can be built and healthy competition can ensue. In the conclusion to this book I will discuss a movement toward more socially responsible business practices, which could have a significant impact on occupational health, as well as on health in the many other domains covered here.

8
Food and Health

Food is obviously essential to our health. The challenge is to eat food that is nutritious, to avoid foods that are harmful or lack nutrients, and to be prudent in the amounts we consume. None of these actions is easy for people living in the United States today because, upstream, the growers, producers, and distributors do not have health as their primary concern.

Overconsumption of unhealthy foods, especially those with high caloric content, characterizes the typical American diet. The consequence is a pervasive state of obesity, which is now a major health concern in our society. But the root cause of obesity is not just excess of consumption; a deeper analysis of causation in this case should encompass the many ways in which people come to eat the wrong types of food—foods that are in themselves harmful to human health. The striking reality is that food is linked to a variety of health issues, of which obesity is only one example. Some of the problems with food are well known, but others are poorly understood or potential hazards created by fast-changing methods of production, seductive products, and effective advertising.

In this discussion attention will be given to the social determinants of food production and food consumption. I will, as usual, look upstream to find the relationships that interconnect food and health in the context of economic forces and the social factors that limit our choices and mediate our behavior when it comes to food. Particular attention will be given to the industries that increasingly dominate the production, processing, distribution, and marketing of the foods people eat. Two rich online sources discussing many of these issues are http://phsj.org/food-safety-issues and www.uconnruddcenter.org.

By the very logic of our capitalist economy, what is central to the food industry's agenda is profit, not public health. Unfortunately the taste for thriving business operations has to a large degree diminished the quality, variety, and nutritional value of food and has even led to risky patterns of consumption. Many argue that we don't take the hazards laid at our door by the food industry seriously enough. For example, an obesity researcher at Yale said:

> As a culture, we've become upset by the tobacco companies advertising to children, but we sit idly by while the food companies do the very same thing. And we could make a claim that the toll taken on public health by a poor diet rivals that taken by tobacco. (Brownell, quoted in Moss 2013: 36)

The food industry can have such a major health impact because it is big and exceedingly concentrated—and becoming even more so. Over the past twenty years "the number of plants in eight important food industries—meatpacking, meat processing, cheese products, fluid milk, flour milling, corn milling, feed, and soybean processing—declined by about one-third" (Ollinger et al. 2005: iv), while the plant size grew and the productivity of employees rose sharply. We now have "massive agribusiness companies" (Brownell and Warner 2009: 263), from growers and butchering plants to food sellers and large restaurant chains, be they fast-food outlets such as McDonald's and Burger King or "casual dining" franchises such as Applebee's and Olive Garden. Food is one of the biggest industries worldwide and a major source of profit (Leahy 2009). Large food companies "dominate markets internationally," concentrating many components of the food industry (Leahy 2009: 67). For example, in 2003 four US companies controlled 80 percent of the world's seed market, and six corporations controlled nearly all (85 percent) of the world market in grain (Leahy 2009: 67–8). In the United States, the largest share (80 percent) of output in the beef-packing industry comes from four companies, as does most flour milling (62 percent) and pork production (57 percent) (Lawrence and Grice 2009: 81). Big players in the food retailer part of the industry include Kraft, General Mills, PepsiCo, and ConAgra, each owning ten or more brands (Brownell and Horgen 2004). Kraft, owned by Philip Morris, has leading brands that include Nabisco, Post Cereals, Oscar Meyer, Maxwell House, Jell-O, Tombstone Pizza, Stove Top, Louis Rich, Philadelphia Cream Cheese, and Bakers' Chocolate (Brownell and Horgen 2004: 11). The concentration is such that, in the United States, the "ten largest food companies control more than half of all food sales" (Moodie et al. 2013: 671). This economic concentration and the resulting power of the food industry raise serious questions about the health of the food supply and warrants a careful examination of the social determinants of unhealthy food. Many writers on this topic, including Brownell quoted above, use the term "Big Food" in discussing the food industry. I will follow their lead.

Food-related health threats are manifested in a variety of public health realms: harmful impacts on the heart, increasing spread and severity of obesity, and prevalence of diseases such as Type 2 diabetes. For instance, important health problems are caused by the trend toward ultra-processed foods, a matter discussed more fully below. These are, typically, ready to consume products that are fatty, sugary or salty, and energy-dense (Steele et al. 2016). Some of the ingredients can be harmful to health in and of themselves. It has been long recognized that the abundant consumption of trans fats may lead to heart disease. Other ingredients, such as sugar and salt, are not necessarily harmful when eaten in moderation but become threats when they are eaten in excess, as is often the case when people's diets contain increasing amounts of ultra-processed foods. Too much sugar increases the likelihood of weight gain, obesity, Type 2 diabetes, hypertension, and cardiovascular disease (Yang et al. 2014), while too much salt increases the chances of raised blood pressure, hypertension, and mortality from cardiovascular heart disease and stroke (Dickinson and Havas 2007).

Big Food's impact on the soundness of the food supply is evident in various aspects of the process that puts food on people's table. Here I will examine the change in the size and nature of the farms where livestock is grown and crops are raised, the change in the types of crops that are grown, in particular the increase in genetically modified organism (GMO) crops, the change to ultra-processed foods, and the unhealthy options offered by popular restaurants.

Raising Livestock and Growing Crops

It is not only the availability of processed food—especially ultra-processed food, which is so unhealthy—that has increased so much in the last fifty years; this period has also seen the progressive dominance of livestock raised and crops grown according to a factory model that puts the health of consumers, the environment, and animals at risk. Focusing for the moment on livestock, one change has been the move from decentralized family farms that raised animals (as in

Thomas Jefferson's vision of America as an agrarian utopia) to fewer and larger producers that raise huge numbers of animals—a change triggered by the postindustrial age (Boehlje and Doering 2000). Instead of cattle grazing in open fields or chickens running around the farmyard, one sees animals being put in small spaces, where their movement is restricted. In the United States, these sights are called concentrated animal feeding operations (CAFOs) or industrial food animal production (IFAP). Two fifths of US animals are now raised in the "largest 2 percent of livestock facilities" (APHA 2007: 3). A major reason for this transition was the mass demand for beef, pork, and chicken. In 1989 the biggest purchaser, Walmart, wanted to apply its successful "big volume–big discount" model to a new grocery section (Roberts 2009; Food and Water Watch 2012). Walmart needed to buy huge quantities of chicken, beef, and pork cheaply, so it pushed for efficiency throughout the production chain. Only the largest producers could survive the Walmart model; and, to do so, they began producing more in less time.

Producing more in less time turned out to mean that one needed to resort to genetics, hormones, and new feeding options in order to grow animals bigger and faster. Chickens are now twice as big as they were in 1975 (Roberts 2009: 69). Twice!! Thanks to the new efficiencies, meat costs have dropped considerably since 1970 and animals have grown faster. In 1950 it took eighty-four days for a chicken to grow to five pounds; in 2005 it only took forty-five days (Pew Commission on Industrial Farm Animal Protection 2008: 5). In fact many animals have grown so huge that they cannot even walk. Gone are the 1950s, when "chickens were raised in small flocks by many farmers; today, most are 'factory-farmed' in massive numbers under contract to a few large companies" (Nestle 2002: 11).

The pork industry has seen similar changes. The concentration of production is impressive. The United States had over 600,000 hog farms in the early 1980s; by 2011 the number was down to 70,000. Hog farms with more than 50,000 heads grew rapidly; those with fewer than 2,000 lost ground steadily (Meyer 2012). The changes for the animals have been dramatic: breeding sows used to deliver an average of fourteen piglets a year; now they are up to twenty-three. A single sow has doubled her output of meat per year (Roberts 2009: 72).

These huge commercial operations put thousands upon thousands of animals in narrow enclosures, for the sake of efficiency. This concentration is concerning for a variety of reasons, one being the fecal output. Hogs in particular are a problem as they typically produce three gallons of feces and urine a day, an enormous amount (Roberts 2009: 77). When you have a lot of hogs in a limited space, the disposal of all of this manure becomes a huge problem.

The old family farm could deal with the manure because it had enough agricultural land to spread it around as fertilizer. As food writer Michael Pollan explains, taking the animals off our farms and putting them in CAFOs "is to take an elegant solution—animals replenishing the fertility that crops deplete—and neatly divide it into two problems: a fertility problem on the farm and a pollution problem on the feedlot. The former problem is remedied with fossil fuel fertilizer; the latter is remedied not at all" (Pollan 2008: 4). One attempt at handling the manure at a CAFO is with a lagoon, and many lagoons have soil-containment banks that can fail. Runoff can cause damage to local lakes and rivers. A PBS Frontline documentary, *Poisoned Water*, shows the runoff from the CAFOs in Delaware causing serious pollution problems in the Chesapeake Bay.

A well-documented case in North Carolina involved an eight-acre, twelve-foot-deep lagoon that broke and released about 25 million gallons of feces and urine into the local water table, causing a huge increase in nutrients, algae, dinoflagellates, and ultimately in fish deaths and threats to human health (Barker 1998: 236) in the form of cognitive impairment, short-term memory loss, kidney dysfunction, blurred vision, and vomiting (Horrigan et al. 2002: 451). Even if the lagoons don't fail, the smell and the gradual leakage into the local soil and water can cause health problems such as neurobehavioral symptoms and respiratory illnesses (Greger and Koneswaran 2010). The manure is typically a concentrated source of nitrogen, phosphorus, or other minerals harmful to the ecology of the area. As one would expect after our discussion of environmental injustice in chapter 4, CAFOs have a disproportionate impact on African Americans and poor people as a result of proximity to their homes (Ladd and Edwards 2002).

A further health concern related to CAFOs is the use of antibiotics, deemed necessary because animals are raised in such close proximity to one another. On a factory farm, antibiotics are used on healthy animals for disease *prevention*. This is not the typical use of an antibiotic, which was developed to fight bacterial infection. "More than 70 percent of all US antibiotics are estimated to be fed to hogs, poultry, and beef cattle for such nontherapeutic reasons" (APHA 2007). Their widespread use increases the risk of antimicrobial resistance—which is especially troubling since food is the major source of this resistance (Pew Commission on Industrial Farm Animal Protection

2008: 408; Aitken et al. 2016). The good news is that consumer pressure is leading to a decrease in antibiotic use in livestock. Walmart's corporate site announced in May of 2015 that they would implement the American Veterinary Medical Association's "Judicious Use Principles of Antimicrobial Use" (corporate.walmart.com).

To further reduce costs of livestock production, processing has become automated and the size of the processing plants has grown. The top four meat-processing and poultry slaughter and processing industries have seen a stunning increase in concentration ratios, up to 50 percent, in a twenty-year period (Ollinger et al. 2005). The result of all of this? Since 1980 the US chicken output has tripled and prices have plummeted (Roberts 2009: 71). This is just what Walmart ordered, and in the process small farming operations became increasingly unprofitable.

Changed agricultural methods have affected not only the raising of animals for food, but also the growing of crops. Family farms have declined and large farms have prospered. The average size of farms in 1900 was about 150 acres while in 2012 it increased to about 430 acres. The number of farms decreased from a high of about 6.8 million in 1935 to 2.1 million in 2012 (USDA 2017). The old model of small farms had many benefits. Small farmers can "intercrop" different types of plants: plants that shade one another, plants that process water at different depths of soil, and plants that use different soil nutrients. The smaller farms are also more productive per acre and use the land, water, and oil more efficiently (McKibben 2007). As noted above, they could also use manure productively and thus had a natural, renewable fertilizer.

Large farms, on the other hand, must operate very differently to be efficient. They tend to practice monoagriculture, decreasing biodiversity among plants and animals (Horrigan et al. 2002; Leahy 2009; Nestle 2012). They use large quantities of nonrenewable fossil fuel-based inputs like fertilizers (APHA 2007). Worldwide fertilizer use has increased more than fourfold a person (Horrigan et al. 2002). Pesticide and herbicide use has also increased, and the runoff and airborne drift from fertilizers, pesticides, and herbicides pollute surface waters and groundwater (Horrigan et al. 2002: 446). Current farming practices are held responsible for 70 percent of the nation's river and stream pollution (Horrigan et al. 2002: 447). They also cause "dead zones" downstream, places where the water does not have enough oxygen to support life. Dead zones impact fisheries and the associated ecosystems (APHA 2007: 2; see chapter 5 for further discussion). In addition, pesticides have the potential for a more direct impact on human health, since they are found on most fresh fruits and vegetables (APHA 2007). Large growing operations that pick and package on an enormous scale are increasingly found to harbor biohazards, for instance the bacterium *Escherichia coli*, in otherwise nutritious foods such as spinach and other leafy greens. While small operations must guard against food safety issues, the opportunity for contamination is much more prevalent in mass operations.

Overall, the food system intrinsic to industrialized farming does not seem sustainable. A sustainable food system must not only provide for people now (which our system does in abundance); it also needs to respect the ecosystem to make sure that food can be provided for future generations (APHA 2007: 1). Practices like overuse of non-renewable fossil fuels, toxic chemicals in pesticides and herbicides, and overuse of water do not bode well. In addition, there is evidence of rather near-range health problems such as "elevated cancer risks and disruption of the body's reproductive, immune, endocrine, and nervous systems" (Horrigan et al. 2002: 450). Cardiovascular disease and diabetes are also implicated (APHA 2007). The health of workers at various stages of the industrial agriculture production cycle is threatened by many current practices and by extensive use of chemicals (see discussion of these health impacts in chapter 7).

Move to GMO crops

Another major change has taken place in the area of what is grown: GMOs—also referred to as gene-altered food, genetically engineered food (GE), or bioengineering—have become dominant in many crops such as corn and soybeans. In contrast to traditional methods of crop improvement, namely through the selection of seeds from crops with desirable characteristics or through the cross-pollination of selected plants, GMOs don't work with complete organisms and don't typically combine traits from related types of plants. Instead, isolated genes are identified and genes from one organism are inserted into another organism. The organisms don't need to be related. You can take a cold-water fish, extract a gene from it, and insert that gene into a strawberry seed; and you will end up with a frost-resistant strawberry. With traditional methods or traditional breeding, the integrity of the organism places limits on what can be done. GMOs are different. As one critic said: "No amount of coaxing could get a flounder to mate with a strawberry to produce berries with 'antifreeze' genes" (Holdrege and Talbott 2001: 2). In the United States the production of bioengineered food has increased rapidly, from zero acres in 1980 to 151.4 million acres in 2009; and, in 2009, 93 percent of US soybeans and 80 percent of the corn crop were grown with seeds containing Monsanto-patented genetics (Food and Water Watch 2013: 3).

GMOs were different enough for many countries to argue that, at a minimum, we should label GMO food, and many do have some form of mandatory labeling. The United States does not. Americans haven't gotten as upset with the idea of GMO food as have people of other countries. The Hungarian government recently destroyed more than 1,000 acres of corn that they discovered were planted with GM seeds, while in California, in 2012, the voters rejected a proposition to label GM foods.

A major reason why people are concerned about GMOs is the possibility that consuming them is unhealthy—concerns that have produced a lively debate, with passionate spokespeople on both sides. Obviously long-term data are not yet available, and the GMO technologies are not only changing but also becoming an increasing part of our daily diet—an estimated 70 percent of processed food contains GMO ingredients (Rubin and Tesmenitsky 2002: 307)—which makes long-term assessments impossible. Space does not permit here a full discussion of this debate about how healthy or unhealthy GMOs are. Much of the pro-GMO literature is, as expected, from the GMO companies themselves, but many scientists do agree that GMOs look harmless at this point. The interested reader is pointed to Nemecek (2006a and 2006b) and to Lawrence and Grice (2009). My point of view on the healthiness of GM food can be characterized by the precautionary principle perspective noted in chapter 4. GMOs are a relatively new food and the percentage of the human diet made up of them is increasing, so to say that GMOs are safe seems premature. We need to keep hearing varied voices and having useful discussions about this new technology; we need to keep the two sides of the discussion engaged.

One unhealthy aspect of GMOs, which has been well documented, is the increase in the use of chemicals in the production process. An important Monsanto product is a seed known as Roundup Ready. Roundup is a Monsanto herbicide and Monsanto's Roundup Ready seeds are protected against Roundup, so when you spray Roundup on a field planted with a Roundup Ready crop only the unwanted weeds are killed. Since the plants that are Roundup Ready resist the herbicide, the farmer can spray Roundup indiscriminately on the field and the crops won't be hurt, even though chemical residue saturates the plant. That is concerning, especially since agrichemicals cannot be fully washed off by the consumer. Nor is it what a farmer interested in sustainable farming would design. Furthermore, with Roundup Ready crops, farmers have increased their use of Roundup or herbicides with the specific chemical in Roundup, namely Glyphosate, which reduces the effectiveness of the herbicide in the long term and causes some weeds to become Glyphosate-resistant. Weeds less susceptible to Glyphosate are increasing (Center for Food Safety 2009; Benbrook 2012; see chapter 5). The current dependence on more and more herbicides is not a long-term sustainable solution.

Seeds

The rise of GMOs has also raised questions about the availability of seeds. Seeds are the bedrock of farming, a hugely important purchase for a farmer.

Traditionally farmers have saved seeds privately and in seed banks, in an effort to protect biodiversity and as a way to save money and produce crops of known origin (Shiva 2000). Consolidation of the seed industry and the increasing use of GMO seeds have changed this tradition, so that the farmer is now paying more and more for new seeds and having less and less choice. For instance, corn seed prices rose by 32 percent in 2009 (Neuman 2010a), and the cost of planting an acre of soybean rose by 325 percent, from $13.32 to $56.56 (Barker et al. 2013: 9). Less choice comes in part from the fact that the seed bank is no longer as large and diverse as it was until recently. In 1981 about 5,000 non-hybrid vegetable varieties were sold through mail order. By 1998, 88 percent of those varieties had disappeared (Horrigan et al. 2002: 448). A plant-rich diet, as recommended by the US Department of Agriculture (USDA), requires a large variety of crops to accommodate the nutritional standards outlined in the current MyPlate guidelines.

Choice is also limited because of the concentration of seed company ownership. Over half (53 percent) of the global commercial seed market is under the control of three agrichemical firms, Monsanto, DuPont, and Syngenta, and the seeds are increasingly GMO seeds: 93 percent of soybean, 86 percent of corn and 64 percent of canola seeds are GMOs (Barker et al. 2013: 2–5). Because companies develop the seeds and then patent them, those seeds cannot be saved by farmers. This patenting power gives a company like Monsanto the ability to sue others with patent infringement if anyone grows a crop with Monsanto seeds without Monsanto's approval. Farmers can become caught in Monsanto's web by deciding one year to buy the seeds, then ending up having to rebuy them each year (Food and Water Watch 2013). In 2013 a case before the Supreme Court (*Bowman v. Monsanto*) tested this idea even further. A farmer planted seeds he legally purchased, but the seeds were a mix, and some were second-generation Monsanto seeds. The question was whether a company's patent extends to the resale of the patented item. Monsanto said the farmer committed a crime by planting them. The court agreed with Monsanto. To discourage supposedly illegal use of Monsanto seeds, Monsanto spreads fear among farmers and seed dealers by spying on farmers and threatening law suits if they saved seeds from one year to the next (Barlett and Steele 2008). Monsanto has been on the winning side of 91 of the 104 lawsuits between it and farmers up to 2007 (Center for Food Safety 2007).

Yet one of the problems for farmers is that it is difficult to keep Monsanto seeds out of one's field. A well-known case involved a Canadian farmer whose field was inadvertently planted with Monsanto seeds when the wind blew seeds off a passing truck. Monsanto took him to court, which ruled against him. He wasn't fined, but had considerable legal fees to pay. In Oregon, a genetically altered wheat test crop that was shut down a decade ago showed up in 2013 in a farmer's field. Monsanto says that the appearance was a "random isolated occurrence," hardly reassuring to farmers who fear expensive litigation if such seeds appear in their fields (Wines 2013).

Big Food also means big lobbying, and Monsanto's push for GMO food is routinely supported in Congress. Although the long-term effects of GMOs are unknown, Monsanto was worried that people might sue them for health issues related to the consumption of GMO seeds. Evidence of Monsanto's powerful connections to political people was evident in a rider in a congressional budget bill passed in 2013. It contained a little-noticed Monsanto Protection Act, which protects genetically modified seeds from litigation suits over health risks posed by the crops' consumption. This is a huge win for the GMO industry. Even if a court rules that there is a health hazard, the crops can be planted and the GMO company can't be sued for any resulting health problems.

Ultra-Processed Food

In addition to food being grown under unusual and less healthy conditions, what is actually available to the consumer has changed greatly. People are increasingly eating stuff that doesn't look much like what used to be grown on the farm. This change in consumption patterns is largely determined by upstream decisions on what should be available. For instance, the food industry is pushing ultra-processed food: this is not minimally processed food such as lettuce that has been washed, cut, and bagged (which is also considered to have been "processed"), but food that bears little resemblance to its purported ingredients. For the last two decades in the United States, about 60 percent of the calories ingested by the public have come from ultra-processed foods (Monteiro and Gannon 2012), which are "concentrated in calories, but deficient in fiber, micronutrients, and phytochemicals (plant substances that may mediate some of the protective effects of vegetables and fruits against diabetes, heart disease, and cancer)" (Ludwig 2011: 1352) and add disproportionately to our daily sugar intake (Eicher-Miller et al. 2012). Most processing does not improve nutritional content; instead it improves palatability, shelf life, and transportability. But all the changes made for this purpose in fact reduce nutritional quality (Stuckler and Nestle 2012). Some researchers call ultra-processed items "products," not food, and describe them as "created from substances extracted from whole foods such as the cheap parts or remnants of animals, inexpensive ingredients such as 'refined' starches, sugars, fats and oils, preservatives, and other additives" (Monteiro and Cannon 2012). One illustrative product, Strawberry Splash Fruit Gushers, "contains highly processed ingredients never before present in the food supply, including 7 variants of sugar and partially hydrogenated fat" (Ludwig 2011: 1352). Simply put, these products do not offer us a nutritious diet. Examine a typical ultra-processed home meal, say, a Hungry Man chicken dinner, and you will find on the package label that the meal has 960 calories and an overload of fat (69 percent of daily requirements) and sodium (120 percent of daily requirements). Even the once healthy choice of the whole fresh chicken—the dominant way in which chicken used to be sold in the United States—has now given way to chicken processed as patties, breaded strips, and nuggets. These forms of chicken now make up the "overwhelming share of the domestic market" (Gereffi et al. 2009: 360). Researchers link consumption of ultra-processed food and sugar-sweetened beverages to health outcomes such as weight gain, cardiovascular disease, Type 2 diabetes, and childhood obesity (Stuckler and Nestle 2012).

An important component of the success of Big Food in reshaping the American diet has been the application of scientific know-how to food design and production. Food scientists have learned how to combine ingredients such that the human palate is easily hooked.

They do careful research on the bliss point—the optimal taste and tactile sensation. They calibrate products so as to maximize cravings and make the products addictive. Salt, sugar, and fat are key to that success. Food items can't be too strong in taste, or too sweet. You need combinations of ingredients that stimulate the taste buds long enough to be alluring but not long enough to leave a flavor "that tells the brain to stop eating" (Moss 2013: 39). Hence the "I can't eat just one" comment that people make (and that Lays potato chips shamelessly adopted as an advertising slogan). That is how the food was engineered.

A former chief food scientist for Frito-Lay commented: "I feel so sorry for the public" (Moss 2013: 48). He felt sorry because he had tried to push for healthier options when he worked for Frito-Lay but failed; and he realized his work had made Americans less healthy. Food scientists hit the jackpot when they designed the Cheetos—cheese-flavored, puffed cornmeal snacks. Cheetos are pure pleasure. They melt down quickly in your mouth and the brain is tricked. The phenomenon is called "vanishing caloric density" (Moss 2013: 46): the mind decides that there can't be many calories because you put *Cheetos* in your mouth and they are instantly gone. You feel you can just keep eating them forever—which is what some people seem to do!

Potato chips, with the salt, fat, and the sugar from the starch of the potato, are another winner. For many people, the combination rewards the brain with instant feelings of pleasure. The starch causes glucose levels in the blood to spike, which leads to a craving for more. Food companies depend on this type of science to make their products. It is a highly competitive market and each food company is competing for what they call "stomach share," the amount of digestive space that a company can grab from the competition (Moss 2013: 36).

Designing unhealthy food: The case of Lunchables

The grocery store sells many products, but one with a particularly interesting history is Lunchables. In the mid-1980s Oscar Meyer was faced with a declining demand for red meats like bologna. The vice-president for development, Bob Drane, was in charge of improving Oscar Meyer's bottom line. He gathered from consumers information on lunch and found mothers stressed about having to provide daily packed lunches for their children. He decided that a prepackaged lunch was the answer; and bologna could be the central feature.

By 1992 Lunchables were earning $8 million for the company, but bigger profits were on the horizon. Following "one of the cardinal rules in processed food: When in doubt, add sugar," (Moss 2013: 40), the company added a dessert. Currently the Bologna and Stacker Lunchable package label shows 390 calories, 198 from fat, 45 percent of the recommended daily allowances (RDAs) of fat, 37 percent of sodium, and 12 grams of sugar. Popular criticism included the line: "If you take Lunchables apart, the most healthy item in it is the napkin" (Moss 2013: 40). The author of a *New York Times Magazine* article on processed food interviewed Bob Drane's daughter. She commented: "I don't think my kids have ever eaten a Lunchable ... They know they exist and that Grandpa Bob invented them. But we eat very healthfully" (Moss 2013: 40). Bob Drane is now a speaker who talks about the obesity epidemic and "holds the entire industry accountable" (Moss 2013: 46).

The food available in restaurants

If we consider reshaping the American diet, it is important to examine the emergence in the last half century of a small number of fast-food chains, each with thousands of outlets, and more recently of chains of casual dining restaurants. The proliferation, convenience, and affordability of these restaurants have shaped what we eat, often in unhealthy ways. Big Food has a large fast-food restaurant component, which has very effectively put its icons in front of us and gotten us to spend a lot of money buying very unhealthy food. The money spent at McDonald's and other similar venues has increased dramatically: since 1970 there has been an eighteen-fold increase (Brownell and Horgen 2004: 8). The food purchased at fast-food restaurants is unhealthy because it is calorie-laden, nutrient-deficient, and often super-sized. Here are some specifics. Baskin Robbins had a chocolate oreo shake with 2,600 calories: this is more calories than an adult male should eat in an entire day. While this menu choice was taken off the market in 2009, high-calorie items are abundant among the selections at all fast-food restaurants. A Big Mac hamburger contains half the calories you are supposed to eat in a day, and many people combine the Big Mac with fries and a drink. Capitalizing on an increased demand for chicken as well as on new meat-processing techniques, McDonald's developed Chicken McNuggets, which became an enormous hit, particularly among children. An irony here is that chicken carries the image of being a healthier "white" meat in comparison to "red" meats. In fact McNuggets has no health

advantage over beef: ounce for ounce, it has more calories, fat, cholesterol, and salt than a Big Mac, yet it remains a popular option for
"happy meals" devoured by our smallest eaters (Roberts 2009: 67).
When people eat out, they tend to eat higher calorie food or to eat
more (USDA 2003: 14), and a quarter of the meals are considered to
belong in the fast-food category (Nestle 2002: 19).

What about those affordable sit-down establishments that lure
folks in with their family-friendly atmosphere? Casual dining restaurants such as Applebee's, the Olive Garden, and Red Lobster may
bring people together, but they emphasize menu items with abundant
cheeses, fried foods, and pastas. Among the popular selections at
these restaurants: the Cheesecake Factory offers Pasta Carbonara at
2,130 calories; Applebee's has a Riblet Platter at 2,100 calories and
Fish and Chips at 1,690 calories; and the Olive Garden has Chicken
Alfredo at 1,440. These calorie totals, of course, do not include the
appetizers and side dishes, and the drinks and perhaps even desserts
that often accompany the meals. The success of such restaurants only
compounds the obesity problem in the United States and contributes
to the array of negative health outcomes associated with excessive
sugar, salt and fat.

As if mirroring the lack of healthy choices in grocery stores and
"food deserts" in poor neighborhoods (discussed in chapter 3), restaurants in those areas provide fewer healthy options, in part because
they are dominated by fast-food chains. Thus poor people are more
likely to have high-calorie, less nutritious, "super-sized" meals than
people who live in other neighborhoods (Lee et al. 2014).

Advertising by a powerful industry

Central to the success of Big Food has been the industry's aggressive
advertising. Big Food gains power and dominance in many ways, but
its effective advertising of profitable foods is certainly key. Big Food
does a lot of advertising of unhealthy food. Marion Nestle, a noted
nutritionist (unrelated to the Nestle food corporation), says: "There's
$34 billion worth of advertising ... that goes to ... foods that are high
in fat and calories, mostly from corn sweeteners and hydrogenated
fats" (Frontline 2003: 1). If you turn on your television or look at the
advertisements that pop up on your tablet or computer screen, you
will see that the advertisements are not for healthy food—only 2.2
percent are for fruits, veggies, grains, or beans (Nestle 2002: 22)—
but for prepared foods and drinks that have little nutritional value.
And most advertising dollars aren't even going for real food. Nearly

70 percent of the food advertising in the United States is for convenience foods, candy, snacks, alcoholic beverages, soft drinks, and desserts. Marketing to children and adolescents is particularly intense (Story and French 2004), as are other inducements for children to develop a desire for non-nutritious food. For instance, many food companies (Kellogg, McDonald's, Burger King, Nabisco, Keebler, and Oscar Meyer) are linked to movie companies like Nickelodeon and Disney, to television and movie actors, and to sports stars by way of cross-promoting their brands (Brownell and Horgen 2004: 107–110; Harris, Schwartz, Brownell 2009). No wonder that 40 percent of kids' calories are from snack foods, if you consider that 20,000 new products are introduced each year and advertised aggressively (Nestle 2012).

Apart from being aggressive, Big Food advertisements can be rather deceptive. For instance, the industry set up a Smart Choices label campaign, putting a Smart Choices logo on packages if a food passed a nutritional standard. The problem was that the so-called nutritional standards were so unhealthy that they allowed Froot Loops Cereal, ice cream, and mayonnaise to get high nutritional marks. In October of 2009 the Food and Drug Administration (FDA) declared the program deceptive and ended it (Blumenthal 2009). Other food manufacturers have also been slapped on the wrist for deceptively pushing unhealthy food. In the summer of 2010, the Federal Trade Commission (FTC) told the Nestle Corporation that it could not boast that its drink Boost Kid Essential was so good that it could keep kids from getting a cold. The FTC ordered Nestle to stop advertising this bogus benefit (Neuman 2010b). Similarly, the FTC forced Heinz to withdraw its tomato ketchup advertisements in 1999, when Heinz made an unauthorized claim that its ketchup "may help reduce the risk of prostate and cervical cancer" (see Nestle 2002: 335 for a picture of the ad).

Pushing unhealthy food: Pouring rights

The advertising of less nutritious food and other techniques used to promote processed food create a particular health problem and illustrate the power of Big Food quite well. While using various media to advertise food products is a major method for Big Food, it is hardly the only method that has been used for the promotion of unhealthy food choices. An extreme example of pushing less nutritious food and beverage items onto the public is "pouring rights," a type of contract between a soda (soft drink) company and an institution, say, school or university, that gives the company exclusive rights to sell its soda to and on the premises of that institution. The health concern is that soda is like a liquid candy (Nestle 2002: 198). It is not nutritious and, in the elementary to high school setting, drinking soda ends up replacing healthy options like drinking water or milk. Contracts typically guarantee that the school will receive a lump-sum up-front payment and then additional payments over five to ten years, all in return for exclusive sales in the school's vending machines and at all school events. The dollar amounts are staggering. North Syracuse in New York, for example, signed a contract for $1.53 million: $900,000 on signing and annual installments of $70,000 (Nestle 2002: 204).

When schools are approached with the possibility of making so much money, many say "yes" because the contracts are an easy way for them to increase their budget for school activities; and, given that schools are increasingly feeling underfunded, such offers are very tempting. Once signed, the contracts mean that students are constantly exposed to the company logo and pressured to buy more. The contracts are set up such that the company can give a bonus to the school if the target amount specified in the contract is exceeded. So some schools decide that it is in their best interests to increase consumption. To do so, they sometimes offer significant rewards to students who are helpful in promoting soda. One school gave away a car. Other schools punish students if they don't support the effort. One school suspended a student for a day because he wore a Pepsi shirt on Coke Day (Nestle 2002: 206).

These arrangements obviously make school administrators push a product that isn't healthy. When a Colorado school administrator announced one such contract, he indicated the ground rules:

> "We must sell 70,000 cases of this product at least once during the first three years of the contract ... Here is how we can do it. Allow students to purchase and consume vended products throughout the day ... the long term benefits are worth it." He signed himself "the Coke Dude." (Nestle 2002: 205)

As pouring rights contracts began to increase in number and value, many people expressed concern over the power of the soft drink industry. In 2006 that public concern led to a national agreement brokered by the Clinton Foundation and the American Heart Association that took sugary drinks out of elementary and middle schools and set limits on portion size in high school vending machines. In addition, the agreement said that states could be more restrictive. Legislation in New York established a restriction: "From the beginning of the school day until the end of the last scheduled meal period, no sweetened soda water, no chewing gum, no candy... shall be sold in any public school in the state of NY" (New York Education Law, Section 915). Despite the positive press for the national agreement, some public health officials feared that it had loopholes, and indeed it had: "modifications to the agreement reintroduced caloric beverages—such as sugary vitamin waters and sports drinks—into schools, thereby limiting the initiative's effectiveness" (Ludwig and Nestle 2008: 1810).

The school setting is important for a young person's health. The school should provide daily healthy nutrition during a critical physical growth period for students; it should help them establish good eating habits. By and large, this hasn't happened in American schools because of pouring rights—and because of school lunch offerings, which we will soon discuss. Obviously the school setting is only one out of many venues that reflect the influence of the food and beverage industry when it comes to forcing unhealthy products onto unsuspecting consumers.

The Government and Food Health

The US government is supposed to protect US citizens, their health, and their general well-being through laws and regulatory agencies. Federal, state, and local governments indeed have many agencies that concerned themselves with food safety. At the national level, the government has claimed an interest in promoting good eating by providing guidelines for an individual's daily diet. This interest began with general food advice in 1894 and was followed by RDAs in the 1940s, by the four basic food groups (dairy, meat, vegetables, cereals) from 1956 to 1992, and finally by the first food pyramid, with which the American public was presented in 1992 (Perelman 2011). The food pyramid is a clever graphic that school children and adults could understand (see Figure 8.1). At the wide base of the pyramid were foods one should have more of, and at the skinny peak foods one should rarely eat. But it turns out that this graphic's nutritional advice was not exactly accurate.

So what happened and where are Americans now? For a long time, the US government's nutritional message was relatively simple. During the early part of the last century, the country's food problem was inadequate nutrition and the government's advice was basically to eat more of a variety of foods. Few prepared foods were available, so variety and "eat more" was good advice. Then, in the 1970s, fast-food options and advertising increased dramatically—as did people's waistlines. Health officials and the government got concerned about chronic disease and the health problems of being overweight. "Eat more" no longer worked; so the government turned its attention to more specific advice about what should be eaten. Various agencies tried to determine the number and the size of portions and the relative amount of different types of food that people should eat.

A very basic idea in this new environment was "eat less": the exact opposite of what had been recommended in the past. But the problem is that "eat less" is not something that Big Food wants people to hear (Nestle 2002: 31). Eating less means that people will buy less, which means that Big Food sells less and makes less money. Lots of interested parties were concerned about the "eat less" message: the Sugar Beet Growers Association, the National Broiler Council, the National Fisheries Institute, the National Milk Producers' Federation, the National Pork Producers Council, the Food Marketing Institute, the National Cattlemen's Beef Association, and the United Egg Producers (Nestle 1993: 487). So the industry worked hard to remove that wording from government publications.

In the late 1980s, Marion Nestle was working in Washington, DC on the Surgeon General's Report on Nutrition and Health. As a well-respected and committed nutritionist, she wanted to give the best and most accurate advice to consumers. She was told that she had to be careful with the words she used when she gave nutritional advice. She wrote: "My first day on the job, I was given the rules: No matter what the research indicated, the report could not recommend 'eat less meat' as a way to reduce intake of saturated fat, nor could it suggest restrictions on the intake of any other category of food" (Nestle 2002: 3).

Since saying "eat less" about any particular item of food was not OK, she couldn't say "eat less sugar"—that would have sent sugar producers right to Congress to complain. The industry did agree to the words: "choose a diet moderate in sugar" (Nestle 2002: 3). "Eat less beef" outraged the beef industry, so the advice on beef had to be worded as "choose lean," which was later changed to "2–3 servings" (Nestle 2002: 4 and 6).

The cattle ranchers were particularly motivated, as there was (and still is) strong agreement that Americans eat too much red meat; and that idea threatened the industry. The industry was able to have the food pyramid not only approve of "2–3 servings" associated with beef, but also put beef in a healthy category, with things like poultry, fish, dry beans and nuts. This is not what nutritionists would have countenanced: their recommendation to eat less red meat should be loud and clear. But in the 1992 food pyramid it was neither.

A major critic of the government's food pyramid has been Walter C. Willett, professor at the Harvard School of Public Health, who stated that the pyramid was based on very shaky science and influenced by politics. He proposed his own food pyramid (Figure 8.2), which (among other changes) placed red meat at the top, along with butter, with a note: "use sparingly." Nutritionally, this location for beef and its pairing with butter made much more sense. Through his treatment of red meat and other food items, Willett gave us a more scientific pyramid, which silenced the power of Big Food (Willett and Stampfer 2003).

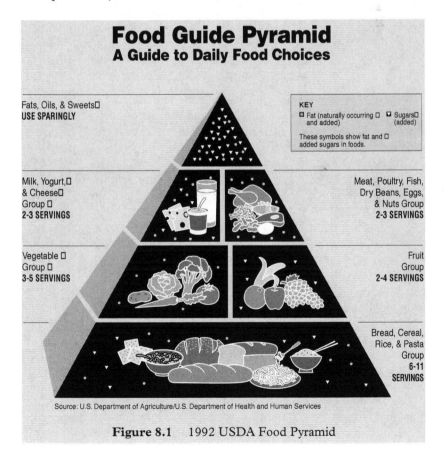

Figure 8.1   1992 USDA Food Pyramid

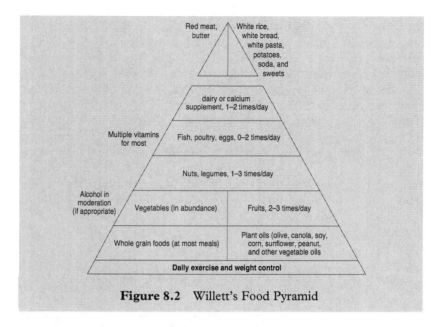

Figure 8.2 Willett's Food Pyramid

Willett's pyramid, however, did not become the official one. Instead, in 2005 a new food pyramid appeared on the web as MyPyramid. Although this pyramid was interactive and endowed with fancy new technology that could customize your food needs by paying heed to age, sex, weight, height, and level of physical activity, the critics argued that it was confusing. The easy graphic of the old-style pyramid clearly said eat more of what is at the bottom. That idea is lost with the upward-facing lines of MyPyramid (which replaced the horizontal divisions). Then in 2011 the American public was presented with MyPlate—a new version of the food pyramid. Like MyPyramid, MyPlate gives no clear and simple nutritional information but only complicated graphics that are not likely to be used, particularly not by poor people who lack easy access to a computer. This is what is mainly wrong with this upgrade. And, quite importantly, Big Food was able to influence MyPlate's recommendations. For instance, the protein recommendations in MyPlate suggest that hamburgers and hot dogs are fine; and there is no indication that red and processed meats may not be healthy (http://www.hsph.harvard. edu/nutritionsource/healthy-eating-plate-vs-usda-myplate).

Historically, the power of the food industry in America was such that the federal government bowed to its influence in important respects, which compromised public health. The citizenry did not get the straightforward advice to "eat less red meat" among other important, scientifically backed recommendations. Even today, this power persists. In January 2016, the new Dietary Guidelines for Americans was scheduled to include a recommendation that people limit the consumption of red meat, especially processed meat. "This advice was deleted from the final guidelines following vehement protests from the National Cattlemen's Beef Association, an industry trade group, and its supporters in Congress" (Brody 2016: 1). In addition to the government, there are also professional nutritionists who could have voiced strong recommendations on what is healthy and what is not, but they too have been influenced by Big Food (Brownell and Warner 2009: 277), as will be discussed below under "Partnerships."

Recognizing the critical importance of food for health and the problem of access to food for many Americans, the federal government has established three important food programs: Food Stamps, WIC (Women, Infants, and Children), and the School Lunch Program. Food Stamps—now called the Supplemental Nutrition Assistance Program (SNAP)—is an income-eligibility program for very poor people. In Connecticut, for example, the program requires a current bank balance of less than $2,001 and an annual household income of less than $14,079 if one person lives in the household. The average monthly benefit is $133.79 (Wilde 2013)—helpful but not generous. SNAP is part of the wildly complicated Farm Bill and provides a good example of "logrolling politics in action" (Nestle 2012: 16). The political power of agricultural states was threatened in the 1970s, prompting the representatives of those states to find allies so that the Farm Bill legislation would pass. They turned to representatives from states with large populations of urban poor, representatives who needed support for Food Stamps and other similar programs. The result was that "they traded votes in an unholy alliance that pleased Big Agriculture as well as advocates for the poor" (Nestle 2012: 16). This "unholy alliance" continues, as the Farm Bill is reauthorized every five years. In consequence SNAP got entangled in a political discussion about ideas that are irrelevant to the needs of poor, hungry people.

The Farm Bill

Poor people have a difficult time finding food and affording it: this is a poverty and distribution problem. When they (and others) do have access to food, they increasingly find that the food is not very nutritious. One of the reasons is the Federal Farm Bill. When the Bill was first passed, it made sense: it stabilized crop prices and kept farmers in business (Angelo 2009). But now a major impact is that it encourages the production of corn, soybeans, and wheat, not that of fresh produce. The various products that contain corn (e.g., corn syrup and processed foods) are relatively inexpensive but not very healthy. In contrast, more nutritious foods, such as fresh fruits and vegetables, get no such subsidy (Pollan 2007; Mortazavi 2011; Nestle 2012) so "producing fruits and vegetables is a risky strategy in an already risky business" (Stull and Patz 2015: 332). The price of fresh fruits and vegetables has increased by a factor of 3.3 since 1985, while the consumer price index has only increased by 2.1 (Brownell and Frieden 2009). The increase is bound to put nutritious whole foods out of the reach of low-income families.

This one piece of legislation essentially governs what is or isn't cultivated on American soil. As food writer Michael Pollan explains:

> The smorgasbord of incentives and disincentives built into the farm bill helps decide what happens on nearly half of the private land in America: whether it will be farmed or left wild, whether it will be managed to maximize productivity (and therefore doused with chemicals) or to promote environmental stewardship. (Pollan 2007: n.p.)

One analysis of the agricultural subsidies shows the relative support for different kinds of food at a national and individual level. Between 1995 and 2011, $18.2 billion tax dollars went to four common junk-food additives: corn syrup, high fructose syrup, corn starch, and soy oils. If subsidies for junk food ingredients and those for fruits and vegetables went directly to taxpayers, each taxpayer would receive $7.58 for junk food and 27 cents for apples: in other words, twenty-one Twinkies snacks, but just half of a Delicious apple (Etherton et al. 2012).

The WIC program recognizes the importance of nutrition for very young children and gives pregnant mothers access to nutritious food if they are at financial and nutritional risk. The mother can get continued help until the baby's first birthday if she is breast feeding, and benefits for the child can be extended up to the fifth birthday. Parents get vouchers for particular kinds of food. The program is, again, helpful but not generous. In Connecticut, for example, allotments for fruits and vegetables recently went up to $10 a month. Critics of the program are concerned that Big Food influences it. Observers notice such an influence when they examine the level of support that the WIC program gives to breastfeeding, which is part of its mandate. They find that the power of infant-formula companies has undermined the mandate, since "formula companies have leveraged WIC as a promotional vehicle" by giving WIC programs "price rebates in exchange for exclusive rights to provide its [= each company's] brand of formula to all WIC participants in the state" (Kaplan and Graff 2008: 497). Providing the best nutrition for babies, mother's milk, loses out to Big Food, as it encourages infant formula through WIC.

Poor children also have access to food through school lunches, but their right to healthy food has not been well protected. The school lunches sponsored by the Department of Agriculture are often less healthy than they should be. This is because the programs serve not only the dietary needs of the students but also the needs of the Department of Agriculture, as it supports farmers with surplus commodities. Decisions about what foods to serve at lunch take these surpluses into account. Therefore it is likely that the foods included in these meal programs are not necessarily the healthiest but rather the cheapest and most available ones, even if they only marginally comply with nutrition standards (as in the infamous push to define ketchup and pickle relish as vegetables, for example). In addition, there are political pressures from Big Food. When nutrition-minded people wanted less beef served at school lunches, the National Cattlemen's Beef Association was not happy and made its objections clear. Fast-food chains were allowed into the school lunchroom in the mid-1990s, so young children were exposed to Pizza Hut, Taco Bell, Subway, McDonald's, and other fast-food establishments. Although the fast food served in the school had to have higher nutritional value than a similar offering at the same fast-food restaurant in the neighborhood, the food was still less healthy than desirable. Serving fast food also generates brand loyalty, which potentially leads to life-long preferences for less healthy food (Levine 2008). So by not being as diligent about the interests of healthy food as it should be, the government has allowed Big Food into the lunchroom.

Local and state governments as well as the national government have many laws and agencies relevant to food safety. Some municipalities have programs, for example farmers' markets that bring healthy food to cities.

Better Food in Urban Neighborhoods

Some municipalities are trying to encourage better eating. For instance, public health organizations and economic development agencies are approaching store owners in Cleveland, Louisville and other towns with offers of new equipment and marketing expertise, in order to encourage them to stock more fresh produce, whole wheat bread, and other healthy offerings. The organizations provide grants and free advertising for the stores as healthy places; they also help change zoning regulations, enabling stores to have fruit and vegetable stands outside, for instance (Granville 2009).

Community-supported agriculture (CSA) has come to many areas. Encouraged by the USDA, the CSA program links local residents to nearby farmers, thereby "eliminating 'the middleman' and increasing the benefits to both the farmer and the consumer" (Wilkinson 2001: 1). There are several types of CSA programs, but the basic design is to sell "farm shares" to local residents, giving them a portion of the farmer's crop when the growing season begins. Farmers have money up front and a guaranteed market at the end. CSA helps small farms to survive and encourages the production of healthier food (Horrigan et al. 2002: 453).

Many communities across the United States also have farmers' markets where local residents have access to fresh food. The food there is typically not cheap, since it does not enjoy the "big volume–big discount" advantages of larger retailers like Walmart. Poor people often find the produce too expensive, but some places have partially solved the problem by enabling recipients of the SNAP to buy food at farmers' markets (Beals 2012).

At the same time, some cities are attempting to decrease people's access to unhealthy food. Los Angeles has banned new fast-food restaurants in South Los Angeles, which is "a huge section of the city that has significantly higher rates of poverty and obesity than other neighborhoods." The councilmen are trying to apply land use laws in order to limit unhealthy food, just as they and other communities do to control bars and liquor stores (Medina 2011).

At the national level, the FDA and the USDA act in myriad ways to address food health issues. Both have websites that give the reader a good idea of their mandates and programs. The specifics of their work are too much to cover in this chapter, but it is important to note (as I did above for the SNAP, the WIC, and the School Lunch Program) that federal agencies are not immune to industry influence.

USDA advisory committees are filled with people who have current or former ties to Big Food. "For example," notes one critic, "on just the 2000 Committee ... members had past or present ties to: two meat associations; four dairy association and five dairy companies; one egg association; one sugar association; one grain association; five other food companies; six other industry-sponsored associations" (Steier 2012: 27). The FDA appeared to become more beholden to Big Food when, in 2009, Monsanto's vice-president for public policy was appointed to an advisory post for the FDA commissioner. This business-regulatory revolving door gives Big Food increased power (Flock 2012). In addition, Big Food successfully influences other aspects of the political process, as noted in the box on the sugar industry.

Big Food Defends Itself

The Sugar Industry Flexed Its Muscle

The sugar industry has been under particular attack because of the obesity epidemic, but our government remains protective of sugar's economic foothold in our diet. When in 2003 the World Health Organization (WHO) planned to highlight the link between sugar and non-communicable diseases (mainly obesity and associated diseases), the Sugar Association went into high gear. A letter-writing campaign ensued, and the Secretary of Health and Human Services sent a twenty-eight-page report that largely echoed the usual defensive comments of Big Food, namely that "personal responsibility should be the emphasis; there should be a stronger focus on physical activity; and there are no good and bad foods" (Brownell and Warner 2009: 275). The final WHO report replaced a specific 10 percent limit on the amount of sugar in a healthy diet with a general statement that urged a reduction in sugar intake (Germov and Williams 2009: 221). The power of the industry prevailed.

The sugar industry has also attacked individual scientists who push for less sugar in the American diet. Marion Nestle, mentioned in the text especially for her role in developing food guidelines, reported receiving several threatening letters from the Sugar Association, which was displeased with her statements about high-sugar food sales (Steier 2012: 28–9).

Even the federal government has been drawn into the web of sugar propaganda. Although the industry knew that sugar causes tooth decay, it convinced the National Institute of Dental Research to develop research programs that focused on enzymes that break up dental plaque and vaccines rather than on reducing sugar consumption (Kearns et al. 2015). They want us to have our cake and eat it too!

Concerns with pouring rights, advertisements to children, super-sized foods, CAFOs, GMOs, excessive sugar and salt in our diets, and obesity have led to considerable public criticism of Big Food. As a result, "the food industry is on the defensive, hit hard by nutrition groups and public health professionals, the press, parent groups, child advocacy organization, and state and national legislators sponsoring bills that could have a powerful impact on business" (Brownell and Warner 2009: 262). As early as 1999, the industry felt so threatened that the CEOs of the largest food companies (including Kraft, Nestle, Nabisco, General Mills, Procter and Gamble, Coca-Cola, and Mars) gathered in Minneapolis to discuss a possible response to the increasing pressure on Big Food to do something about America's growing weight problem. The vice-president of Kraft, Michael Mudd, challenged the group to respond to the perception of the processed-food industry as a "public health menace" (Moss 2013: 36). He recommended that the industry admit to some culpability and then decrease the use of sugar, fat, and salt in its products. Others at the meeting did not agree with such voluntary industry standards. In an interview, Pillsbury's chief technical officer said that the basic reaction was of this sort: "Look, we're not going to screw around with the company jewels here and change the formulations because a bunch of guys in white coats are worried about obesity" (Moss 2013: 37).

Instead, Big Food has found other ways to respond. Its use of other strategies is particularly sophisticated and parallels the tobacco playbook developed by the tobacco industry, which is "unsurprising in view of the flow of people, funds, and activities across these industries, which also have histories of joint ownership—e.g., Philip Morris owned both Kraft and Miller Brewing: Altria is a lead shareholder in tobacco and food companies that have shared directorships" (Moodie et al. 2013: 674). Along these lines, Big Food has defended itself in other ways, by pushing favorable legislation, discrediting researchers, establishing front groups, building partnerships, developing corporate responsibility campaigns, and popularizing arguments that suggest that any problem with food isn't the fault of the industry. Let us look briefly at some examples of each of these defenses.

Legislation

Big Food has been powerful enough to be largely successful about pushing legislation advantageous to its practices. A case in point is that of food disparagement laws, which exist in many states and prohibit people from making unproven claims about a food and its safety or its negative health impacts. Such laws sound reasonable. Why would anyone champion the right to make unproven claims? Yet, early in the process of worrying about the safety of a particular food, the claims are likely to be exactly that: unproven. The impact of the law is to restrict the free flow of questions about food safety.

Food Disparagement Laws

In February 1989 the CBS in-depth news program *60 Minutes* focused on Alar, a chemical sprayed on apples to regulate growth and enhance color. We have long used pesticides in agriculture to control pests and herbicides to control weeds. Alar wasn't much different—a sprayed-on chemical—but the *60 Minutes* program said that it was a major health risk for kids. The claim was that Alar was carcinogenic. The TV program instigated demands that Alar apples be taken off the market immediately. Public pressure made it happen, and overnight the apples were off the shelves.

The evidence, then and now, indicates that Alar is harmful but that the harm comes from *long-term* exposure. Very little is ingested in a single season. The public health need is really to stop Alar on all future crops. A bit more exposure in 1989 wouldn't have made a difference. Clearly the media coverage led public health officials to overreact, and this caused Big Food to panic. The concern wasn't just about Alar; it was that a similar scenario could repeat itself. Some claim would be made about a perishable food, society would react, and the food would be withdrawn from the shelves. Since we are talking about fresh and perishable food, the financial damage would be great. You can't store fresh food indefinitely while people figure out whether there is a problem or not, because the food spoils. So a recall means that the producers and middlemen lose lots of money.

In consequence Big Food lobbied several states to minimize the possibility of this happening again. The intention was to make it very hard to recall perishable foods. Big Food was successful in getting food disparagement laws passed. These laws ensured that a person can't speak disrespectfully about a food: you can't

disseminate the view that perishable farm products are unsafe—
not on the basis of unproven claims.

These types of laws were tested in 1999, when Oprah had a
show about the mad cow disease. By saying that beef was unsafe,
she was speaking disrespectfully of cattle. Texas cattlemen sued
her under the Texas food disparagement law. She won, but the law
was left on the books in Texas and in thirteen other states. Such
laws intimidate people who want to raise food safety issues. Even if
a person thinks that s/he will win in court, going to court is costly
and few have Oprah's time or money. This means that the laws
have weakened, if not silenced, the voices of those concerned with
some food safety issues (Negin 1996).

A second example is the response to the undercover videotaping at CAFOs that reveals the horrible conditions of the animals.
Big Food persuaded the legislatures in several states to consider a
"gag" rule of some kind that would prohibit covert videotaping.
The American Legislative Exchange Council, a member organization with hundreds of representatives from farm states, drafted a
model bill—the Animal and Ecological Terrorism Act—that prohibits filming that could defame either the owner or the operations
at the facility. Violators could be placed on a registry of terrorists
(Oppel 2013). All eleven of these "ag-gag" bills proposed in 2013
died before being passed, but they were seriously considered. Six
states do have ag-gag laws. Three were passed in 2012, when Iowa,
Utah, and Missouri adopted them. North Dakota, Montana, and
Kansas were the first states to adopt such provisions into law back
in 1990–1 (Flynn 2013).

Discrediting researchers

A particularly concerning and sophisticated defensive strategy was
employed in 2002 by Monsanto when it attacked scientists who
address the issue of possible dangers in agricultural biotechnology.
Two researchers published an article in *Nature* that raised concerns
that the introduction of trans genes could adversely affect genetic
diversity. The two came under attack, finding themselves charged
with laboratory incompetence in major newspapers. A public relations firm with ties to Monsanto (the Bivings Group) "created false
Internet identities and spread rumors" that further attacked these
scientists. "In that assault, otherwise unknown individuals with
e-mail addresses that were traced to the Bivings Group posted mes-

sages containing unsupported claims including that the *Nature* paper had not been peer reviewed" (Worthy et al. 2005: 136). This kind of attitude hampers the search for understanding and could prolong the public's exposure to potential health risks. A lively research community that feels free to raise questions and to find scientific answers is critical in all areas of society, particularly one that can have a direct impact on health outcomes.

Front groups

Industry front groups attempt to control public discourse on a particular issue by making it difficult to discover who their backers, funders, or board members are. Their names are often deceptive and public comments that group members make about the front group give the appearance that the group is neutral or represents public interests, not corporate agendas. The hope is to "create a positive public impression that hides their funders' economic motives" (Center for Food Safety 2013: 4). For instance, such groups might appear to represent small farmers when in fact they are funded by big farmers. They work hard to discredit critics, and sometimes "buy" science by "paying for research, hiring scientific experts as spokespeople, placing science stories in media, all without disclosing the conflict of interest" (Center for Food Safety 2013: 4). One such powerful front group is the US Farmers and Ranchers Alliance, which debuted in 2011. According to its website,

> US Farmers and Ranchers Alliance (USFRA) consists of more than 80 farmer- and rancher-led organizations and agricultural partners representing virtually all aspects of agriculture, working to engage in dialogue with consumers who have questions about how today's food is grown and raised. USFRA is committed to supporting US farmers' and ranchers' efforts to increase confidence and trust in today's agriculture. (http://www.fooddialogues.com/about-usfra)

On closer inspection, the group's members include the National Pork Board and the American Egg Board—industry coalitions promoting products, not the best practices of farmers and ranchers. Other front groups include the International Food Information Council Foundation, which seeks to communicate science-based information on health while being funded by Kraft, McDonald's, Monsanto, and others; the Alliance to Feed the Future, whose mission is to understand the benefits of modern food technology and whose partners include the American Meat Institute, the Grocery Manufacturers' Association and the United Egg Producers; the Center for Food Integrity, which works to build trust in our food system and has board members from Monsanto, the National Restaurant Association, and Tyson Foods; and the Bell Institute of Health and Nutrition, which seeks to develop products that contribute to healthy living but is funded by General Mills, the leading producer of sugary cereals for children (Center for Food Safety 2013: 5, 10–15). Finally, the Center for Consumer Freedom (CCF) has a $3 million budget that it uses to lobby against obesity-related public health campaigns and against legislation that would regulate the marketing of junk food to children. "The CCF boasts that '[our] strategy is to shoot the messenger ... We've got to attack [activists'] credibility as spokespersons'" (Ludwig and Nestle 2008: 1809). This is an organization funded by Tyson Foods, Coca-Cola, and Wendy's, among others.

Partnerships

Food companies have also established formal partnerships with various health organizations in order to promote their public image and minimize scrutiny of their products in the name of supporting public health. There was an unlikely partnership, for example, between the Nestle Company and the International Diabetes Federation (Moodie et al. 2013: 675), one between the American Academy of Family Physicians and Coca-Cola, Inc. (Anderson 2010), and one between Coca-Cola and the Academy of Pediatrics (O'Connor 2015). Even the nation's largest association of nutrition professionals, the Academy of Nutrition and Dietetics (AND), whose declared goal is to maximize "the nation's health through food and nutrition" (Simon 2013: 3), has increasingly had sponsors from the food industry (the number went up from 10 in 2001 to 38 in 2011). The National Cattlemen's Beef Association, General Mills, and Kellogg, for example, have been sponsors of AND for at least nine of the past twelve years. In addition, food industry sponsors even provide continuing education seminars for AND, allowing Coca-Cola to give a course on how sugar is not harmful to children. Nearly a quarter of the speakers at AND's annual meetings have industry ties. The result is that, "to date, AND has not supported controversial nutrition policies that might upset corporate sponsors, such as limits on soft drink sizes, soda taxes, or GMO labels" (Simon 2013: 2).

Similarly, the American Heart Association (AHA) established a cozy relationship with several food companies. It decided to raise funds by labeling with an AHA logo foods that met some nutritional standards. "The association planned to collect fees from food companies that made approved products ... and expected to benefit from company advertising and promotion of the partnership" (Nestle 2001: 1017). The program was widely criticized and ended almost immediately. Such industry connections with hospitals may seem unlikely, but they, too, happen; for example, "the soft drink industry gave the Children's Hospital of Philadelphia a US $10 million gift— at a critical time the city of Philadelphia was considering a soda tax" (Brownell 2012). Charitable organizations have also forged partnerships; the Save the Children charity, for example, reversed its support of soda taxes at the same time as it received a $5-million grant from PepsiCo and sought a grant from Coke (Freedhoff and Hébert 2011). The President's Council on Physical Fitness and Sport partnered with General Mills, which produces Lucky Charms cereal, Pillsbury cookies, and Haagen Dazs ice cream (Steier 2012: 13).

Many experts in nutrition argue that partnerships won't work because public health interests do not align with the interests of the food companies. The companies are all about "expanding markets to reach more people, increasing people's sense of hunger so that they buy more food, and increasing profit margins through encouraging consumption of products with higher price/cost surpluses" (Stuckler and Nestle 2012: e1001242). One obesity researcher boldly states: "When the history of the world's attempt to address obesity is written, the greatest failure may be collaboration with and appeasement of the food industry" (Brownell 2012: e1001254).

Corporate responsibility campaigns

Big Food has developed a variety of social responsibility campaigns in order to improve its image. Thus both Pepsi and Coca-Cola undertook major media campaigns to associate their brand with good works. Pepsi began the Pepsi Refresh Project, which supports community-based projects, and Coca-Cola began its Live Positively campaign, which includes educational aspects called "Balanced Living" and "Exercise Is Medicine" (Dorfman et al. 2012). Such programs might sound good, but they are often just public relations campaigns designed to attach a positive message to products with potential negative health outcomes (Ludwig and Nestle 2008). PepsiCo also donated over $11 million to the Young Men's Christian Association (YMCA) to encourage kids to get excited about physical activity. Nutritionists point out: "This focus on physical activity, characteristically without commensurate attention to diet quality, appears disingenuous" (Ludwig and Nestle 2008: 1809).

Arguments Big Food makes

Embedded in the many public activities of Big Food are themes suggesting that foods and beverages are not the cause of health problems or obesity; rather individuals are to blame for the choices they make (Koplan and Brownell 2010). The classic statement of this "personal responsibility script" came in a tobacco setting when, at an annual meeting of RJR Nabisco, a woman in the audience asked "whether he would want people smoking around his children and grandchildren." The chair of RJR Nabisco responded: "If the children don't like to be in a smoky room ... they will leave." When the woman made the observation that infants don't have the option of leaving the room, the chair said: "At some point they learn to crawl, okay? And then they begin to walk" (Brownell and Warner 2009: 266).

Coca-Cola's "Exercise Is Medicine" educational campaign (mentioned above) has a personal responsibility message, as does the company's full-page advertisement in the *New York Times* of May 8, 2013, which states: "At Coca-Cola, we believe active lifestyles lead to happier lives. That's why we are committed to creating awareness around choice and movement, to help people make the most informed decisions for themselves and their families." The oft-repeated themes are stated clearly; "the importance of individual responsibility, the right of consumers to choose their own lifestyles, and the value of voluntary guidelines to govern corporate behavior" (Freudenberg 2012: 248). Placing the emphasis on the importance of physical exercise and self-control about one's diet is a technique for deflecting criticism from Big Food and placing it squarely on the consumer (Brownell and Warner 2009: 265).

Public health experts and doctors have a united voice when they express concern about such messages and the *Journal of Public Health Policy* went so far as to editorialize that research on individual responsibility hurts the cause of anti-obesity efforts. The editors said: "research studies concentrating on personal behavior and responsibility as causes of the obesity epidemic do little but offer cover to an industry seeking to downplay its own responsibility" (Robbins and Nestle 2011: 145).

Conclusion

Everyone needs access to healthy food. Although poor people's access to any food is a serious problem, given their poverty and the failures of distribution, access to healthy food is a problem for all of us. Our increasingly limited access to nutrition-rich food grown in sustainable ways is the result of upstream actions: the increasing concentration, economic power, political connections, and sophistication of players in many areas of Big Food, from the raising of livestock and the growing of crops to the manufacturing of new food choices, many of which are ultra-processed and unhealthy. In addition to being an unhealthy part of our daily diet, this food is produced in ways that hurt the environment by polluting soil, water, and air and by overusing nonrenewable fossil fuel-based inputs. All of these impacts ultimately affect human health. They are neither sustainable nor desirable. Although the government works in many ways to protect people's health, Big Food has been more powerful than the government (e.g., in the case of the food pyramid) and has influenced nutritionists, policy makers, and regulators to the extent that healthy food initiatives have lost out. Big Food has used many strategies to protect itself by implementing the tobacco playbook; and it has been extraordinarily effective.

Although most people could make healthier choices about the food they eat, the choices are limited by Big Food. It is as though "unhealthy food choices are the default" (Freudenberg 2012: 247). They are cheaper, ubiquitous, constantly advertised, and seductively delicious, hitting our "bliss point" again and again. Before we know it we are hooked and swept into a pattern of eating that is driven by our corporate culture. Unfortunately this pattern can have devastating health consequences for individuals and large costs for the healthcare system and for society at large.

9

Conclusion

This book has challenged readers to look upstream. We have long thought that the primary solution to poor health is the healthcare system; and we have allowed the biomedical model to reign supreme. This old model said, "diagnose the problem, treat it, and you have improved health." Throughout this book I have frequently used the river imagery to reinforce a different and more sociological perspective. I have argued that, when people drown, we should not focus on the water in their lungs when we diagnose or treat them; we should look instead to the stream itself (a metaphor for the conditions of life), recognize its power to kill those who fall into it (or are pushed), and work to change its course (that is, change those conditions). I then argued that my task here is to look further upstream, searching for the drivers or triggers of the conditions of life and asking what made our victims fall into the river. Or, stated differently, what power, structure, policies, and actions expose people to unhealthy conditions of life?

This upstream view has a strong history among researchers, clinical practitioners, activists, and others who identify unhealthy conditions of life and find ways to mitigate them, some of which I noted briefly. But, since I said so little about the important contribution of healthcare providers, I will do so now, focusing on doctors. The final chapter is an opportune place for it.

Unlike fifty years ago, nowadays doctors understand that health is typically achieved only when the provider goes beyond a biomedical understanding of the patient. They recognize the importance of the social determinants of health (SDoH) and want the healthcare system to address them; in one survey, 76 percent of doctor-respondents say that the healthcare system should cover the costs of connecting patients to services that can address their social needs.

More specifically, they wish they could write prescriptions for fitness programs (75 percent), nutritional food (64 percent), transportation (47 percent), and housing assistance (43 percent) (Robert Wood Johnson Foundation 2011a). The American Academy of Pediatrics has moved beyond the biomedical model by recognizing the health toll, on children, of being exposed to toxic stress and talks about the need to "strengthen the social and economic fabric of society" and about the devastating impact of poverty and discrimination on children (Shonkoff et al. 2012). American medical schools have changed their curriculum to reflect this heightened concern with SDoH. The Association of American Medical Colleges now talks about health as "the product of the interactions among biology, genetics, behavior, relationships, cultures, and environments" (Pelletier 2015), and the new Medical College Admission Test (MCAT) exam for students seeking admission to medical school includes sections on sociology and psychology. Occupational health, long missing from the medical curriculum, is a more typical part of the medical student's exposure and more recently there has been an increase in environmental education (Pelletier 2015). Some medical schools, like Tulane, have even enrolled their students in culinary courses in order to impress on them the importance of healthy food in one's diet.

Clinical settings have also changed over the years. One doctor in charge of an emergency room found that his trauma victims were often repeat patients who presented each time similar gun shot or knife wounds. The doctor decided that the best medical care, alone, wasn't enough and turned to offering general educational development (GED) courses and workshops on conflict resolution, which resulted in a decline in medical "recidivism" (Cooper et al. 2006). Several other health settings have demonstrated the viability and importance of doctors' having access to legal and social work professionals. In Boston two groups, Boston Legal Eagles and Health Leads, make sure that lawyers are on hand to provide legal assistance if a patient needs help in bringing a landlord to justice so that housing health standards can be followed or referrals for social services can be easily made (see www.medical-legalpartnership.org). As he describes in his TED Talk, Dr. Rishi Manchanda has established clinics with "upstream doctors." These doctors not only know the importance of SDoH but also have connections to community health workers and public interest lawyers who can resolve the conditions of life that are a primary cause of the patient's poor health (www.ted.com/talks/rishi_manchanda_what_makes_us_get_sick_look_upstream?language=en).

For doctors, nurses, and other healthcare providers who are not in upstream clinics, an increasing number of screening tools, community resources, and incentives have made the job of becoming an upstream provider easier. Healthcare providers typically lack the time and expertise to ask about conditions of living that are key SDoH. Having a publicly available social screening tool (e.g., HealthBeginsSocialScreeningTool.pdf) encourages providers to learn about non-medical aspects of a patient's life that affect personal health. Boston Children's Hospital has customized an online screening tool (helpsteps.com) that is completed by the client before the appointment with the provider. The results are given to the provider and, when leaving the facility, the client receives a hardcopy listing of appropriate resources in the community. In other communities many providers are now using the 211 infoline (www.211.org), a constantly updated search engine that connects people to local resources 24/7. A provider learning of unhealthy conditions of living does not need to respond as a deer in the headlights. There is instead an easily accessible and helpful resource to help address the patient's needs.

In addition to having access to screening tools and knowledge of community resources, healthcare providers have new incentives to think about SDoH. Our healthcare reimbursement system is on a hopeful trajectory in which outcomes matter and SDoH are acknowledged. Thus, the latest version of the International Classification of Diseases (ICD-10)—which is used for Medicare and Medicaid reimbursement and will soon be the foundation for other health insurance reimbursement—includes eighty-three "Z codes" that assess many SDoH. For example, providers can use the Z codes to note threat of job loss, stressful work schedule, occupational exposure to various toxins, homelessness, inadequate housing, lack of adequate food and safe drinking water, and low income. These conditions are then incorporated into a risk assessment model for the patient that can in turn generate increased reimbursements for any provider who takes care of a patient with social vulnerabilities.

Other transitions in healthcare—such as the turn to patient-centered medical homes, the movement away from the strict fee-for-service model, and the emphasis on greater team work that should incorporate community health workers (CHW), social workers, and others—all bode well for the serious incorporation of SDoH into the clinical setting. These changes are also a reminder of the mission of the original community health centers—now often referred to as federally qualified health centers (FQHCs)—begun as a War on Poverty initiative in the 1960s. The current "practice transformations" will bring back many features of those original community health centers, which prioritized team work with doctors, nurses, social workers, nutritionists, and even community residents: together, all these attempted to establish community priorities for health and to provide culturally appropriate interdisciplinary care. Furthermore, such teams went beyond traditional medical screening and treatment, asking for instance whether the patient had access to enough food. If not, the team prescribed food or even established a community garden.

Making Communities Healthier

A variety of other initiatives have successfully worked to mitigate unhealthy conditions of life without necessarily identifying or stopping the source of the problem (the driver of the condition). Though too numerous to list, a few examples serve to suggest that optimism is realistic. A major unhealthy condition of life comes from the use of fossil fuel. The dependence of human societies on fossil fuels has polluted the planet's air, water, and soil and is a major contributor to climate change. Any change that can reduce the level of pollution or clean up existing pollution could improve our unhealthy conditions of life. School buses and their diesel emissions are an important polluter, so evidence that school bus retrofits can reduce bronchitis, asthma, and pneumonia is encouraging (Beatty and Shimshack 2011). A 2015 Environmental Protection Agency (EPA) "Clean Power Plan" (https://www.epa.gov/cleanpowerplan/clean-power-pl an-existing-power-plants) established the first national standards ever to address carbon pollution from power plants. Clearly this initiative does not end the impact of carbon pollution but is a step toward a serious reduction.

Another approach is to make fossil fuels more expensive to use. In Canada, British Columbia appears to have been successful with a tax on the carbon content of fossil fuels. Others are finding ways to develop alternative sources of energy by using food waste. In Colorado, a company is experimenting with anaerobic digestion to turn food into methane gas which is captured and turned into electricity (Runyon 2016).

Cleaning up trash and pollution in general could make a significant impact on our conditions of living, and several ideas are being implemented. One includes figuring out combinations of microbial communities that can mitigate harmful environmental impacts of wastewater while at the same time extracting useful products. Kartik Chandran, a MacArthur Foundation fellow at Columbia University, has figured out a way to remove nitrogen from waste and to transform bio-generated methane gas into methanol, a chemical that is useful in industry (https://www.macfound.org/fellows/930). Two recent University of Pennsylvania graduates are testing a way to clean up water using a natural seed which, when crushed, produces a coagulant protein which binds together with bacteria, other toxins, clay, and silt (Lazos 2015). In Baltimore, the city has purchased solar-powered trash collectors which use solar panels and water current to remove 50,000 pounds of trash a day from the harbor (Wang 2014). And in San Francisco there is a recycling plant that uses both humans and optical sorters to cull and classify household waste with such efficiency that 80 percent of waste otherwise headed to landfills is diverted. It is referred to as the "Silicon Valley of Recycling" (Richtel 2016).

The effectiveness of communities organizing around toxic trash dumps has been the subject of many reports since the early days of Love Canal, Woburn, Massachusetts, Pensacola, Florida ("Mt Dioxin"), and Warren County, North Carolina (Bullard 1990; Gibbs 2002; Brown 2007). The environmental justice movement has been effective in many communities:

> Although boundless problems remain, average people have shown that they can achieve many things: buyout of contaminated areas, economic settlements from polluting companies, control and abolition of dangerous chemicals, government and corporate toxics use reduction, health monitoring for people in toxics-affected areas, regulation of oil refinery flaring, substitution of cleaner emission buses, participation in decision making about siting of hazardous facilities, membership on peer review panels for environmental health research, and a host of other actions. (Brown 2007: xiii–xiv)

Such community activism likely provided a model for the recent work of a high school senior, Destiny Watford, whose activism led the state of Maryland to revoke a permit for the incineration of lead- and mercury-laden trash in her community, and led to Watford's receipt of an international award (Fears 2016).

The abundance and advertising of unhealthy foods is another condition of life that has dramatically contributed to a myriad of poor health outcomes. Small-scale but innovative efforts to reform include profitable models for the return of smaller farm, healthy-food operations. In North Carolina, for example, where CAFO-raised hogs are the rule, one farmer and his university partners are working to demonstrate that a 142-animal operation can profitably raise hogs without antibiotics and without putting waste in open-air lagoons (Rivin 2016). Limiting access to unhealthy food is the plan behind a city initiative in South Los Angeles where town officials turned to land-use laws to prohibit new fast-food establishments in poor neighborhoods (Medina 2011). Increasing access to healthy food is the goal of initiatives in several cities such as Cleveland and Louisville, where public health organizations and economic development agencies have approached store owners with offers of new equipment and marketing expertise to encourage them to stock more fresh produce. They help the store owners with grants, free advertising, and help in changing zoning regulations (Granville 2009). Additional healthy food initiatives include support of local farmers' markets by many cities and the federal government's promotion of Community Supported Agriculture (CSA) through their website (http://afsic. nal.usda.gov/community-supported-agriculture-3) and various data collecting efforts. Typically, members of the CSA pledge in advance to cover the anticipated costs of the farm operation. In return, they receive allotments of the food grown. The farmer reduces his risk by acquiring working capital in advance, receives better prices for his crops, and gains some financial security.

Resistance to Change and Challenges to Resistance

But stopping at the conditions of life, as we have noted throughout the book, does not solve the problem of an unhealthy populace. We must look further upstream to the drivers of the conditions of life—a harder but more broadly effective task. We noted in the first two chapters why it is harder to look upstream and commented on two major reasons. One is that we tend to gaze downward and look at genes and individual behaviors. The director of the Human Genome Project, for example, suggested that genome-based tools could mitigate health disparities and the United States responded with $1 billion a year into genomics research, producing virtually no useful information about disparities since they are not caused by "the twists of the double helix, but the grinding inequality of the environment" (Silverstein 2015). The second reason is that a focus on the drivers of the conditions threatens the status quo of powerful industries, and these industries resist, often quite successfully. They have learned and refined the "tobacco playbook," the strategies used by the tobacco industry for decades to avoid the truth about the harmful impact of tobacco on health. They use doubt and denial, public relations firms, front groups, and attacks on legitimate researchers to deflect attention from the problems they are causing, offering solutions that often call solely for individual responsibility and more rational individual choices. Much of this book has analyzed precisely these tactics and argued that our health has been seriously compromised by decades of deceptive practices.

Despite considerable resistance, however, many individuals, communities, and social movements have been successful in drawing attention to these drivers. One of the big victories at the end of the last century was the litigation against the Tobacco Industry. After years of denying the scientific evidence, the industry was finally made to stop many of their practices, pay billions, and work to educate people about the health problem they had manufactured. Unfortunately, that victory meant that some of the pressure to smoke was exported overseas where many countries saw rates of smoking increase. Litigation has been used in other situations and has been effective in changing corporate behavior. Pending litigation includes a landmark case in which twenty-one plaintiffs, aged eight to nineteen, have sued the federal government "for violating their constitutional rights to life, liberty and property, and their right to essential public trust resources, by permitting, encouraging, and otherwise enabling continued exploitation, production, and combustion of fossil fuels" (Children's Trust 2016). A US Magistrate Judge in the federal District Court in Eugene, Oregon has decided in their favor. Sometimes the threat of litigation can produce enough bad press to force changes before any court makes a decision. When Kraft was sued for marketing Oreo cookies to children without disclosing known harm from trans-fat, media attention forced Kraft to reduce trans-fats in their products (Freudenberg 2014: 221).

Indeed, changes in public policies could make a significant difference in regulating the power of industry over consumers. Since economic inequality is an obvious factor in so many outcomes related to poor health, as chapter 3 illustrated, addressing economic policies that privilege an already privileged few is an important start. Some people are pushing for a reduction in the kind of inequality that produces disparate health outcomes by means of changing tax rates, so that rich people pay in proportion to their large share of income and wealth. A group of forty millionaires in New York wrote to the governor, suggesting that increasing their taxes could help address poverty and rebuild failing infrastructure (Klepper 2016).

Even Charles G. Koch, CEO of Koch Industries and perennial high donor to conservative causes, suggested that corporate welfare was a problem: "Consider the regulations, handouts, mandates, subsidies and other forms of largesse our elected officials dole out to the wealthy and well-connected. The tax code alone contains $1.5 trillion in exemptions and special-interest carve-outs" (Koch 2016). A California Equal Opportunity Plan takes a different angle on inequality and poverty: it proposes to identify critical points when a child does not have the same access to high-quality training and education as his peers and suggests that, if provided, such training and education would dramatically change that child's life and health outcomes (Parker 2015). Potentially supporting such efforts are campaigns like "Giving Pledge," a commitment by the wealthy families of the world to give most of their wealth to philanthropy (www.givingpledge.org).

In a different realm, discussed at length in chapter 6, several government- and community-based initiatives have changed the contemporary asphalt- and cement-covered landscape. With a vision not limited by car-dependent blinders, which see streets merely as places for moving one's car rapidly and efficiently, and with the help of ideas of "smart growth" and "complete streets" (http://www.smart-growthamerica.org/complete-streets), people are finding ways to transform urban areas into spaces that serve not just vehicles but also pedestrians, cyclists, and people who like to sit and enjoy being out of doors. The Transportation Alternatives movement in New York City (https://www.transalt.org) is an excellent example. It is rebuilding community, decreasing pollution, and increasing social interaction, all of which are important for people's health. Vision Zero, active in many US cities such as Boston (http://www.visionzeroboston.org), has the goal of zero deaths of pedestrians, bikers, and car drivers and passengers. Many cities have worked to increase bicycle use through bike-sharing programs. The number of such programs is increasing: recently it has doubled in just one year (Malouff 2014). Internationally, the Sophia project in Barcelona is a more inclusive urban renewal project focused on improving various health outcomes of residents in disadvantaged neighborhoods by transforming infrastructure and transportation options (Mehdipanah et al. 2014).

Housing is another key area in which policy changes can work to improve health outcomes. In an attempt to encourage the building of homes for poor people and to decrease segregation—both key structural changes that have an impact on health—states can offer tax credits to developers. How they set up the tax credits is critical, and luckily a 2015 Supreme Court decision has made it clear that the process must not contribute to structural racism. The decision found that a Texas process did exactly that, by "allocating too many tax credits to housing in predominantly black inner-city areas, and too few in predominantly white suburban neighborhoods" (Alito 2015: 1). The Court-mandated system will change such disparities. The government also gives housing subsidies directly to people; at present, however, the bulk of these subsidies goes to people who are not poor. This is the result of a significant income tax break that home owners receive for interest paid on mortgages. In one year, as data show, direct housing assistance for poor people was barely over $40 billion while tax benefits for home owners exceeded $171 billion (Desmond 2016: 312). A change in government policy on housing and in the tax code could improve housing quality and affordability for poor people in significant ways. Subsidies in other arenas could be altered as well, to the benefit of public health. Presently, the US government (and other governments) subsidizes fossil fuels. The United States gives annual subsidies on the order of $37.5 billion, including $21 billion for exploration and production. While such subsidies keep current prices low for consumers, they discourage the development and implementation of renewable energy sources and forestall a sustainable future (Schwartz 2015; also visit http://priceofoil.org/fossil-fuel-subsidies). On a large scale, a change in government subsidies could affect our carbon footprint and reduce climate change.

Changing Institutional Practices

Changes in regulatory agencies could lead to improved health. Some people argue that agencies like the EPA are not independent enough from political and economic pressure to make decisions that truly value human health. A staff member working in the EPA for more than twenty years has recommended giving the EPA an independence more like that of the Federal Reserve by selecting a scientist as director for a ten-year term, by making any contact between the EPA and industrial lobbyists illegal, and by setting up rules to prohibit career moves from the EPA to private industry without a five-year gap (Vallianatos and Jenkins 2014: 228–9). Contributing to the problem of corporate bias is the burden on regulatory agencies when potential harm is assessed. In chapter 4 we have seen how the manufacturer of a new industrial chemical notifies the EPA and then leaves it with the task of documenting the potential risk. This process makes the "presumption of innocence" the operative rule by putting an onerous burden of evidence-gathering on the EPA. The Occupational Safety and Health Administration (OSHA)'s annual publication of a list of "suspected carcinogens" is a more even-handed, health-promoting approach.

In general, government agencies have rules for scientific evidence that are not robust. Many research journals do better. A former assistant secretary of Energy for Environment, Safety, and Health, David Michaels, argues that the data used for regulatory decisions need to be at least comparable to the research integrity guidelines of biomedical journals. Conflict of interest must be transparent and researchers should declare if they were permitted to publish findings without the permission of the sponsor (Michaels 2008b: 102–3). Without such permission, publications of harm are suppressed and societal knowledge about a chemical is biased and incomplete.

Also, government agencies need to be more up-to-date in their safety standards. For instance, while the government has long known that silica is a very toxic occupational hazard, it took until the spring of 2016 for OSHA to come out with a rule that could effectively protect workers (Hopkins 2016). The current standards for too many toxic chemicals—far too many—were set decades ago. New knowledge about the health impact of these chemicals means that new standards are imperative.

Another important source of change in the drivers of our health is the private sector and the corporations themselves. Many have already moved in the direction of health-improving changes. Early in our history we learned that exposing decision makers (like CEOs) to the actual conditions for which they were responsible could have a powerful impact. In the early 1900s, Alice Hamilton insisted on not just writing a report on occupational health, but actually taking the CEO of the company to the plant so he could see the horrendous working conditions firsthand (https://www.youtube.com/watch?v=E75pST2QTEM). Recently Jeffrey Dunn, Coca Cola's president and chief operating officer in North and South America, had a similar experience. He was tasked to market Coke in smaller containers, so that poor people would be more likely to buy it. When he visited the favelas of Brazil to imagine how he might design this campaign, he was so taken by the conditions of poverty that he had an epiphany. "A voice in my head says, 'These people need a lot of things, but they don't need a Coke.' I almost threw up" (Moss 2013: 48). He was fired as a consequence, but the episode made clear the power of making executives feel the consequences of their actions. Similarly, as I noted in chapter 6, when GM Vice-President Lutz got personal emails about his reluctance to support an electric car, he changed his mind and supported the development of the Chevy Volt, an electric hybrid.

But such individual changes of heart will not significantly alter the drivers of the conditions of life. Importantly, more systemic changes are appearing in the corporate world. One change is called "impact investing," which establishes funds for social change. One group has proposed a model to promote more sustainable, healthier food systems "offering small growers and retailers an alternative to reliance on agribusiness and mainstream financial institutions and investors an opportunity to make money while doing good" (Freudenberg 2014: 232). Another approach is to leverage the power of institutional investors so as to make companies more environmentally responsible. The Carbon Disclosure Project, with its more than 300 institutional investors, asks the 500 largest companies to report annually on their greenhouse gas emissions (Freudenberg 2014: 233).

Change is also coming from what *Fortune Magazine* calls a "quiet corporate revolution": the move from corporate social responsibility as window dressing, often in the form of limited philanthropy, to addressing important social problems as a core part of a business plan. In support of such efforts, one group, formed by two Harvard professors, is working with businesses through the Sustainability and Health Initiative for NetPositive Enterprise (SHINE) to help companies understand their impact on health (both occupational and environmental) and to factor that understanding into all business decisions (McNeely 2015). One approach to implement this idea has been the certification of existing for-profit companies. A nonprofit "B lab" evaluates a business in order to determine whether it is meeting standards of social and environmental performance, accountability, and transparency. Currently 1,600 businesses in forty-two countries are B-certified with the unifying slogan: "better for workers, better for communities, and better for the environment" (www.bcorporation.net). A potentially more significant change could come with the spread of legal entities defined outside the dualism of for-profit corporations and not-for-profit corporations. Such hybrid entities are starting to be called low-profit limited-liability companies, benefit corporations, and flexible-purpose corporations. Each has a profit-making side combined with a social goal mandate. Various US states, including Maryland, Vermont, California, Hawaii, New Jersey, and Virginia, now recognize these benefit corporations as legal entities (Sabeti 2011; Cummings 2012). For instance, in 2010, Maryland's governor signed into law the nation's first benefit corporation legislation. A Maryland state senator commented: "We are giving companies a way to do good and do well at the same time" (Resor 2012: 91). Other people talk about a new accounting framework called "the triple bottom line," which expands performance evaluation by examining impacts not just on profits, the traditional bottom line, but on people, profit, and the planet (Slaper and Hall 2011).

This chapter should provide reasonable hope that we can follow a trajectory that reduces the harm produced by SDoH. I have clearly not documented all of the positive work that has been completed or is planned on altering the conditions of life and the drivers of those conditions. As this text was being written, the National Park Service announced the full remediation of the Krejci dump, a highly toxic dump that contains "among the nation's most toxic materials, including polychlorinated biphenyls (PCB's), polycyclic aromatic hydrocarbons (PAH's), arsenic, and other carcinogenic wastes" (https://www.nps.gov/cuva/learn/news/krejci.htm) sited amid the Cuyahoga Valley National Park—a popular recreation destination, a vibrant ecosystem, and a national treasure. Examples like this serve to illustrate the variety of possibilities for positive change in the SDoH. My analysis has focused on the behavior of corporations, which are responsible for the lion's share of negative SDoH, so let me offer a few concluding remarks on the corporate world and then recall the overarching principles behind the concerns addressed in this book.

Health as a Human Right

Capitalism has long been the foundation of a strong American economic system. The creativity, ingenuity, and risk taking of corporations have enabled amazing improvements in people's life comforts. Throughout history, the public and the government have also recognized that corporations can be brutal in their treatment of workers and the environment. Early in American history, citizens worked to smooth the rough edges of capitalism by passing child labor laws and laws that fixed the length of the working day. In the 1970s various regulations were passed and agencies were established to protect workers and the environment from the actions of corporations. Still, corporations had considerable latitude and many did create externalities that were costly to society. When a corporation releases toxins into the air, the ground, and the water, ordinary people end up paying the price. A recent article in the *Harvard Business Review* concludes: "Our current model of capitalism has generated prosperity and improved the quality of life, but not without undesirable environmental and social consequences" (Sabeti 2011: 7). We need a compassionate capitalism with reasonable regulations.

This book has argued for better health, built on a foundation of principles such as democracy, responsibility, health as a human right, upstream public health, and social justice. The move forward to a healthier society and world must first fully respect the idea and original meaning of a country of the people, by the people, and for the people. For too long the voices of a handful of powerful people have decided the fate of Americans. The illustrations of the effectiveness of the tobacco playbook clearly document this. Second, the public must demand that corporations are held accountable to the same standards of responsibility they often suggest for the customers of their unhealthy products. With externalities, corporations clearly have shunned their responsibilities. If a corporate action leads to disease, injury, or death, sometimes there is no significant penalty for the parties responsible. Thus, when GM knowingly produced a faulty ignition switch and people died, no one at GM was accused of a crime. To the extent that responsibility has been assigned and people have paid for their actions, this has not been brought about by regulatory agencies enforcing policies, but typically by district attorneys seeking justice. In 1981, one official at a chicken-processing plant was sentenced to twenty years in prison; in 1998 the owner of a company was fined half a million dollars and sent to jail for over a year when two workers died; and the CEO of Massey Energy, Don Blankenship, was tried in 2015 on charges of mine safety violations and for the cover-up of a mine explosion that killed twenty-nine miners. Although he was acquitted on charges that could have led to thirty years in jail, he is expected to spend up to a year in jail. Significantly, since the 1970s there has been an increase in "the number of manslaughter and murder charges brought against corporations and their executives" (Rosner 2000: 535). And now environmental harm is seeing some justice: in Flint, Michigan, charges are pending against the officials who made the decisions and covered up the harm from lead-polluted water in 2015. So we can be hopeful that US society is moving in the direction of making high-level decision makers assume responsibility for harmful actions.

Third, the wisdom behind the precautionary principle seems more evident each day, as harm to workers and the environment is increasingly yet belatedly discovered. Given the decades-long latency period after which many toxins begin to produce recognizable symptoms in people and in the ecosystem, we are slow to learn of many harmful actions. One needs to exercise more care when one approves of government and corporate actions, new chemicals, and new processes for raising food. Reasonable regulations applied to all can ensure a level playing field for the various relevant companies.

Fourth, people need to respect health as a human right, push for a more upstream public health vision and practice, and use a social justice lens as they work for change and evaluate impacts. These three arenas impacting research, policy, and action—human rights, public health, and social justice—are complementary and interconnected and overlap considerably with the SDoH. Perhaps most well-known is the human rights arena set forth in the 1948 Universal Declaration of Human Rights and in various UN treaties and agreements since then. The UN mentions most of the SDoH I have discussed in this book, as well as some I have not, when discussing the right to health. It notes that the human right to health is interwoven with other human rights:

> Human rights are interdependent, indivisible and interrelated. This means that violating the right to health may often impair the enjoyment of other human rights, such as the rights to education or work, and vice versa. The importance given to the "underlying determinants of health," that is, the factors and conditions which protect and promote the right to health beyond health services, goods and facilities, shows that the right to health is dependent on, and contributes to, the realization of many other human rights. These include the rights to food, to water, to an adequate standard of living, to adequate housing, to freedom from discrimination, to privacy, to access to information, to participation, and the right to benefit from scientific progress and its applications. (WHO 2008b: 6)

At times the emphasis in the field of human rights has been more on political and civic rights, but increasingly it focuses on social and economic rights, including the right to health. The connectivity of human rights and SDoH is growing. There is also a strong connection between human rights and public health, as the research and practice of public health evolved from using a lens defined by the biomedical model to using a lens that increasingly sees the need to change societal conditions (Markowitz and Rosner 2013b: 3–5). The first editor of the *Health and Human Rights* journal discussed how powerful this connectivity is by using a human rights framework to present a public health concern. He argues that "there is a vital, societal, legal and personal difference between saying 'If you think it is all right, it would be nice if I could'" have some clean water and saying "'I am human—I have a right to'" clean water (Mann 1996: 231). The latter is a powerful claim on government action rather than a plea for basic rights. Thus there is strong synergy between SDoH, human rights, and public health.

Linking SDoH not only to human rights and public health but also to social justice—the third arena of research, policy, and action— stems in part from the human rights concern with vulnerable individuals whose health suffers precisely because of systemic discrimination and lack of power in society. Writing in 1998, Nancy Krieger began an article with the sentence "Social justice is the foundation of public health" and then continued:

> To declare that social justice is the foundation of public health is to call upon and nurture that invincible human spirit that led so many of us to enter the field of public health in the first place: a spirit that has a compelling desire to make the world a better place, free of misery, inequity, and preventable suffering, a world in which we all can live, love, work, play, ail, and die with our dignity intact and our humanity cherished. (Krieger and Birn 1998: 1603)

While a "walk upstream implies a radical shift" (Brown 2007: 58) and bringing the very different fields of human rights, social justice, and public health together with an emphasis on SDoH is not an easy task, recent institutional developments suggest that this trajectory is not a fantasy. Many schools of public health are already establishing centers or tracks of study that take the walk upstream and work to bring these arenas together. The Center for Public Health and Human Rights at the Johns Hopkins Bloomberg School of Public Health works to advance fundamental human rights through research, teaching, and advocacy; the Boston University School of Public Health sponsored a 2016 symposium on public health and human rights; and the website of the Columbia University Mailman School of Public Health notes: "Increasingly, the public health field is recognizing that integrating human rights approaches into public health practices and policies can provide a powerful force for social justice and improved health" (https://www.mailman.columbia.edu/become-student/degrees/masters-programs/masters-public-health/columbia-mph/certificates/health-and). Various initiatives at Harvard, stimulated in part by the work of Paul Farmer and Partners in Health, provide strong additional evidence of the academic vibrancy and efficacious community health actions that result when a concern for human rights, social justice, and public health force a vision that looks upstream.

References

Abramsky, Sasha. 2013. *The American Way of Poverty: How the Other Half Still Lives*. New York: Nation Books.

Adeola, Francis O. 2012. "Hazardous and Toxic Wastes: Modern Social Problem or Plague of Our Time?" In Francis O. Adeola, *Industrial Disasters, Toxic Waste, and Community Impact: Health Effects and Environmental Justice Struggles Around the Globe*, 15–26. Lanham, MD: Lexington Books.

Adeola, Francis O. 2012 [1997]. "Sociology of Hazardous Wastes Unnatural Disasters, and Health Risks." In Francis O. Adeola, *Industrial Disasters, Toxic Waste, and Community Impact*, 3–14. Lanham, MD: Lexington Books.

Adler, Jonathan H. 2015. "Sixth Circuit Puts Controversial 'Waters of the United States' (WOTUS) Rule on Hold." *Washington Post*, October 9. https://www.washingtonpost.com/news/volokh-conspiracy/wp/2015/10/09/sixth-circuit-puts-controversial-waters-of-the-united-states-wotus-rule-on-hold.

Adler, Robert W., Jessica C. Landman, and Diane M. Cameron. 1993. *The Clean Water Act: 20 Years Later*. Washington, DC: Island Press.

Ahern, Melissa M. et al. 2011. "The Association between Mountaintop Mining and Birth Defects among Live Births in Central Appalachia, 1996–2003." *Environmental Research* 111(6): 838–46.

Aitken, Samuel L., Thomas J. Dilworth, Emily L. Heil, and Michael D. Nailor. 2016. "Agricultural Applications for Antimicrobials: A Danger to Human Health: An Official Position Statement of the Society of Infectious Diseases Pharmacists." *Pharmacotherapy: The Journal of Human Pharmacology and Drug Therapy* 36(4): 422–32.

Alfonzo, Mariela, Marlon G. Boarnet, Kristen Day, Tracy Mcmillan, and Craig L. Anderson. 2008. "The Relationship of Neighbourhood Built Environment Features and Adult Parents' Walking." *Journal of Urban Design* 13(1): 29–51.

Alito, J. 2015. *Texas Department of Housing and Community Affairs v. Inclusive Communities Project, INC.* Washington, DC: United States Supreme Court.

Altman, Rebecca G. et al. 2011. "Pollution Comes Home and Gets Personal: Women's Experience of Household Chemical Exposure." In *Contested Illnesses: Citizens, Science, and Health Social Movements,* edited by Phil Brown, Rachel Morello-Frosch, and Stephen Zavestoski, 123–46. Berkeley: University of California Press.

Altschuler, Andrea, Carol P. Somkin, and Nancy E. Adler. 2004. "Local Services and Amenities, Neighborhood Social Capital, and Health." *Social Science & Medicine* 59(6): 1219–29.

Alvaredo, Facundo, Anthony B. Atkinson, Thomas Piketty, and Emmanuel Saez. 2013. *The Top 1 Percent in International and Historical Perspective.* National Bureau of Economic Research. http://www.nber.org/papers/w19075.

American Cancer Society. 2011. *Cancer Facts and Figures 2011.* Atlanta: American Cancer Society. https://www.cancer.org/content/dam/cancer-org/research/cancer-facts-and-statistics/annual-cancer-facts-and-figures/2011/cancer-facts-and-figures-2011.pdf.

American Lung Association. 2001. "Urban Air Pollution and Health Inequities: A Workshop Report." *Environmental Health Perspectives* 109(S3): 357–74.

American Lung Association. 2013. "A Penny for Prevention: The Case for Cleaner Gasoline and Vehicle Standards." http://www.lung.org/healthy-air/outdoor/defending-the-clean-air-act/interactive-presentations/cleaner-gasoline-and-vehicles-report-2013.pdf.

American Water Works Association. 2010. *Buried No Longer: Confronting America's Water Infrastructure Challenge.* Water Utility Council. http://www.awwa.org/Portals/0/files/legreg/documents/BuriedNoLonger.pdf.

Anderson, Matthew. 2010. "Sleeping with the Enemy: 'More Doctors Smoke Camels' Revisited." *Social Medicine* 5(2): 85–9.

Andreen, William L. 2004. "Water Quality Today: Has the Clean Water Act Been a Success?" *Alabama Law Review* 55(3): 537–93.

Andreen, William L. 2013. "Success and Backlash: The Remarkable (Continuing) Story of the Clean Water Act." *George Washington Journal of Energy and Environmental Law* 4(1): 25–37.

Andrews, Bonnie K., Susan Karcz, and Beth Rosenberg. 2008. "Hooked on a Feeling: Emotional Labor as an Occupational Hazard of the Post-Industrial Age." *New Solutions* 18(2): 245–55.

Angelo, Mary Jane. 2009. "Corn, Carbon, and Conservation: Rethinking US Agricultural Policy in a Changing Global Environment." *George Mason Law Review* 17 (593). http://scholarship.law.ufl.edu/facultypub/32.

APHA (American Public Health Association). 2007. "Policy Statement Database: Toward a Healthy Sustainable Food System." APHA. https://

www.apha.org/policies-and-advocacy/public-health-policy-statements/po
licy-database/2014/07/29/12/34/toward-a-healthy-sustainable-food-sys
tem.

APHA (American Public Health Association). 2010. "Backgrounder: The Hidden Health Costs of Transportation." National Academies of Sciences, Engineering, Medicine. http://trid.trb.org/view.aspx?id=919815.

Arnold, Emily and Janet Larsen. 2006. "Bottled Water: Pouring Resources Down the Drain." Earth Policy Institute. http://www.earth-policy.org/plan_b_updates/2006/update51.

Arnold, Tony. 2007. "Planning for Environmental Justice." *Planning & Environmental Law* 59(3): 3–12.

Assadourian, Erik. 2010. "The Rise and Fall of Consumer Cultures." In *State of the World 2010: Transforming Cultures: From Consumerism to Sustainability*, edited by Worldwatch Institute, 3–20. Washington, DC: Island Press.

Athar, Heba M., Man-Huei Chang, Robert A. Hahn, Eric Walker, and Paula Yoon. 2013. "Unemployment: United States, 2006 and 2010." *CDC Centers for Disease Control and Prevention* 62(3): 27–33. https://www.cdc.gov/mmwr/preview/mmwrhtml/su6203a5.htm.

ATSDR (Agency for Toxic Substances and Disease Registry). 2011. "Toxic Substance Portal: Arsenic." CDC. http://www.atsdr.cdc.gov/substances/toxsubstance.asp?toxid=3.

ATSDR (Agency for Toxic Substances and Disease Registry). 2014. "Toxic Substances Portal-Polychlorinated Biphenyls (PCBs)." http://www.atsdr.cdc.gov/toxfaqs/tf.asp?id=140&tid=26.

Aviv, Rachel. 2014. "A Valuable Reputation." *New Yorker*, February 6, 53–73. http://www.newyorker.com/magazine/2014/02/10/a-valuable-rep utation.

Baer, Hans A. and Merrill Singer. 2009. *Global Warming and the Political Ecology of Health: Emerging Crises and Systemic Solutions*. Walnut Creek, CA: Left Coast Press.

Balazs, Carolina, Rachel Morello-Frosch, Alan Hubbard, and Isha Ray. 2011. "Social Disparities in Nitrate-Contaminated Drinking Water in California's San Joaquin Valley." *Environmental Health Perspectives* 119(9): 1272–8.

Banerjee, Neela. 2013. "Message Is Mixed on Fracking." *Los Angeles Times*, July 28. http://www.latimes.com/nation/nationnow/la-na-epa-dimock-20130728-m-story.html#page=1.

Barker, Debbie, Bill Freese, and George Kimbrell. 2013. "Seed Giants vs. US Farmers." *Center for Food Safety*. http://www.centerforfoodsafety.org/reports/1770/seed-giants-vs-us-farmers.

Barker, Rodney. 1998. *And the Waters Turned to Blood: The Ultimate Biological Threat*. New York: Simon & Schuster.

Barlett, Donald L. and James B. Steele. 2008. "Monsanto's Harvest of Fear." *Vanity Fair* 4: 1–9.

Barlow, Maude and Tony Clarke. 2002. *Blue Gold: The Fight to Stop the Corporate Theft of the World's Water*. New York: New Press.

Baron, Sherry and Theodore M. Brown. 2009. "Alice Hamilton (1869–1970): Mother of US Occupational Medicine." *American Journal of Public Health* 99(S3): S548.

Baron, Sherry et al. 2011. "The Health of the Low-Income Workforce: Integrating Public Health and Occupational Health Approaches." Issue paper presented for discussion at the conference "Eliminating Health and Safety Disparities at Work," Chicago, September 14–15.

Barry, Michele and James M. Hughes. 2008. "Talking Dirty: The Politics of Clean Water and Sanitation." *New England Journal of Medicine* 359(8): 784–7.

Bashir, Samiya A. 2002. "Home Is Where the Harm Is: Inadequate Housing as a Public Health Crisis." *American Journal of Public Health* 92(5): 733–8.

Bassett, Mary T. 2015. "#BlackLivesMatter: A Challenge to the Medical and Public Health Communities." *New England Journal of Medicine* 372(12): 1085–7.

Bassett, Mary T. 2016. "Public Health Meets the 'Problem of the Color Line.'" Speech in acceptance of the Calderone Prize, October 25, Columbia University Mailman School of Public Health. https://www.mailman.columbia.edu/public-health-now/events/calderone-prize/2016-winner-dr-mary-t-bassett.

Baugher, John E. and J. Timmons Roberts. 2004. "Workplace Hazards, Unions, and Coping Styles." *Labor Studies Journal* 29(2): 83–106.

Bayer, Ronald. 1988. *The Health and Safety of Workers: Case Studies in the Politics of Professional Responsibility*. New York: Oxford University Press.

Bayliss, Kate. 2014. "The Financialization of Water." *Review of Radical Political Economics* 46(3): 292–307.

Beals, Shawn R. 2012. "SNAP at Farmers' Market to Grow." *Hartford Courant*, November 23.

Beatty, Timothy K. M. and Jay P. Shimshack. 2011. "School Buses, Diesel Emissions, and Respiratory Health." *Journal of Health Economics* 30(5): 987–99.

Beder, Sharon. 1998. "Public Relations' Role in Manufacturing Artificial Grass Roots Coalitions." *Public Relations Quarterly* 43(2): 20–3.

Benach, Joan, Carles Muntaner, Orielle Solar, Vilma Santana, and Michael Quinlan. 2010. "Introduction to the WHO Commission on Social Determinants of Health Employment Conditions Network (EMCONET) Study, with a Glossary on Employment Relations." *International Journal of Health Services* 40(2): 195–207.

Benbrook, Charles M. 2012. "Impacts of Genetically Engineered Crops on Pesticide Use in the US: The First Sixteen Years." *Environmental Sciences Europe* 24(24). doi: 10.1186/2190-4715-24-24.

Benfield, F. Kaid, Matthew Raimi, and Donald D. T. Chen. 1999. *Once There Were Greenfields: How Urban Sprawl Is Undermining America's*

Environment, Economy, and Social Fabric. New York: Natural Resources Defense Council.

Bernstein, Andrea and Nancy Solomon, with Laura Yuen and Casey Miner. 2012. "Back of the Bus: Race, Mass Transit and Inequality." Transportation Nation. http://project.wnyc.org/backofthebus.

Bernstein, Jake. 2005. "Don't Drink the Water." *The Texas Observer*. http://www.texasobserver.org/2090-dont-drink-the-water-in-the-urban-colonias-of-the-greater-houston-area-the-water-stinks.

Bezruchka, Stephen. 2015. "Early Life or Early Death: Support for Child Health Lasts a Lifetime." *International Journal of Child, Youth and Family Studies* 6(2): 204–29.

Bingham, Eula and Celeste Monforton. 2013. *The Pesticide DBCP and Male Infertility*. European Environment Agency. http://www.eea.europa.eu/publications/late-lessons-2/late-lessons-chapters/late-lessons-ii-chapter-9.

Biodiversity Research Institute. 2013. *Global Mercury Hotspots: New Evidence Reveals Mercury Contamination Regularly Exceeds Health Advisory Levels*. Biodiversity Research Institute. http://www.briloon.org/uploads/BRI_Doc uments/Mercury_Center/BRI-IPEN-report-update-102214%20for%20 web.pdf.

Bitton, Asaf, Mark D. Neuman, and Stanton A. Glantz. 2002. *Tobacco Industry Attempts to Subvert European Union Tobacco Advertising Legislation*. Center for Tobacco Control Research and Education, University of California, San Francisco. http://escholarship.org/uc/item/3r1334mz.

Blair, Aaron, Patricia Stewart, Jay H. Lubin, and Francesco Forastiere. 2007. "Methodological Issues Regarding Confounding and Exposure Misclassification in Epidemiological Studies of Occupational Exposures." *American Journal of Industrial Medicine* 50(3): 199–207.

Blair, Benjamin D., Jordan P. Crago, Curtis J. Hedman, and Rebecca D. Klaper. 2013. "Pharmaceuticals and Personal Care Products Found in the Great Lakes above Concentrations of Environmental Concern." *Chemosphere* 93(9): 2116–23.

Blanding, Michael. 2011. *The Coke Machine: The Dirty Truth behind the World's Favorite Soft Drink*. New York: Penguin.

BLS (Bureau of Labor Statistics). 2015. *Census of Fatal Occupational Injuries Summary, 2014*. http://www.bls.gov/news.release/cfoi.nr0.htm.

Blumenthal, Richard. 2009. "Food-Makers Promote Bad Eating Habits." *Hartford Courant*, November 10.

Blumenthal, Ricky N. et al. 2008. "Alcohol Availability and Neighborhood Characteristics in Los Angeles, California and Southern Louisiana." *Journal of Urban Health* 85(2): 191–205.

Boehlje, Michael and Otto Doering. 2000. "Farm Policy in an Industrialized Agriculture." *Journal of Agribusiness* 18(1): 53–60.

Boehmer, Tegan K., Stephanie L. Foster, Jeffrey R. Henry, and Efomo L. Woghiren-Akinnifesi. 2013. "Residential Proximity to Major Highways: United States, 2010." *Morbidity and Mortality Weekly Report* 62(3): 46–50.

Bohme, Susanna Rankin, John Zorabedian, and David S. Egilman. 2005. "Maximizing Profit and Endangering Health: Corporate Strategies to Avoid Litigation and Regulation." *International Journal of Occupational and Environmental Health* 11(4): 338–48.

Bolin, Bob, Sara Grineski, and Timothy Collins. 2005. "The Geography of Despair: Environmental Racism and the Making of South Pheonix, Arizona, USA." *Human Ecology Review* 12(2): 156–68. http://www. humanecologyreview.org/pastissues/her122/bolingrineskicollins.pdf.

Bongers, Paulien M., Anja M. Kremer, and Jolanda ter Laak. 2002. "Are Psychosocial Factors, Risk Factors for Symptoms and Signs of the Shoulder, Elbow, or Hand/wrist? A Review of the Epidemiological Literature." *American Journal of Industrial Medicine* 41(5): 315–42.

Boothe, Vickie L. and Derek G. Shendell. 2008. "Potential Health Effects Associated with Residential Proximity to Freeways and Primary Roads: Review of Scientific Literature, 1999–2006." *Journal of Environmental Health* 70(8): 33–41, 55–6.

Borkowski, Liz and Celeste Monforton. 2014. *The Year in US Occupational Health and Safety: Fall 2013–Summer 2014.* Public Welfare Foundation. http://defendingscience.org/sites/default/files/Year_in_US_Occupational_ Health_Safety_2014.pdf.

Bose-O'Reilly, Stephan, Kathleen M. McCarty, Nadine Steckling, and Beate Lettmeier. 2010. "Mercury Exposure and Children's Health." *Current Problems in Pediatric and Adolescent Health Care* 40(8): 186–215.

Bosworth, Barry, Gary Burtless, and Kan Zhang. 2014. *Later Retirement, Inequality in Old Age, and the Growing Gap in Longevity between Rich and Poor.* The Brookings Institute. https://www.brookings.edu/wp-content/ uploads/2016/02/BosworthBurtlessZhang_retirementinequalitylongev- ity_012815.pdf.

Bradsher, Keith. 2002. *High and Mighty: SUVs: The World's Most Dangerous Vehicles and How They Got That Way.* New York: PublicAffairs.

Braveman, Paula A., Susan A. Egerter, and Robin E. Mockenhaupt. 2011. "Broadening the Focus: The Need to Address the Social Determinants of Health." *American Journal of Preventive Medicine* 40(1) (Suppl. 1): S4–18.

Braveman, Paula A., Susan Egerter, and David R. Williams. 2011. "The Social Determinants of Health: Coming of Age." *Annual Review of Public Health* 32(1): 381–98.

Breast Cancer Fund. 2013. *Disrupted Development: The Dangers of Prenatal BPA Exposure.* San Francisco, CA: Breast Cancer Fund.

Brody, Jane E. 2016. "What's New in the Dietary Guidelines." *New York Times*, January 18.

Brown, Jeffrey R., Eric A. Morris, and Brian D. Taylor. 2009a. "Paved with Good Intentions: Fiscal Politics, Freeways and the 20th Century American City." *ACCESS Magazine* 1(35). http://www.accessmagazine. org/wp-content/uploads/sites/7/2016/01/access35_Paved_with_Good_ Intentions_Fiscal_Politics_.pdf.

Brown, Jeffrey R., Eric A. Morris, and Brian D. Taylor. 2009b. "Planning for Cars in Cities: Planners, Engineers, and Freeways in the 20th Century." *Journal of the American Planning Association* 75(2): 161–77.

Brown, Phil. 2002. "Preface." *The Annals of the American Academy of Political and Social Science* 584(11): 7–12.

Brown, Phil. 2007. *Toxic Exposures: Contested Illnesses and the Environmental Health Movement*. New York: Columbia University Press.

Brown, Phil. 2008. "Environmental Health as a Core Public Component." In *The Contested Boundaries of American Public Health*, edited by James Colgrove, Gerald Markowitz, and David Rosner, 85–109. New Brunswick, NJ: Rutgers University Press.

Brown, Phil et al. 2003. "The Health Politics of Asthma: Environmental Justice and Collective Illness Experience in the United States." *Social Science & Medicine* 57(3): 453–64.

Brown, Phil and Edwin J. Mikkelsen. 1997. *No Safe Place: Toxic Waste, Leukemia, and Community Action*. Berkeley: University of California Press.

Brown, Thomas C. and Pamela Froemke. 2012. "Nationwide Assessment of Nonpoint Source Threats to Water Quality." *BioScience* 62(2): 136–46.

Brownell, Kelly D. 2012. "Thinking Forward: The Quicksand of Appeasing the Food Industry." *PLoS Medicine* 9(7): e1001254.

Brownell, Kelly D. and Thomas R. Frieden. 2009. "Ounces of Prevention: The Public Policy Case for Taxes on Sugared Beverages." *New England Journal of Medicine* 360(18): 1805–8.

Brownell, Kelly D. and Katherine Battle Horgen. 2004. *Food Fight: The Inside Story of the Food Industry, America's Obesity Crisis, and What We Can Do About It*. Chicago: McGraw-Hill Education.

Brownell, Kelly D. and Kenneth E. Warner. 2009. "The Perils of Ignoring History: Big Tobacco Played Dirty and Millions Died. How Similar Is Big Food?" *Milbank Quarterly* 87(1): 259–94.

Buckley, Cara and Dan Frosch. 2007. "Mine Safety Leader Loses Some Respect for Actions in Utah." *New York Times*, August 24.

Bullard, Robert D. 1990. *Dumping in Dixie: Race, Class, and Environmental Quality*. Boulder, CO: Westview Press.

Bullard, Robert D. 2005. "All Transit Is Not Created Equal." *Race, Poverty & the Environment* 12(1): 9–12.

Bullard, Robert D. and Glenn S. Johnson. 2000. "Environmental Justice: Grassroots Activism and Its Impact on Public Policy Decision Making." *Journal of Social Issues* 56(3): 555–78.

Bullard, Robert D., Paul Mohai, Robin Saha, and Beverly Wright. 2008. "Toxic Wastes and Race at Twenty: Why Race Still Matters after All of These Years." *Environmental Law* 38: 371–411.

Burkholder, JoAnn et al. 2007. "Impacts of Waste from Concentrated Animal Feeding Operations on Water Quality." *Environmental Health Perspectives* 115(2): 308–12.

Burt, Martha R. 2006. *Characteristics of Transitional Housing for Homeless Families: Final Report*. Washington, DC: Urban Institute.

Burton, Lloyd and Paul Stretesky. 2014. "Wrong Side of the Tracks: The Neglected Human Costs of Transporting Oil and Gas." *Health and Human Rights Journal* 16(1): 82–92.

Calavita, Kitty. 1983. "The Demise of the Occupational Safety and Health Administration: A Case Study in Symbolic Action." *Social Problems* 30(4): 437–48.

Cannon, Ben and Lew Frederick. 2011. "Columbia River Crossing: Pollution or Salvation in North and Northeast Portland?" *OregonLive.com*, June 5.

Carson, Rachel. 1962. *Silent Spring*. Boston, MA: Houghton Mifflin.

Casey, Joan A. et al. 2015. "Unconventional Natural Gas Development and Birth Outcomes in Pennsylvania, USA." *Epidemiology* 27(2): 163–72.

CDC (Centers for Disease Control and Prevention). 1999. "Achievements in Public Health, 1900–1999 Motor-Vehicle Safety: A 20th Century Public Health Achievement." *Morbidity and Mortality Weekly Report* 48(18): 369–74.

CDC (Centers for Disease Control and Prevention). 2011. "Social Determinants of Health: Frequently Asked Questions." http://www.cdc.gov/nchhstp/socialdeterminants/faq.html.

CDC (Centers for Disease Control and Prevention). 2012. "NIOSH Backgrounder: Alice's Mad Hatter and Work-Related Illness." http://www.cdc.gov/niosh/updates/upd-03-04-10.html.

CDC (Centers for Disease Control and Prevention). 2013. "Motor Vehicle Injuries." http://www.cdc.gov/winnablebattles/motorvehicleinjury.

CDC (Centers for Disease Control and Prevention). 2015a. "Global WASH Fast Facts." http://www.cdc.gov/healthywater/global/wash_statistics.html.

CDC (Centers for Disease Control and Prevention). 2015b. "Therapeutic Drug Use." http://www.cdc.gov/nchs/fastats/drug-use-therapeutic.htm.

Center for Food Safety. 2007. "Monsanto vs. US Farmers: November 2007 Update." http://www.centerforfoodsafety.org/reports/1411/monsanto-vs-us-farmers-november-2007-update.

Center for Food Safety. 2009. "New Report Reveals Dramatic Rise in Pesticide Use on Genetically Engineered (GE) Crops Due to the Spread of Resistant Weeds." http://www.centerforfoodsafety.org/video/2519/cfs-videos/press-releases/1184/new-report-reveals-dramatic-rise-in-pesticide-use-on-genetically-engineered-ge-crops-due-to-the-spread-of-resistant-weeds.

Center for Food Safety. 2013. *Best Public Relations That Money Can Buy: A Guide to Industry Front Groups*. Washington, DC: Center for Food Safety. http://www.centerforfoodsafety.org/files/front_groups_final_84531.pdf.

Center for Responsive Politics. n.d. "Oil and Gas: Money to Congress." Open Secrets. https://www.opensecrets.org/industries/summary.php?ind=E01&cycle=2016&recipdetail=M&sortorder=U.

Ceres. 2015. "Companies and Investors Come Out in Support of the EPA's

New Carbon Pollution Standards." Ceres. http://www.ceres.org/press/ press-releases/major-u.s.-companies-and-investors-support-carbon-pollu tion-standards-for-new-power-plants.

Chang, Jung. 1991. *Wild Swans: Three Daughters of China.* New York: Anchor Books.

Charles, Luenda E., Dana Loomis, and Zewditu Demissie. 2009. "Occupational Hazards Experienced by Cleaning Workers and Janitors: A Review of the Epidemiologic Literature." *Work* 34(1): 105–16.

Charney, William and Joseph Schirmer. 2007. "Nursing Injury Rates and Negative Patient outcomes: Connecting the Dots." *AAOHN* 55(11): 470–5.

Cheung, Paul T., Jennifer L. Wiler, Robert A. Lowe, and Adit A. Ginde. 2012. "National Study of Barriers to Timely Primary Care and Emergency Department Utilization among Medicaid Beneficiaries." *Annals of Emergency Medicine* 60(1): 4–10.

Children's Trust. 2016. *Federal Court Affirms Constitutional Rights of Kids and Denies Motions of Government and Fossil Fuel Industry in Youth's Landmark Climate Change Case.* Our Children's Trust. http://www.commondreams. org/newswire/2016/04/08/federal-court-affirms-constitutional-rights-kids-landmark-climate-case.

Cho, Charles H., Jennifer C. Chen, and Robin W. Roberts. 2008. "The Politics of Environmental Disclosure Regulation in the Chemical and Petroleum Industries: Evidence from the Emergency Planning and Community Right-to-Know Act of 1986." *Critical Perspectives on Accounting* 19(4): 450–65.

Cho, Charles H., Dennis M. Patten, and Robin W. Roberts. 2006. "Corporate Political Strategy: An Examination of the Relation between Political Expenditures, Environmental Performance, and Environmental Disclosure." *Journal of Business Ethics* 67(2): 139–54.

Chung, Mei et al. 2015. "Association of PNC, BC, and PM2.5 Measured at a Central Monitoring Site with Blood Pressure in a Predominantly Near Highway Population." *International Journal of Environmental Research and Public Health* 12(3): 2765–80.

Clapp, Jennifer. 2001. *Toxic Exports: The Transfer of Hazardous Wastes from Rich to Poor Countries.* Ithaca, NY: Cornell University Press.

Clapp, Jennifer. 2011. *Food.* Cambridge: Polity.

Clapp, Richard, Polly Hoppin, and David Kriebel. 2006. "Erosion of the Integrity of Public Health Science in the USA." *Occupational and Environmental Medicine* 63(6): 367–8.

Clougherty, Jane E., Kerry Souza, and Mark R. Cullen. 2010. "Work and Its Role in Shaping the Social Gradient in Health." *Annals of the New York Academy of Sciences* 1186(1): 102–24.

Cohen, Deborah A. et al. 2003. "Neighborhood Physical Conditions and Health." *American Journal of Public Health* 93(3): 467–71.

Cohen, Susan and Christine Cosgrove. 2009. *Normal at Any Cost: Tall Girls,*

Short Boys, and the Medical Industry's Quest to Manipulate Height. New York: Tarcher.

Cohn, Barbara A. et al. 2015. "DDT Exposure in Utero and Breast Cancer." *Journal of Clinical Endocrinology & Metabolism* 100(8): 2865–72.

Colborn, Theo, Dianne Dumanoski, and John Peter Meyers. 1996. *Our Stolen Future: Are We Threatening Our Fertility, Intelligence, and Survival? A Scientific Detective Story.* New York: Plume.

Cole, Luke W. and Caroline Farrell. 2006. "Structural Racism, Structural Pollution and the Need for a New Paradigm." *Washington University Journal of Law & Policy* 20(1): 265–82.

Collomb, Jean-Daniel. 2014. "The Ideology of Climate Change Denial in the United States." *European Journal of American Studies* 9(1): 1–17.

Cooper, Carnell, Dawn M. Eslinger, and Paul D. Stolley. 2006. "Hospital-Based Violence Intervention Programs Work." *The Journal of Trauma: Injury, Infection, and Critical Care* 61(3): 534–40.

Corlin, Laura. 2015. "Cardiovascular and Cognitive Health Effects Associated with Ultrafine Particulate Matter Exposure among Adults in the Boston Puerto Rican Health Study." Tufts University, Massachusetts. http://pqdtopen.proquest.com/pubnum/1589411.html?FMT=AI.

Costello, Anthony et al. (2009). "Managing the Health Effects of Climate Change." *Lancet* 373(9676): 1693–733.

Cranor, Carl F. 2008. *Toxic Torts: Science, Law and the Possibility of Justice.* Cambridge: Cambridge University Press.

Crow, Ben and Farhana Sultana. 2002. "Gender, Class, and Access to Water:Three Cases in a Poor and Crowded Delta." *Society and Natural Resources* 15: 709–24.

Cullingford, Benita. 2003. *Chimneys and Chimney Sweeps.* Princes Risborough, Buckinghamshire: Shire Publications.

Cummings, Briana. 2012. "Benefit Corporations: How to Enforce a Mandate to Promote the Public Interest." *Columbia Law Review* 112(3): 578–627.

Cummings, Steven R., Xu Ling, and Katie Stone. 1997. "Consequences of Foot Binding among Older Women in Beijing, China." *American Journal of Public Health* 87(10): 1677–9.

Cunningham, Peter J. 2002. *Mounting Pressures: Physicians Serving Medicaid Patients and the Uninsured, 1997–2001.* Washington, DC: Center for Studying Health System Change.

Cutchin, Malcolm P., Kathryn Remmes Martin, Steven V. Owen, and James S. Goodwin. 2008. "Concern about Petrochemical Health Risk before and after a Refinery Explosion." *Risk Analysis: An Official Publication of the Society for Risk Analysis* 28(3): 589–601.

Cutts, Bethany B., Kate J. Darby, Christopher G. Boone, and Alexandra Brewis. 2009. "City Structure, Obesity, and Environmental Justice: An Integrated Analysis of Physical and Social Barriers to Walkable Streets and Park Access." *Social Science & Medicine* 69(9): 1314–22.

Dankelman, Irene et al. 2008. *Gender, Climate Change and Human Security:*

Lessons from Bangladesh, Ghana, and Senegal. Women's Environmental Development Organization. http://www.wedo.org/wp-content/uploads/hsn-study-final-may-20–2008.pdf.

Darvill, Thomas, Edward Lonky, Jacqueline Reihman, Paul Stewart, and Jim Pagano. 2000. "Prenatal Exposure to PCBs and Infant Performance on the Fagan Test of Infant Intelligence." *Neurotoxicology* 21(6): 1029–38.

Davis, Devra Lee. 2002. *When Smoke Ran Like Water: Tales of Environmental Deception and the Battle Against Pollution.* New York: Basic Books.

Davis, Devra Lee. 2007. *The Secret History of the War on Cancer.* Philadelphia: Basic Books.

Davis, Devra Lee et al. 2007. "Declines in Sex Ratio at Birth and Fetal Deaths in Japan, and in US Whites but Not African Americans." *Environmental Health Perspectives* 115(6): 941–6.

Davis, Devra Lee and Pamela S. Webster. 2002. "The Social Context of Science: Cancer and the Environment." *Annals of the American Academy of Political and Social Science* 584: 13–34.

Delva, Jorge, Patrick M. O'Malley, and Lloyd D. Johnston. 2007. "Availability of More-Healthy and Less-Healthy Food Choices in American Schools: A National Study of Grade, Racial/Ethnic, and Socioeconomic Differences." *American Journal of Preventive Medicine* 33(4): S226–39.

DeMatteo, Robert et al. 2012. "Chemical Exposures of Women Workers in the Plastics Industry with Particular Reference to Breast Cancer and Reproductive Hazards." *New Solutions* 22(4): 427–48.

Denison, Richard A. 2009. "Ten Essential Elements in TSCA Reform." Environmental Law Reporter. https://elr.info/news-analysis/39/10020/ten-essential-elements-tsca-reform.

Desmond, Matthew. 2016. *Evicted: Poverty and Profit in the American City.* New York: Crown.

Dickinson, Barry D. and Stephen Havas. 2007. "Reducing the Population Burden of Cardiovascular Disease by Reducing Sodium Intake: A Report of the Council on Science and Public Health." *Archives of Internal Medicine* 167(14): 1460–8.

Diez Roux, Ana V. and Christina Mair. 2010. "Neighborhoods and Health." *Annals of the New York Academy of Sciences* 1186(1): 125–45.

Dockery, Douglas W. and James H. Ware. 2015. "Cleaner Air, Bigger Lungs." *New England Journal of Medicine* 372(10): 970–2.

Donohoe, Martin. 2008. "Flowers, Diamonds, and Gold: The Destructive Public Health, Human Rights, and Environmental Consequences of Symbols of Love." *Human Rights Quarterly* 30(1): 164–82.

Donohoe, Martin and Claire Robinson. 2010. "Corporations and Public Health: Overview and Case Study of GE Healthcare: Most Admired Company or Foe of Public Health?" *Social Medicine* 5(4): 237–9.

Dorfman, Lori, Andrew Cheyne, Lissy C. Friedman, Asiya Wadud, and Mark Gottlieb. 2012. "Soda and Tobacco Industry Corporate Social

Responsibility Campaigns: How Do They Compare?" *Public Library of Science Medicine* 9(6): e1001241.

Douglas, Margaret J., Stephen J. Watkins, Dermot R. Gorman, and Martin Higgins. 2011. "Are Cars the New Tobacco?" *Journal of Public Health* 33(2): 160–9.

Doyle, Scott, Alexia Kelly-Schwartz, Marc Schlossberg, and Jean Stockard. 2006. "Active Community Environments and Health: The Relationship of Walkable and Safe Communities to Individual Health." *Journal of the American Planning Association* 72(1): 19–31.

Drajem, Mark. 2013. "Pennsylvania Residents Ask EPA to Reopen Fracking Probe." *Bloomberg Business*, August 13. http://www.bloomberg.com/news/articles/2013-08-13/pennsylvania-residents-ask-epa-to-reopen-fracking-probe.

Draper, Elaine. 2003. *The Company Doctor: Risk, Responsibility, and Corporate Professionalism*. New York: Russell Sage Foundation.

Draper, Elaine, Joseph Ladou, and Dan J. Tennenhouse. 2011. "Occupational Health Nursing and the Quest for Professional Authority." *New Solutions* 21(1): 57–88.

Duggan, Jennifer, et al. 2013. "Closing the Floodgates: How the Coal Industry Is Poisoning Our Water and How We Can Stop It." http://earthjustice.org/sites/default/files/ClosingTheFloodgates-Final.pdf.

Duhigg, Charles. 2009a. "Clean Water Laws Are Neglected, at a Cost in Suffering." http://www.nytimes.com/2009/09/13/us/13water.html.

Duhigg, Charles. 2009b. "Cleansing the Air at the Expense of Waterways." http://www.nytimes.com/2009/10/13/us/13water.html.

Duhigg, Charles. 2009c. "Debating How Much Weed Killer Is Safe in Your Water Glass." http://www.nytimes.com/2009/08/23/us/23water.html.

Duhigg, Charles. 2009d. "That Tap Water Is Legal but May Be Unhealthy." http://www.nytimes.com/2009/12/17/us/17water.html.

Eakin, Joan M., Danièle Champoux, and Ellen MacEachen. 2010. "Health and Safety in Small Workplaces: Refocusing Upstream." *Canadian Journal of Public Health* 101(S1): S29–33.

Ebner, Paul. 2007. "CAFOs and Public Health: Pathogens and Manure." *Purdue University Extension: Public Health*. https://www.extension.purdue.edu/extmedia/id/cafo/id-356.pdf.

Edelstein, Michael R. 1988. *Contaminated Communities: Coping with Residential Toxic Exposure* (2nd edn.). Boulder, CO: Westview Press.

Edin, Kathryn J. and H. Luke Shaefer. 2015. *$2.00 a Day: Living on almost Nothing in America*. Boston, MA: Houghton Mifflin Harcourt.

Egilman, David S. and Marion A. Billings. 2005. "Abuse of Epidemiology: Automobile Manufacturers Manufacture a Defense to Asbestos Liability." *International Journal of Occupational and Environmental Health* 11(4): 360–71.

Egilman, David S. and Susanna Rankin Bohme. 2005. "Over a Barrel: Corporate Corruption of Science and Its Effects on Workers and the

Environment." *International Journal of Occupational and Environmental Health* 11(4): 331–7.

Egilman, David, Wes Wallace, and Candace Hom. 1998. "Corporate Corruption of Medical Literature: Asbestos Studies Concealed by W. R. Grace & Co." *Accountability in Research* 6(1–2): 127–47.

Ehrenreich, Barbara. 1992. "Stamping Out a Dread Scourge." *Time*, February 17.

Eicher-Miller, Heather A., Victor L. Fulgoni, and Debra R. Keast. 2012. "Contributions of Processed Foods to Dietary Intake in the US from 2003–2008: A Report of the Food and Nutrition Science Solutions Joint Task Force of the Academy of Nutrition and Dietetics, American Society for Nutrition, Institute of Food Technologists, and International Food Information Council." *Journal of Nutrition* 142(11): 2065S–72S.

Emmons, Karen M., Ichiro Kawachi, and Gillian Barclay. 1997. "Tobacco Control: A Brief Review of Its History and Prospects for the Future." *Hematology/Oncology Clinics of North America* 11(2): 177–95.

EPA (Environmental Protection Agency). 2010. *National Lakes Assessment Fact Sheet: Summary Results of the First National Lakes Assessment.* http://water.epa.gov/type/lakes/lakessurvey_index.cfm.

EPA (Environmental Protection Agency). 2012. *Love Canal: Niagara Falls, NY.* Washington, DC: Environmental Protection Agency.

EPA (Environmental Protection Agency). 2013a. "Basic Information about Arsenic in Drinking Water." http://water.epa.gov/drink/contaminants/basicinformation/arsenic.cfm.

EPA (Environmental Protection Agency). 2013b. "Basic Information about Beryllium in Drinking Water." http://water.epa.gov/drink/contaminants/basicinformation/beryllium.cfm.

EPA (Environmental Protection Agency). 2013c. "EPA Survey Finds More Than Half of the Nation's River and Stream Miles in Poor Condition." http://yosemite.epa.gov/opa/admpress.nsf/0/C967210C37CFFB6885257B3A004CFAF6.

EPA (Environmental Protection Agency). 2014a. "Mercury." https://www.epa.gov/mercury.

EPA (Environmental Protection Agency). 2014b. "Nonpoint Source Pollution: The Nation's Largest Water Quality Problem." http://water.epa.gov/polwaste/nps/outreach/point1.cfm.

EPA (Environmental Protection Agency). 2015a. "Animal Waste Terms." http://www3.epa.gov/region9/animalwaste/terms.html.

EPA (Environmental Protection Agency). 2015b. "Green Power Partnership." https://www3.epa.gov/greenpower/documents/partner100_jul2015.pdf.

EPA (Environmental Protection Agency). n.d. "Drinking Water Contaminants." http://water.epa.gov/drink/contaminants/index.cfm.

Epstein, Paul R. et al. 2011. "Full Cost Accounting for the Life Cycle of Coal." *Annals of the New York Academy of Sciences* 1219: 73–91.

Epstein, Samuel. 1985. "Environmental Issues in Medicine: A Dissenting View." In *Dissent in Medicine: Nine Doctors Speak Out*, edited by Robert Mendelsohn, 35–53. Chicago, IL: Contemporary Books.

Esch, Laura and Michael Hendryx. 2011. "Chronic Cardiovascular Disease Mortality in Mountaintop Mining Areas of Central Appalachian States." *Journal of Rural Health* 27(4): 350–7.

Eslami, Mohammad H., Maksim Zayaruzny, and Gordon A. Fitzgerald. 2007. "The Adverse Effects of Race, Insurance Status, and Low Income on the Rate of Amputation in Patients Presenting with Lower Extremity Ischemia." *Journal of Vascular Surgery* 45(1): 55–9.

Estache, Antonio and Lourdes Trujillo. 2003. *Efficiency Effects of "Privatization" in Argentina's Water and Sanitation Services*. Rochester, NY: Social Science Research Network. http://papers.ssrn.com/abstract=412942.

Etherton, Laura, Mike Russo, and Nasima Hossain. 2012. "Apples to Twinkies 2012: Comparing Taxpayer Subsidies for Fresh Produce and Junk Food." US PIRG Education Fund. http://www.uspirg.org/sites/pirg/files/reports/Apples%20to%20Twinkies%20vUS_2.pdf.

Evans, Gary W. and Susan Saegert. 2012. "Residential Crowding in the Context of Inner City Poverty." In *Theoretical Perspectives in Environment-Behavior Research: Underlying Assumptions, Research Problems, and Methodologies*, edited by Seymour Wapner, Jack Demick, C. Takiji Yamamoto, and Hirofumi Minami, 247–68. New York: Springer Science & Business Media.

Evans, Gary W. and Elyse Kantrowitz. 2002. "Socioeconomic Status and Health: The Potential Role of Environmental Risk Exposure." *Annual Review of Public Health* 23: 303–31.

Evens, Anne et al. 2015. "The Impact of Low-Level Lead Toxicity on School Performance among Children in the Chicago Public Schools: A Population-Based Retrospective Cohort Study." *Environmental Health* 14(21). doi: 10.1186/s12940-015-0008-9.

Ewing, Reid and Richard Kreutzer. 2006. *Understanding the Relationship Between Public Health and the Built Environment: A Report Prepared for the LEED-ND Core Committee*. US Green Building Council. http://www.usgbc.org/sites/default/files/public-health-built-environment.pdf.

Fackler, Eliot Henry. 2009. "Protesting Portland's Freeways: Highway Engineering and Citizen Activism in the Interstate Era." University of Oregon. http://hdl.handle.net/1794/9842.

Fagan, Kevin and Thaai Walker. 1997. "Factory That Leaked Acid Was 'Good Job' for Some: It Provided Work for Many Immigrants." *San Francisco Chronicle*, October 2. http://www.sfgate.com/bayarea/article/PAGE-ONE-Factory-That-Leaked-Acid-Was-Good-2804199.php.

Fagin, Dan. 2013. *Toms River: A Story of Science and Salvation*. New York: Random House.

Farmer, Paul E., Bruce Nizeye, Sara Stulac, and Salmaan Keshavjee. 2006.

"Structural Violence and Clinical Medicine." *PLOS Medicine* 3(10): 1686–91.

Fawell, John and Mark J. Nieuwenhuijsen. 2003. "Contaminants in Drinking Water Environmental Pollution and Health." *British Medical Bulletin* 68(1): 199–208.

Fears, Darryl. 2016. "This Baltimore 20-Year-Old Just Won a Huge International Award for Taking Out a Giant Trash Incinerator." *Washington Post*, April 18.

Federal Healthy Homes Work Group. 2013. *Advancing Healthy Housing: A Strategy for Action*. Housing and Urban Development. http://portal.hud.gov/hudportal/documents/huddoc?id=ExecSummary013113.pdf.

Fields, Ally. 2015. *Polluting Politics: Political Spending by Companies Dumping Toxics into Our Waters*. Environment America. http://www.environment america.org/sites/environment/files/reports/Polluting%20Politics%20AME %202.pdf.

Finnegan, William. 2002. "Leasing the Rain." *The New Yorker*, April 8. http://www.newyorker.com/magazine/2002/04/08/leasing-the-rain.

Fiscella, Kevin and David R. Williams. 2004. "Health Disparities Based on Socioeconomic Inequities: Implications for Urban Health Care." *Academic Medicine* 79(12): 1139–47.

Fitzgerald, Edward F. et al. 2007. "Environmental Exposures to Polychlorinated Biphenyls (PCBs) among Older Residents of Upper Hudson River Communities." *Environmental Research* 104(3): 352–60.

Flock, Elizabeth. 2012. "Monsanto Petition Tells Obama: 'Cease FDA Ties to Monsanto.'" *Washington Post*, January 30. https://www.washing tonpost.com/blogs/blogpost/post/monsanto-petition-tells-obama-cease-fda -ties-to-monsanto/2012/01/30/gIQAA9dZcQ_blog.html?utm_term=.eeb 94e9f9b01.

Flocks, Joan. 2012. "The Environmental and Social Injustice of Farmworker Pesticide Exposure." *Georgetown Journal on Poverty Law and Policy* 19(2): 255–82.

Flynn, Dan. 2013. "2013 Legislative Season Ends with 'Ag-Gag' Bills Defeated in 11 States." *Food Safety News*. http://www.foodsafetynews. com/2013/07/2013-legislative-season-ends-with-ag-gag-bills-defeated-in-11-states.

Food and Water Watch. 2012. "Why Walmart Can't Fix the Food System." *Food & Water Watch*. http://www.foodandwaterwatch.org/news/why-walmart-can%E2%80%99t-fix-food-system.

Food and Water Watch. 2013. "Monsanto: A Corporate Profile." *Food & Water Watch*. http://www.foodandwaterwatch.org/insight/monsanto-corporate-profile.

Forkenbrock, David J. 2001. "Comparison of External Costs of Rail and Truck Freight Transportation." *Transportation Research Part A* 35(4): 321–37.

Fox, Steve. 1991. *Toxic Work: Women Workers at GTE Lenkurt*. Philadelphia, PA: Temple University Press.

Frank, Lawrence D. and Peter O. Engelke. 2001. "How Land Use and Transportation Systems Impact Public Health: A Literature Review of the Relationship between Physical Activity and Built Form." Active Community Environments Initiative Working Paper 1. https://www.cdc.gov/nccdphp/dnpa/pdf/aces-workingpaper1.pdf.

Freedhoff, Yoni and Paul C. Hébert. 2011. "Partnerships between Health Organizations and the Food Industry Risk Derailing Public Health Nutrition." *Canadian Medical Association Journal* 183(3): 291–2.

Freilla, Omar. 2004. "Burying Robert Moses's Legacy in New York City." In *Highway Robbery: Transportation Racism and New Routes to Equity*, edited by Robert D. Bullard, Glenn S. Johnson, and Angel O. Torres, 75–98. Boston, MA: South End Press.

Freudenberg, Nicholas. 2012. "The Manufacture of Lifestyle: The Role of Corporations in Unhealthy Living." *Journal of Public Health Policy* 33(2): 244–56.

Freudenberg, Nicholas. 2014. *Lethal but Legal: Corporations, Consumption, and Protecting Public Health*. Oxford: Oxford University Press.

Freund, Peter and George Martin. 2007. "Moving Bodies: Injury, Dis-Ease, and the Social Organisation of Space." In *Critical Perspectives in Public Health*, edited by Judith Green and Ronald Labonté, 228–35. New York: Routledge.

Freund, Peter and Meredith McGuire. 1999. *Health, Illness, and the Social Body: A Critical Sociology*. Upper Saddle River, NJ: Prentice Hall.

Freyman, Monika and Ryan Salmon. 2013. *Hydraulic Fracturing and Water Stress: Growing Competitive Pressures for Water*. Ceres. https://www.ceres.org/resources/reports/hydraulic-fracturing-water-stress-growing-competitive-pressures-for-water/view.

Friedman, Lissy C., Andrew Cheyne, Daniel Givelber, Mark A. Gottlieb, and Richard A. Daynard. 2015. "Tobacco Industry Use of Personal Responsibility Rhetoric in Public Relations and Litigation: Disguising Freedom to Blame as Freedom of Choice." *American Journal of Public Health* 105(2): 250–60.

Friedman-Jimenez, George. 1989. "Occupational Disease among Minority Workers: A Common and Preventable Public Health Problem." *AAOHN* 37(2): 64–70.

Frontline. 2003. "Interview: Marion Nestle." http://www.pbs.org/wgbh/pages/frontline/shows/diet/interviews/nestle.html.

Frosch, Dan. 2014. "Amid Toxic Waste, a Navajo Village Could Lose Its Land." *New York Times*, February 20.

Fry, Carolyn. 2008. "Tread Lightly: Give Up Bottled Water." *The Guardian*, March 20. http://www.theguardian.com/environment/2008/mar/21/water.pledges.

Fung, Archon and Dara O'Rourke. 2000. "Reinventing Environmental

Regulation from the Grassroots Up: Explaining and Expanding the Success of the Toxics Release Inventory." *Environmental Management* 25(2): 115–27.

Geiger, H. Jack. 2006. "Medical Care." In *Social Injustice and Public Health*, edited by Barry S. Levy and Victor W. Sidel, 207–19. Oxford: Oxford University Press.

Gennaro, Valerio and Lorenzo Tomatis. 2005. "Business Bias: How Epidemiologic Studies May Underestimate or Fail to Detect Increased Risks of Cancer and Other Diseases." *International Journal of Occupational and Environmental Health* 11(4): 356–9.

Gentner, Drew R. et al. 2012. "Elucidating Secondary Organic Aerosol from Diesel and Gasoline Vehicles through Detailed Characterization of Organic Carbon Emissions." *Proceedings of the National Academy of Sciences* 109(45): 18318–23.

Gereffi, Gary, Joonkoo Lee, and Michelle Christian. 2009. "US-Based Food and Agricultural Value Chains and Their Relevance to Healthy Diets." *Journal of Hunger & Environmental Nutrition* 4(3–4): 357–74.

Germov, John and Lauren Williams, eds. 2009. *A Sociology of Food and Nutrition: The Social Appetite* (3rd edn.). South Melbourne: Oxford University Press.

Geronimus, Arline T. 2000. "To Mitigate, Resist, or Undo: Addressing Structural Influences on the Health of Urban Populations." *American Journal of Public Health* 90(6): 867–72.

Gibbs, Lois. 2002. "Citizen Activism for Environmental Health: The Growth of a Powerful New Grassroots Health Movement." *Annals of the American Academy of Political and Social Science* 584(1): 97–109.

Gleick, Peter H. 2011. *Bottled and Sold: The Story Behind Our Obsession with Bottled Water*. Washington, DC: Island Press.

Gleick, Peter H. 2015. "Keynote Address." Paper presented at the UNESCO Chair and Institute of Comparative Human Rights 16th Annual International Conference, October 20, University of Connecticut.

Gleick, Peter H., Gary Wolff, and Rachel Reyes Chalecki. 2002. *The New Economy of Water: The Risks and Benefits of Globalization and Privatization of Fresh Water*. Oakland, CA: Pacific Institute for Studies in Development, Environment and Security.

Glicksman, Robert and Matthew R. Batzel. 2010. "Science, Politics, Law, and the Arc of the Clean Water Act: The Role of Assumptions in the Adoption of a Pollution Control Landmark." *Washington University Journal of Law & Policy* 32(1): 99–138.

Gochfeld, Michael. 2005. "Occupational Medicine Practice in the United States since the Industrial Revolution." *Journal of Occupational and Environmental Medicine* 47(2): 115–31.

Goldenberg, Suzanne. 2015. "Exxon Knew of Climate Change in 1981, Email Says: But It Funded Deniers for 27 More Years." *The Guardian*, July 8.

Grandjean, Philippe and Philip J. Landrigan. 2014. "Neurobehavioural Effects of Developmental Toxicity." *Lancet Neurology* 13(3): 330–8.

Granville, Kevin. 2009. "Bringing Fresh Produce to the Corner Store." *New York Times*, October 30.

Greenberg, Jerald. 2010. "Organizational Injustice as an Occupational Health Risk." *The Academy of Management Annals* 4(1): 205–43.

Greger, Michael and Gowri Koneswaran. 2010. "The Public Health Impacts of Concentrated Animal Feeding Operations on Local Communities." *Family & Community Health* 33(1): 11–20.

Gregson, Sarah. 2008. "'Titanic' 'Down Under': Ideology, Myth and Memorialization." *Social History* 33(3): 268–83.

Grossman, Elizabeth. 2011. "Toxics in the 'Clean Rooms': Are Samsung Workers at Risk?" *Yale Environment 360*, June 9.

Grumbach, Kevin and Thomas Bodenheimer. 2002. "A Primary Care Home for Americans: Putting the House in Order." *Journal of the American Medical Association* 288(7): 889–93.

Grunwald, Michael. 2002. "Monsanto Hid Decades of Pollution." *Common Dreams*. http://www.commondreams.org/headlines02/0101–02.htm.

Gudsnuk, Kathryn and Frances A. Champagne. 2012. "Epigenetic Influence of Stress and the Social Environment." *Ilar Journal* 53(3–4): 279–88.

Haiken, Elizabeth. 1997. *Venus Envy: A History of Cosmetic Surgery by Professor Elizabeth Haiken*. Baltimore, MD: Johns Hopkins University Press.

Hakim, Danny. 2015. "Big Tobacco's Staunch Friend in Washington: US Chamber of Commerce." *New York Times*, October 9. https://www.nytimes.com/2015/10/10/business/us-chamber-of-commerces-focus-on-advocacy-a-boon-to-tobacco.html?_r=0.

Hall, Noah D. 2009. "Protecting Freshwater Resources in the Era of Global Water Markets: Lessons Learned from Bottled Water." *University of Denver Water Law Review* 13(1): 1–53.

Hall, Shannon. 2015. "Exxon Knew about Climate Change almost 40 Years ago." *Scientific American*. http://www.scientificamerican.com/article/exxon-knew-about-climate-change-almost-40-years-ago.

Halonen, Jaana I. et al. 2015. "Road Traffic Noise Is Associated with Increased Cardiovascular Morbidity and Mortality and All-Cause Mortality in London." *European Heart Journal* 36(39): 2653–62. doi: 10.1093/eurheartj/ehv216.

Hansen, Steffen and Joel A. Tickner. 2013. "The Precautionary Principle and False Alarms." In *Late Lessons from Early Warnings: Science, Precaution, Innovation: European Environment Agency* (EEA Report), edited by European Environment Agency, 17–45. Luxembourg: Publication Offices of the European Union.

Hardell, Lennart, Martin J. Walker, Bo Walhjalt, Lee S. Friedman, and Elihu D. Richter. 2007. "Secret Ties to Industry and Conflicting Interests in Cancer Research." *American Journal of Industrial Medicine* 50(3): 227–33.

Harrington, Michael. 1962. *The Other America: Poverty in the United States*. Baltimore, MD: Penguin Books.

Hayden, Dolores. 2012. "'I Have Seen the Future': Selling the Unsustainable City." *Journal of Urban History* 38(1): 3–15.

Hayes, Tyrone B. 2011. "Atrazine Has Been Used Safely for 50 Years?" In *Wildlife Ecotoxicology*, *Emerging Topics in Ecotoxicology*, edited by J. E. Elliott, C. A. Bishop, and C. A. Morrissey, 301–24. New York: Springer.

Heffernan, Andrea, Theresa Galluzo, and Will Hoyer. 2010. *Solution to Pollution: It Starts on the Farm*. Iowa Policy Project. http://www.iowapoli cyproject.org/2010docs/100927-nutrients.pdf.

Hemenway, David. 2001. "The Public Health Approach to Motor Vehicles, Tobacco, and Alcohol, with Applications to Firearms Policy." *Journal of Public Health Policy* 22(4): 381–402.

Hendryx, Michael and Keith J. Zullig. 2009. "Higher Coronary Heart Disease and Heart Attack Morbidity in Appalachian Coal Mining Regions." *Preventive Medicine* 49(5): 355–9.

Henry, Antonia J., Nathanael D. Hevelone, Michael Belkin, and Louis L. Nguyen. 2011. "Socioeconomic and Hospital-Related Predictors of Amputation for Critical Limb Ischemia." *Journal of Vascular Surgery* 53(2): 330–9.

Hernández, Antonio F. et al. 2013. "Toxic Effects of Pesticide Mixtures at a Molecular Level: Their Relevance to Human Health." *Toxicology* 307: 136–45.

Hilts, Phillip J. 1991. "US Fines 500 Mine Companies for False Air Tests." *New York Times*, April 5.

Hoffman, Catherine and Julia Paradise. 2008. "Health Insurance and Access to Health Care in the United States." *Annals of the New York Academy of Sciences* 1136(1): 149–60.

Hofrichter, Richard, ed. 2003a. *Health and Social Justice: Politics, Ideology, and Inequity in the Distribution of Disease*. San Francisco, CA: Jossey-Bass.

Hofrichter, Richard. 2003b. "The Politics of Health Inequalities: Contested Terrain." In *Health and Social Justice: Politics, Ideology, and Inequity in the Distribution of Disease*, edited by Richard Hofrichter, 1–56. San Francisco, CA: Jossey-Bass.

Holdrege, Craig and Steve Talbott. 2001. "Brave New Nature: Sowing Technology." *Sierra Magazine*, July/August.

Holford, Theodore R. et al. 2014. "Tobacco Control and the Reduction in Smoking-Related Premature Deaths in the United States, 1964–2012." *Journal of the American Medical Association* 311(2): 164–71.

Hollaender, Kim and Tom Storrer. 2014. "The Progression from Tetra-Ethyl Lead to MTBE to Ethanol: Hidden Dangers and Unforeseen Risk." *Environmental Claims Journal* 26(4): 333–47.

Holzman, David C. 2011. "Mountaintop Removal Mining: Digging into Community Health Concerns." *Environmental Health Perspectives* 119(11): a476–83.

Hooks, Gregory and Chad L. Smith. 2004. "The Treadmill of Destruction: National Sacrifice Areas and Native Americans." *American Sociological Review* 69(4): 558–75.

Hopkins, Jamie Smith. 2016. "Forty-Two Years Later, OSHA OKs Rule Protecting Workers from Silica." *Center for Public Integrity*. https://www.publicintegrity.org/2016/03/24/19486/forty-two-years-later-osha-oks-rule-protecting-workers-silica.

Horrigan, Leo, Robert S. Lawrence, and Polly Walker. 2002. "How Sustainable Agriculture Can Address the Environmental and Human Health Harms of Industrial Agriculture." *Environmental Health Perspectives* 110(5): 445–56.

Howarth, Robert W., Anthony Ingraffea, and Terry Engelder. 2011. "Natural Gas: Should Fracking Stop?" *Nature* 477(7364): 271–5.

Hribar, Carrie and Mark Schultz. 2010. *Understanding Concentrated Animal Feeding Operations and Their Impact on Communities*. Bowling Green, OH: National Association of Local Boards of Health.

Huff, James. 2011. "Primary Prevention of Cancer." *Science* 332(6032): 916–17.

Human Rights Watch. 2002. "Human Rights in the United States: Labor Rights." *International Journal of Health Services* 32(4): 755–80.

Imbus, Harold R. 2004. "Fifty Years of Hope and Concern for the Future of Occupational Medicine." *Journal of Occupational and Environmental Medicine* 46(2): 96–103.

International Bottled Water Association. 2014. "Bottled Water Sales and Consumption Projected to Increase in 2014, Expected to Be the Number One Packaged Drink by 2016." http://www.bottledwater.org/bottled-water-sales-and-consumption-projected-increase-2014-expected-be-number-one-packaged-drink.

Israel, Brett. 2012. "Dirty Soil and Diabetes: Anniston's Toxic Legacy." *Environmental Health News*. http://www.environmentalhealthnews.org/ehs/news/2012/pollution-poverty-people-of-color-day-6-diabetes.

Jacobs, David E. et al. 2002. "The Prevalence of Lead-Based Paint Hazards in US Housing." *Environmental Health Perspectives* 110(10): A599–606.

Jaffee, Daniel and Soren Newman. 2013. "A Bottle Half Empty: Bottled Water, Commodification, and Contestation." *Organization & Environment* 26(3): 318–35.

Jayaraman, Saru, Jonathan Dropkin, Sekou Siby, Laine Romero Alston, and Steven Markowitz. 2011. "Dangerous Dining: Health and Safety in the New York City Restaurant Industry." *Journal of Occupational and Environmental Medicine* 53(12): 1418–24.

Jehl, Douglas. 2003. "As Cities Move to Privatize Water, Atlanta Steps Back." *New York Times*, February 10. http://www.nytimes.com/2003/02/10/us/as-cities-move-to-privatize-water-atlanta-steps-back.html.

Jepson, Wendy. 2014. "Measuring 'No-Win' Waterscapes: Experience-Based Scales and Classification Approaches to Assess Household

Water Security in Colonias on the US–Mexico Border." *Geoforum* 51: 107–20.

Johnson, Kirk. 2015. "Cleaning Up a Legacy of Pollution on an Alaskan Island." *New York Times*, August 3. https://www.nytimes.com/2015/08/04/us/native-alaskans-study-and-clean-up-a-legacy-of-pollution.html.

Kaplan, Deborah L. and Kristina M. Graff. 2008. "Marketing Breastfeeding: Reversing Corporate Influence on Infant Feeding Practices." *Journal of Urban Health* 85(4): 486–504.

Kassotis, Christopher D. et al. 2015. "Endocrine-Disrupting Activity of Hydraulic Fracturing Chemicals and Adverse Health Outcomes After Prenatal Exposure in Male Mice." *Endocrinology* 156(12): 4458–73. doi: 10.1210/en.2015-1375.

Kasten, Robert. 2000. "Federal Government Pollution." *Congressional Record* 146(17): 25396–9.

Katz, Bruce K. and Margery Austin Turner. 2006. "Rethinking US Rental Housing Policy. (Report No. RR07-10)." *Harvard University Joint Center for Housing Studies*. http://www.jchs.harvard.edu/sites/jchs.harvard.edu/files/rr07-10_turner_katz.pdf.

Kay, Jane Holtz. 1997. *Asphalt Nation: How the Automobile Took Over America, and How We Can Take It Back*. New York: Crown Publishers.

Kearns, Cristin E., Stanton A. Glantz, and Laura A. Schmidt. 2015. "Sugar Industry Influence on the Scientific Agenda of the National Institute of Dental Research's 1971 National Caries Program: A Historical Analysis of Internal Documents." *PLoS Medicine* 12(3): e1001798.

Kessler, Sarah. 2015. "Is Big Coal Buying 'Likes?'" *Sierra* 100(2): 32.

Kickbusch, Ilona. 2015. "The Political Determinants of Health: 10 Years on." *British Medical Journal* 350: 1–2.

Kinney, Patrick L., Maneesha Aggarwal, Mary E. Northridge, Nicole A. H. Janssen, and Peggy Shepard. 2000. "Airborne Concentrations of PM(2.5) and Diesel Exhaust Particles on Harlem Sidewalks: A Community-Based Pilot Study." *Environmental Health Perspectives* 108(3): 213–18.

Kivimaki, Mika et al. 2004. "Organisational Justice and Change in Justice as Predictors of Employee Health: The Whitehall II Study." *Journal of Epidemiology and Community Health* 58(11): 931–7.

Klepper, David. 2016. "Asking for a Tax Hike: Letter Sent to NY Governor." *Hartford Courant*, March 22, A7.

Kneebone, Elizabeth, Carey Nadeau, and Alan Berube. 2011. *The Re-Emergence of Concentrated Poverty*. Brookings Institution. http://www.brookings.edu/~/media/Files/rc/papers/2011/1103_poverty_kneebone_nadeau_berube/1103_poverty_kneebone_nadeau_berube.pdf.

Kniesner, Thomas J. and John D. Leeth. 1995. "Abolishing OSHA." *Regulation* 18(4): 46–56.

Knotts, Jamie. 1999. "A Brief History of Drinking Water Regulations." *On Tap* 8(4): 1.

Koch, Charles G. 2016. "Charles Koch Feeling the Bern? Not Quite." *Hartford Courant*, February 22, A9.

Koplan, Jeffrey P. and Kelly D. Brownell. 2010. "Response of the Food and Beverage Industry to the Obesity Threat." *Journal of the American Medical Association* 304(13): 1487–8.

Korfmacher, Katrina Smith, Maria Ayoob, and Rebecca Morley. 2012. "Rochester's Lead Law: Evaluation of a Local Environmental Health Policy Innovation." *Environmental Health Perspectives* 120(2): 309–15.

Kotelchuck, David. 2000. "Worker Health and Safety at the Beginning of a New Century." In *Perspectives in Medical Sociology*, edited by Phil Brown, 182–92. Long Grove, IL: Waveland Press.

Krieger, James and Donna L. Higgins. 2002. "Housing and Health: Time again for Public Health Action." *American Journal of Public Health* 92(5): 758–68.

Krieger, James, Janice Rabkin, Denise Sharify, and Lin Song. 2009. "High Point Walking for Health: Creating Built and Social Environments That Support Walking in a Public Housing Community." *American Journal of Public Health* 99(S3): S593–9.

Krieger, Nancy. 2003. "Theories for Social Epidemiology in the Twenty-First Century: An Ecosocial Perspective." In *Health and Social Justice: Politics, Ideology, and Inequity in the Distribution of Disease*, edited by Richard Hofrichter, 428–52. San Francisco, CA: Jossey–Bass.

Krieger, Nancy. 2008a. "Ladders, Pyramids and Champagne: The Iconography of Health Inequities." *Journal of Epidemiology and Community Health* 62(12): 1098–104.

Krieger, Nancy. 2008b. "Proximal, Distal, and the Politics of Causation: What's Level Got to Do with It?" *American Journal of Public Health* 98(2): 221–30.

Krieger, Nancy. 2010. "Workers Are People Too: Societal Aspects of Occupational Health Disparities: An Ecosocial Perspective." *American Journal of Industrial Medicine* 53(2): 104–15.

Krieger, Nancy et al. 2006. "Social Hazards on the Job: Workplace Abuse, Sexual Harassment, and Racial Discrimination: A Study of Black, Latino, and White Low-Income Women and Men Workers in the United States." *International Journal of Health Services* 36(1): 51–85.

Krieger, Nancy and Anne-Emanuelle Birn. 1998. "A Vision of Social Justice as the Foundation of Public Health: Commemorating 150 Years of the Spirit of 1848." *American Journal of Public Health* 88(11): 1603–6.

Kubicek, Bettina, Christian Korunka, Matea Paskvan, Roman Prem, and Cornelia Gerdenitsch. 2014. "Changing Working Conditions at the Onset of the Twenty-First Century: Facts from International Datasets." In *The Impact of ICT on Quality of Working Life*, edited by Christian Korunka and Peter Hoonakker, 25–42. New York: Springer Science & Business.

Kumar, Supriya. 2013. "The Looming Threat of Water Scarcity." *Vital Signs*. http://vitalsigns.worldwatch.org/node/180.

Kuper, Hannah and Michael G. Marmot. 2003. "Job Strain, Job Demands, Decision Latitude, and Risk of Coronary Heart Disease within the Whitehall II Study." *Journal of Epidemiology and Community Health* 57(2): 147–53.

Kwate, Naa Oyo A., Ji Meng Loh, Kellee White, and Nelson Saldana. 2013. "Retail Redlining in New York City: Racialized Access to Day-to-Day Retail Resources." *Journal of Urban Health: Bulletin of the New York Academy of Medicine* 90(4): 632–52.

Kwitny, Jonathan. 1981. "The Great Transportation Conspiracy: A Juggernaut Named Desire." *Harper's Magazine*, n.d., 14–15, 18, 20, 21.

Ladd, Anthony E. and Bob Edwards. 2002. "Corporate Swine and Capitalist Pigs: A Decade of Environmental Injustice and Protest in North Carolina." *Social Justice* 29(3): 26–46.

LaDou, Joseph. 2002. "The Rise and Fall of Occupational Medicine in the United States." *American Journal of Preventive Medicine* 22(4): 285–95.

LaDou, Joseph. 2005. "Occupational Medicine: The Case for Reform." *American Journal of Preventive Medicine* 28(4): 396–402.

LaDou, Joseph et al. 2007. "American College of Occupational and Environmental Medicine (ACOEM): A Professional Association in Service to Industry." *International Journal of Occupational and Environmental Health* 13(4): 404–26.

LaDou, Joseph and Sandra Lovegrove. 2008. "Export of Electronics Equipment Waste." *International Journal of Occupational and Environmental Health* 14(1): 1–10.

Landsbergis, Paul A., Joseph G. Grzywacz, and Anthony D. LaMontagne. 2014. "Work Organization, Job Insecurity, and Occupational Health Disparities." *American Journal of Industrial Medicine* 57(5): 495–515.

LaPlante, John and Barbara McCann. 2008. "Complete Streets: We Can Get There from Here." *Institute of Technology Engineers Journal* 78(5): 24–8.

Lavelle, Marianne and Marcia Coyle. 1992. "Unequal Protection: The Racial Divide in Environmental Law." *National Law Review* 15(3): 567–88.

Lawrence, Geoffry and Janice Grice. 2009. "Agribusiness, Genetic Engineering and the Corporation of Food." In *A Sociology of Food and Nutrition: The Social Appetite*, edited by John Germov and Lauren Williams, 78–93. Melbourne: Oxford University Press.

Laws, M. Barton, Julia Whitman, Diana M. Bowser, and Laura Krech. 2002. "Tobacco Availability and Point of Sale Marketing in Demographically Contrasting Districts of Massachusetts." *Tobacco Control* 11(S2): ii71–3.

Lazos, Pam. 2015. "The Seed Guys: Saving the World, One Seed at a Time." *Green Life Blue Water*. https://greenlifebluewater.wordpress.com/2015/08/11/the-seed-guys-saving-the-world-one-seed-at-a-time.

Le Bodo, Yann, Marie-Claude Paquette, Maggie Vallières, and Natalie Alméras. 2015. "Is Sugar the New Tobacco? Insights from Laboratory

Studies, Consumer Surveys and Public Health." *Current Obesity Reports* 4(1): 111–21.

Leahy, Terry. 2009. "Unsustainable Food Production: Its Social Origins and Alternatives." In *A Sociology of Food and Nutrition: The Social Appetite*, edited by John Germov and Lauren Williams, 58–77. Melbourne: Oxford University Press.

Lee, Rebecca E. et al. 2014. "Obesogenic and Youth Oriented Restaurant Marketing in Public Housing Neighborhoods." *American Journal of Health Behavior* 38(2): 218–24.

Leventhal, Tama and Sandra Newman. 2010. "Housing and Child Development." *Children and Youth Services Review* 32(9): 1165–74.

Levine, Susan. 2008. *School Lunch Politics: The Surprising History of America's Favorite Welfare Program*. Princeton, NJ: Princeton University Press.

Levy, Barry S. and Jonathan Patz. 2015. *Climate Change and Public Health*. Oxford: Oxford University Press.

Levy, Barry S. and Victor W. Sidel. 2013. *Social Injustice and Public Health*. New York: Oxford University Press.

Levy, Barry S., David H. Wegman, Sherry L. Baron, and Rosemary K. Sokas. 2011. "Occupational and Environmental Health: Twenty-First Century Challenges and Opportunities." In *Occupational and Environmental Health: Recognizing and Preventing Disease and Injury*, edited by Barry S. Levy, David H. Wegman, Sherry L. Baron, and Rosemary K. Sokas, 3–22. New York: Oxford University Press.

Link, Bruce G. 2008. "Epidemiological Sociology and the Social Shaping of Population Health." *Journal of Health and Social Behavior* 49(4): 367–84.

Lombardi, Kristen, Talia Buford, and Ronnie Green. 2015. "Environmental Racism Persists, and the EPA Is One Reason Why." *Center for Public Integrity*. https://www.publicintegrity.org/2015/08/03/17668/environmental-racism-persists-and-epa-one-reason-why.

Ludwig, David S. 2011. "Technology, Diet, and the Burden of Chronic Disease." *Journal of the American Medical Association* 305(13): 1352–3.

Ludwig, Jens et al. 2011. "Neighborhoods, Obesity, and Diabetes: A Randomized Social Experiment." *New England Journal of Medicine* 365(16): 1509–19.

Ludwig, David S. and Marion Nestle. 2008. "Can the Food Industry Play a Constructive Role in the Obesity Epidemic?" *Journal of the American Medical Association* 300(15): 1808–11.

Luger, Stan. 2000. *Corporate Power, American Democracy, and the Automobile Industry*. New York: Cambridge University Press.

Lupien, Sonia J., Bruce S. McEwen, Megan R. Gunnar, and Christine Heim. 2009. "Effects of Stress throughout the Lifespan on the Brain, Behaviour and Cognition." *Nature Reviews Neuroscience* 10(6): 434–45.

Lynch, Michael J. and Paul Stretesky. 2001. "Toxic Crimes: Examining Corporate Victimization of the General Public Employing Medical and Epidemiological Evidence." *Critical Criminology* 10(3): 153–72.

Lyons, Brendan J. 2014. "Dredging up the Truth." *Times Union*. http://www.timesunion.com/local/article/Dredging-up-the-truth-5294643.php.

Maag, Christopher. 2009. "From the Ashes of '69, a River Reborn." June 21. http://www.nytimes.com/2009/06/21/us/21river.html.

Maas, Jolanda et al. 2009. "Morbidity Is Related to a Green Living Environment." *Journal of Epidemiology and Community Health* 63(12): 967–73.

Macartney, Suzanne, Alemayehu Bishaw, and Kayla Fontenot. 2013. *Poverty Rates for Selected Detailed Race and Hispanic Groups by State and Place: 2007–2011*. US Census Bureau. http://www.mrclotzman.com/handouts/acsbr11–17.pdf.

MacLennan, Carol A. 1988. "From Accident to Crash: The Auto Industry and the Politics of Injury." *Medical Anthropology Quarterly* 2(3): 233–50.

Maine Supreme Judicial Court. 2014. "Mallinckrodt US LLC v. Dep't of Envtl. Prot." *Justia Law*. http://law.justia.com/cases/maine/supreme-court/2014/2014-me-52.html.

Malouff, Dan. 2014. "Here Are America's Largest Bikesharing Systems in 2013." *Greater Greater Washington*. http://greatergreaterwashington.org/post/21260/here-are-americas-largest-bikesharing-systems-in-2013.

Mann, Jonathan. 1996. "Human Rights and the New Public Health." *Health and Human Rights* 1(3): 229–33.

Markowitz, Gerald E. and David Rosner. 2003. *Deceit and Denial: The Deadly Politics of Industrial Pollution*. Berkeley: University of California Press.

Markowitz, Gerald E. and David Rosner. 2013a. *Deceit and Denial: The Deadly Politics of Industrial Pollution*. Berkeley: University of California Press.

Markowitz, Gerald and David Rosner. 2013b. *Lead Wars: The Politics of Science and the Fate of America's Children*. Berkeley: University of California Press.

Marmot, Michael G. 2005. "Social Determinants of Health Inequalities." *Lancet* 365(9464): 1099–104.

Marmot, Michael G. 2006. "Status Syndrome: A Challenge to Medicine." *Journal of the American Medical Association* 295(11): 1304–7.

Marmot, Michael G. 2010. "Fair Society, Healthy Lives: The Marmot Review Executive Summary." *Strategic Review of Health Inequalities in England post-2010*. http://discovery.ucl.ac.uk/111743.

Marmot, Michael G. et al. 1991. "Health Inequalities among British Civil Servants: The Whitehall II Study." *The Lancet* 337(8754): 1387–93.

Marmot, Michael and Jessica J. Allen. 2014. "Social Determinants of Health Equity." *American Journal of Public Health* 104(S4): S517–19.

Marmot, M. G., H. Bosma, H. Hemingway, E. Brunner, and S. Stansfeld. 1997. "Contribution of Job Control and Other Risk Factors to Social Variations in Coronary Heart Disease Incidence." *Lancet* 350(9073): 235–9.

Marmot, Michael G., Martin J. Shipley, and Geoffrey Rose. 1984. "Inequalities in Death: Specific Explanations of a General Pattern?" *The Lancet* 323(8384): 1003–6.s

Marras, William S., Robert G. Cutlip, Susan E. Burt, and Thomas R. Waters. 2009. "National Occupational Research Agenda (NORA): Future Directions in Occupational Musculoskeletal Disorder Health Research." *Applied Ergonomics* 40(1): 15–22.

Mascarenhas, Michael. 2007. "Where the Waters Divide: First Nations, Tainted Water and Environmental Justice in Canada." *Local Environment* 12(6): 565–77.

Mather, Mark, Kevin Pollard, and Linda Jacobsen. 2011. *Reports on America: First Results from the 2010 Census*. Washington, DC: Population Reference Bureau.

Mayer, Brian. 2009. "Blue-Green Coalitions: Fighting for the Right to Know." *New Solutions* 19(1): 59–80.

Mayer, Brian, Phil Brown, and Meadow Linder. 2002. "Moving Further Upstream: From Toxics Reduction to the Precautionary Principle." *Public Health Reports* 117(6): 574–86.

Mayer, Brian, Phil Brown, and Rachel Morello-Frosch. 2012. "Labor-Environment Coalition Formation: Framing and the Right to Know." In *Contested Illnesses: Citizens, Science, and Health Social Movements*, edited by Phil Brown, Rachel Morello-Frosch, Stephen Zavestoski, and the Contested Illness Research Group, 189–208. Berkeley: University of California Press.

McCann, Barbara. 2013. *Completing Our Streets: The Transition to Safe and Inclusive Transportation Networks*. Washington, DC: Island Press.

McCulloch, Jock. 2005. "Mining and Mendacity, or How to Keep a Toxic Product in the Marketplace." *International Journal of Occupational and Environmental Health* 11(4): 398–403.

McDermott-Levy, Ruth, Nina Kaktins, and Barbara Sattler. 2013. "Fracking, the Environment, and Health." *American Journal of Nursing* 113(6): 45–51.

McKibben, Bill. 2007. *Deep Economy: The Wealth of Communities and the Durable Future*. New York: Macmillan.

McKinlay, John B. 1979. "A Case for Refocusing Upstream: The Political Economy of Illness." In *Patients, Physicians and Illness: A Sourcebook in Behavioral Science and Health*, edited by E. G. Jaco, 9–25. New York: Free Press.

McKinlay, John B. and Sonja M. McKinlay. 1977. "The Questionable Contribution of Medical Measures to the Decline of Mortality in the United States in the Twentieth Century." *Milbank Memorial Fund Quarterly: Health and Society* 55(3): 405–28.

McNeely, Eileen. 2015. "Bridging the Gap Between Health and Environmental Sustainability." *Huffington Post*, May 27.

The Medical Bag. 2014. "The Radium Girls." *The Medical Bag*, January

1. http://www.medicalbag.com/profile-in-rare-diseases/the-radium-girls/article/472385.

Medina, Jennifer. 2011. "New Fast-Food Restaurants Are Banned from South LA." *New York Times*, January 15.

Mehdipanah, Roshanak et al. 2014. "The Effects of an Urban Renewal Project on Health and Health Inequalities: A Quasi-Experimental Study in Barcelona." *Journal of Epidemiology and Community Health* 68(9): 811–17.

Mesnage, Robin, Nicolas Defarge, Joël Spiroux de Vendômois, and Gilles-Eric Séralini. 2014. "Major Pesticides Are More Toxic to Human Cells Than Their Declared Active Principles." *BioMed Research International.* http://www.ncbi.nlm.nih.gov/pmc/articles/PMC3955666.

Messing, Karen. 2014. *Pain and Prejudice: What Science Can Learn about Work from the People Who Do It.* Toronto: Between the Lines.

Meyer, Steve. 2012. "Why the Hog Farm Count Has Stabilized." http://nationalhogfarmer.com/business/why-hog-farm-count-has-stabilized.

Michaels, David. 2008a. *Doubt Is Their Product: How Industry's Assault on Science Threatens Your Health.* New York: Oxford University Press.

Michaels, David. 2008b. "Manufactured Uncertainty: Contested Science and the Protection of the Public's Health and Environment." In *Agnotology: The Making and Unmaking of Ignorance,* edited by Richard N. Proctor and Linda L. Schiebinger, 90–107. Stanford, CA: Stanford University Press.

Michaels, David and Celeste Monforton. 2005. "Manufacturing Uncertainty: Contested Science and the Protection of the Public's Health and Environment." *American Journal of Public Health* 95(S1): S39–48.

Michaels, David, Celeste Monforton, and Peter Lurie. 2006. "Selected Science: An Industry Campaign to Undermine an OSHA Hexavalent Chromium Standard." *Environmental Health* 5(5). doi: 10.1186/1476-069X-5-5.

Milazzo, Paul Charles. 2006. *Unlikely Environmentalists: Congress and Clean Water, 1945–1972.* Lawrence, Kansas: University Press of Kansas.

Miller, Wilhelmine D., Craig E. Pollack, and David R. Williams. 2011. "Healthy Homes and Communities: Putting the Pieces Together." *American Journal of Preventive Medicine* 40(1): S48–57.

Mitloehner, Frank M. and Michelle Sara Calvo. 2008. "Worker Health and Safety in Concentrated Animal Feeding Operations." *Journal of Agricultural Safety and Health* 14(2): 163–87.

Mohl, Raymond A. 2004. "Stop the Road: Freeway Revolts in American Cities." *Journal of Urban History* 30(5): 674–706.

Monteiro, Carlos A. and Geoffrey Cannon. 2012. "The Impact of Transnational 'Big Food' Companies on the South: A View from Brazil." *PLoS Medicine* 9(7): e1001252.

Moodie, Rob et al. 2013. "Profits and Pandemics: Prevention of Harmful Effects of Tobacco, Alcohol, and Ultra-Processed Food and Drink Industries." *Lancet* 381(9867): 670–79.

Moore, Latetia and Ana V. Diez Roux. 2006. "Associations of Neighborhood Characteristics with the Location and Type of Food Stores." *American Journal of Public Health* 96(2): 325–31.

Moore, Latetia V., Ana V. Diez Roux, Kelly R. Evenson, Aileen P. McGinn, and Shannon J. Brines. 2008. "Availability of Recreational Resources in Minority and Low Socioeconomic Status Areas." *American Journal of Preventive Medicine* 34(1): 16–22.

Morland, Kimberly, Ana V. Diez Roux, and Steve Wing. 2006. "Supermarkets, Other Food Stores, and Obesity: The Atherosclerosis Risk in Communities Study." *American Journal of Preventive Medicine* 30(4): 333–9.

Morland, Kimberly B. and Kelly R. Evenson. 2009. "Obesity Prevalence and the Local Food Environment." *Health & Place* 15(2): 491–5.

Mortazavi, Melissa D. 2011. "Are Food Subsidies Making Our Kids Fat? Tensions between the Healthy Hunger-Free Kids Act and the Farm Bill." *Washington and Lee University School of Law* 68(4): 1699–735.

Moss, Michael. 2013. "'I Feel So Sorry for the Public': Inside the Hyperengineered, Savagely Marketed, Addiction-Creating Battle for American 'Stomach Share.'" *New York Times Magazine*, February 24.

Mostafalou, Sara and Mohammad Abdollahi. 2013. "Pesticides and Human Chronic Diseases: Evidences, Mechanisms, and Perspectives." *Toxicology and Applied Pharmacology* 268(2): 157–77.

Murray, Patty. 2009. *Dangerous Dust: Is OSHA Doing enough to Protect Workers?* Washington, DC: US Government Printing Office. gpoaccess. gov/congress/senate.

National Association of Water Companies. 2011. "Private Water Service Providers: Quick Facts." *National Association of Water Companies.* http://www.nawc.org/uploads/documents-and-publications/documents/docume nt_ecf5b3ac-c222–4b6c-b99f-a0128ae1e9aa.pdf.

Navarro, Vincente and Leiyu Shi. 2003. "The Political Context of Social Inequality and Health." In *Health and Social Justice: Politics, Ideology, and Inequity in the Distribution of Disease,* edited by Richard Hofrichter, 195–216. San Francisco, CA: Jossey-Bass.

Ndumele, Chima D., Heather J. Baer, Shimon Shaykevich, Stuart R. Lipsitz, and Leroi S. Hicks. 2012. "Cardiovascular Disease and Risk in Primary Care Settings in the United States." *American Journal of Cardiology* 109(4): 521–26.

Nega, Tsegaye Habte, Laura Chihara, Kimberly Smith, and Mallika Jayaraman. 2013. "Traffic Noise and Inequality in the Twin Cities, Minnesota." *Human and Ecological Risk Assessment: An International Journal* 19(3): 601–19.

Negin, Elliott. 1996. "The 'Alar' Scare Was for Real: And so Is That 'Veggie Hate-Crime' Movement." *Columbia Journalism Review* 35(3): 13–16.

Nemecek, Sasha. 2006a. "Does the World Need GM Foods? NO." *Scientific American Special Edition* 16(4): 38–9.

Nemecek, Sasha. 2006b. "Does the World Need GM Foods? YES." *Scientific American Special Edition* 16(4): 36–7.

Nestle, Marion. 1993. "Food Lobbies, the Food Pyramid, and US Nutrition Policy." *International Journal of Health Services* 23(3): 483–96.

Nestle, Marion. 2001. "Food Company Sponsorship of Nutrition Research and Professional Activities: A Conflict of Interest?" *Public Health Nutrition* 4(5): 1015–22.

Nestle, Marion. 2002. *Food Politics: How the Food Industry Influences Nutrition and Health.* Berkeley: University of California Press.

Nestle, Marion. 2012. "Utopian Dream: A New Farm Bill." *Dissent* 59(2): 15–19.

Neuman, William. 2010a. "A Growing Discontent." *New York Times*, March 12.

Neuman, William. 2010b. "Nestlé Will Drop Claims of Health Benefit in Drink." *New York Times*, July 14.

NHTSA (National Highway Traffic Safety Administration). 2012. *2010 Motor Vehicle Crashes: Overview.* http://www-nrd.nhtsa.dot.gov/Pubs/811552.pdf.

Novak, Scott P., Sean F. Reardon, Stephen W. Raudenbush, and Stephen L. Buka. 2006. "Retail Tobacco Outlet Density and Youth Cigarette Smoking: A Propensity-Modeling Approach." *American Journal of Public Health* 96(4): 670–6.

O'Connor, Anahad. 2015. "Coke Spends Lavishly on Pediatricians and Dietitians." *New York Times*, September 28.

OECD (Organisation for Economic Cooperation and Development) Health Statistics. 2015. *Focus on Health Spending.* http://www.oecd.org/els/health-systems/health-data.htm.

Okechukwu, Cassandra A., Kerry Souza, Kelly D. Davis, and A. Butch de Castro. 2013. "Discrimination, Harassment, Abuse, and Bullying in the Workplace: Contribution of Workplace Injustice to Occupational Health Disparities." *American Journal of Industrial Medicine* 57(5): 573–86.

Ollinger, Michael, Sang V. Nguyen, Donald Blayney, Bill Chambers, and Ken Nelson. 2005. *Structural Change in the Meat, Poultry, Dairy, and Grain Processing Industries.* US Department of Agriculture, Economic Research Service. http://www.ers.usda.gov/media/850597/err3.pdf.

Olso, Erik D., with Diane Poling and Gina Solomon. 1999. "Bottled Water: Pure Drink or Pure Hype?" Natural Resources Defense Council (NRDC). https://www.nrdc.org/sites/default/files/bottled-water-pure-drink-or-pure-hype-report.pdf.

O'Neil, Sandra George. 2007. "Superfund: Evaluating the Impact of Executive Order 12898." *Environmental Health Perspectives* 115(7): 1087–93.

Ong, Elsa K. and Stanton A. Glantz. 2001. "Constructing 'Sound Science' and 'Good Epidemiology': Tobacco, Lawyers, and Public Relations Firms." *American Journal of Public Health* 91(11): 1749–57.

Oppel, Richard A., Jr. 2013. "Taping of Farm Cruelty Is Becoming the Crime." *The New York Times*, April 6.

Oreskes, Naomi and Erik M. Conway. 2010. *Merchants of Doubt: How a Handful of Scientists Obscured the Truth on Issues from Tobacco Smoke to Global Warming*. New York: Bloomsbury Publishing.

OSAHA (Occupational Safety and Health Administration). 2013. *Caring for Our Caregivers: Facts about Hospital Worker Safety*. Occupational Safety and Health Administration. https://www.osha.gov/dsg/hospitals/documents/1.2_Factbook_508.pdf.

Osborn, Stephen G., Avner Vengosh, Nathaniel R. Warner, and Robert B. Jackson. 2011. "Methane Contamination of Drinking Water Accompanying Gas-Well Drilling and Hydraulic Fracturing." *Proceedings of the National Academy of Sciences* 108(20): 8172–76.

Overmann, Stephen. 2015. "Water Pollution by Agricultural Chemicals." *Regional Updates*. http://wps.prenhall.com/wps/media/objects/1027/1052055/Regional_Updates/update30.htm.

Owens, David. 2014. "Last of Waterbury's Radium Girls Dies." *The Courant*, March 3.

Pamuk, Elsie, Diane Makuc, Katherine E. Heck, Cynthia Reuben, and Kimberly Lochner, eds. 1999. *Socioeconomic Status and Health Chart Book*. Hyattsville, MD: National Center for Health Statistics.

Parker, Clifton. 2015. "Stanford Scholars Issue Plan to Reduce Poverty." *Stanford News*. http://news.stanford.edu/2015/05/18/poverty-plan-grusky-051815.

Parker, Lynn. 2008. *Commodity Foods and the Nutritional Quality of the National School Lunch Program: Historical Role, Current Operations, and Future Potential*. Food Research and Action Center, Washington, DC. http://citeseerx.ist.psu.edu/viewdoc/download?doi=10.1.1.675.4024&rep=rep1&type=pdf.

Parodi, Stefano, Valerio Gennaro, Marcello Ceppi, and Pierluigi Cocco. 2007. "Comparison Bias and Dilution Effect in Occupational Cohort Studies." *International Journal of Occupational and Environmental Health* 13(2): 143–52.

Parsad, Basmat, Laurie Lewis, and Bernard Greene. 2006. *Calories In, Calories Out: Food and Exercise in Public Elementary Schools, 2005*. National Center for Education Statistics, Institute of Education Sciences, US Department of Education.

Passchier-Vermeer, Willy and Wim F. Passchier. 2000. "Noise Exposure and Public Health." *Environmental Health Perspectives* 108(S1): 123–31.

Pasternak, Judy. 2011. *Yellow Dirt: A Poisoned Land and the Betrayal of the Navajos*. New York: Free Press.

Paulson, Jerome A. 2011. "Chemical-Management Policy: Prioritizing Children's Health." *Pediatrics* 127(5): 983–90.

Payán-Rentería, Rolando et al. 2012. "Effect of Chronic Pesticide Exposure in Farm Workers of a Mexico Community." *Archives of Environmental & Occupational Health* 67(1): 22–30.

Pearce, Neil. 2008. "Corporate Influences on Epidemiology." *International Journal of Epidemiology* 37(1): 46–53.

Pelletier, Stephen G. 2015. "Experts See Growing Importance of Adding Environmental Health Content to Medical School Curricula." In *Achieving Health Equity: How Academic Medicine Is Addressing Social Determinants of Health*, edited by the Association of American Medical Colleges, 21–2. Washington, DC: AAMC. https://www.aamc.org/download/460392/data/sdoharticles.pdf.

Pellow, David Naguib and Lisa Sun-Hee Park. 2002. *The Silicon Valley of Dreams: Environmental Injustice, Immigrant Workers, and the High-Tech Global Economy*. New York: NYU Press.

Perelman, Alison. 2011. "The Pyramid Scheme: Visual Metaphors and the USDA's Pyramid Food Guides." *Design Issues* 27(3): 60–71.

Peters, Gerhard and John T. Wooley. 1976. "Gerald R. Ford: Veto of the Electric and Hybrid Vehicle Research, Development and Demonstration Bill." http://www.presidency.ucsb.edu/ws/?pid=6329.

Pew Commission on Industrial Farm Animal Protection. 2008. *Putting Meat on the Table: Industrial Farm Animal Production America*. Baltimore, MD: Johns Hopkins Bloomberg School of Public Health.

Pflanz, Mike. 2010. "World Water Day: Dirty Water Kills More People than Violence, Says UN." *Christian Science Monitor*, March 22. http://www.csmonitor.com/World/Africa/2010/0322/World-Water-Day-Dirty-water-kills-more-people-than-violence-says-UN.

Pickett, Kate E. and Richard G. Wilkinson. 2015. "Income Inequality and Health: A Causal Review." *Social Science & Medicine* 128: 316–26.

Pimentel, D. et al. 2007. "Ecology of Increasing Diseases: Population Growth and Environmental Degradation." *Human Ecology* 35(6): 653–68.

PLoS Medicine Editorial. 2009. "Clean Water Should Be Recognized as a Human Right." *PLoS Medicine* 6(6): e1000102.

Pollan, Michael. 2007. "You Are What You Grow." *New York Times*, April 22.

Pollan, Michael. 2008. "An Open Letter to the Next Farmer in Chief." *New York Times*, October 9.

Postel, Sandra. 2014. "A Sacred Reunion: The Colorado River Returns to the Sea." *National Geographic*. http://newswatch.nationalgeographic.com/2014/05/19/a-sacred-reunion-the-colorado-river-returns-to-the-sea.

Powell, Lisa M., Sandy Slater, Donka Mirtcheva, Yanjun Bao, and Frank J. Chaloupka. 2007. "Food Store Availability and Neighborhood Characteristics in the United States." *Preventive Medicine* 44(3): 189–95.

Proctor, Robert N. 2011. *Golden Holocaust: Origins of the Cigarette Catastrophe and the Case for Abolition*. Berkeley: University of California Press.

Prud'homme, Alex. 2011. *The Ripple Effect: The Fate of Freshwater in the Twenty-First Century.* New York: Simon & Schuster.

Quinn, Margaret M. 2003. "Occupational Health, Public Health, Worker Health." *American Journal of Public Health* 93(4). doi: 10.2105/AJPH.93.4.526.

Raj, Sean D. 2005. "Bottled Water: How Safe Is It?" *Water Environment Research* 77(7): 3013–18.

Ranganathan, Malini and Carolina Balazs. 2015. "Water Marginalization at the Urban Fringe: Environmental Justice and Urban Political Ecology across the North–South Divide." *Urban Geography* 36(3): 403–23.

Raphael, Dennis. 2003. "Toward the Future: Policy and Community Actions to Promote Population Health." In *Health and Social Justice: Politics, Ideology, and Inequity in the Distribution of Disease,* edited by Richard Hofrichter, 453–68. San Francisco, CA: Jossey-Bass.

Ratcliff, Kathryn Strother. 2002. *Women and Health: Power, Technology, Inequality, and Conflict in a Gendered World.* Boston, MA: Allyn & Bacon.

Ratcliff, Kathryn Strother. 2013. "Power of Poverty: Individual Agency and Structural Constraints." In *Poverty and Health: A Crisis Among America's Most Vulnerable,* vol. 1: *Risks and Challenges,* edited by Kevin Michael Fitzpatrick: 5–30. Santa Barbara, CA: Praeger.

Rechtschaffen, Clifford L. 2004. "Enforcing the Clean Water Act in the Twenty-First Century: Harnessing the Power of the Public Spotlight." *Alabama Law Review* 55(3): 775–814.

Resor, Felicia R. 2012. "Benefit Corporation Legislation." *Wyoming Law Review* 12 (91). http://repository.uwyo.edu/wlr/vol12/iss1/5.

Revkin, Andrew C. 2009. "Industry Ignored Its Scientists on Climate." *New York Times,* April 23.

Richmond, Caroline. 2012. "Lester Breslow." *Lancet* 380(9838): 212.

Richtel, Matt. 2016. "San Francisco, 'The Silicon Valley of Recycling.'" *New York Times,* March 25.

Richter, Elihu, Colin L. Soskolne, and Joseph LaDou. 2001. "Efforts to Stop Repression Bias by Protecting Whistleblowers." *International Journal of Occupational and Environmental Health* 7(1): 68–71.

Rivin, Gabe. 2016. "Another Kind of Hog Farm." *North Carolina Health News,* February 22.

Robbins, Anthony and Marion Nestle. 2011. "Obesity as Collateral Damage: A Call for Papers on the Obesity Epidemic." *Journal of Public Health Policy* 32(2): 143–5.

Robert Wood Johnson Foundation. 2010. "A New Way to Talk about the Social Determinants of Health." Vulnerable Populations Portfolio. http://www.rwjf.org/content/dam/farm/reports/reports/2010/rwjf63023.

Robert Wood Johnson Foundation. 2011a. "Health Care's Blind Side: The Overlooked Connection between Social Needs and Good Health." http://www.rwjf.org/en/library/research/2011/12/health-care-s-blind-side.html.

Robert Wood Johnson Foundation. 2011b. "Work, Workplaces and Health." http://www.rwjf.org/en/library/research/2011/05/work-and-health-.html.

Robert Wood Johnson Foundation. 2012. "How Does Transportation Impact Health?" http://www.rwjf.org/en/library/research/2012/10/how-does-transportation-impact-health-.html.

Roberts, Andrea L. et al. 2013. "Perinatal Air Pollutant Exposures and Autism Spectrum Disorder in the Children of Nurses' Health Study II Participants." *Environmental Health Perspectives* 121(8): 978–84.

Roberts, J. Timmons and Melissa M. Toffolon-Weiss. 2001. "Media Savvy Cajuns and Houma Indians: Fighting an Oilfield Waste Dump in Grand Bois." In *Chronicles from the Environmental Justice Frontline*, edited by J. Timmons Roberts and Melissa M. Toffolon-Weiss, 137–64. New York: Cambridge University Press.

Roberts, Paul. 2009. *The End of Food*. Boston, MA: Mariner Books.

Robin, Marie-Monique. 2010. *The World According to Monsanto: Pollution, Corruption, and the Control of the World's Food Supply*. New York: New Press.

Romley, John A., Deborah Cohen, Jeanne Ringel, and Roland Sturm. 2007. "Alcohol and Environmental Justice: The Density of Liquor Stores and Bars in Urban Neighborhoods in the United States." *Journal of Studies on Alcohol and Drugs* 68(1): 48–55.

Rosner, David. 2000. "When Does a Worker's Death Become Murder?" *American Journal of Public Health* 90(4): 535–40.

Rosner, David and Gerald E. Markowitz. 2005. *Deadly Dust: Silicosis and the On-Going Struggle to Protect Workers' Health*. Ann Arbor: University of Michigan Press.

Rosner, David and Gerald E. Markowitz. 2009. "The Trials and Tribulations of Two Historians: Adjudicating Responsibility for Pollution and Personal Harm." *Medical History* 53(2): 271–92.

Ross, Gilbert. 2004. "The Public Health Implications of Polychlorinated Biphenyls (PCBs) in the Environment." *Ecotoxicology and Environmental Safety* 59(3): 275–91.

Rothman, Barbara Katz. 2001. *The Book of Life: A Personal and Ethical Guide to Race, Normality and the Human Gene Study*. Boston, MA: Beacon Press.

Royte, Elizabeth. 2008. *Bottlemania: Big Business, Local Springs, and the Battle over America's Drinking Water*. New York: Bloomsbury Publishing.

Rubin, Jill and Anna Tesmenitsky. 2002. "Selling before Telling: Why the Government Needs to Take a Second Look at Genetically Engineered Foods." *New Solutions* 12(3): 297–316.

Ruckart, Perri Z., Frank J. Bove, Edwin Shanley, and Morris Maslia. 2015. "Evaluation of Contaminated Drinking Water and Male Breast Cancer at Marine Corps Base Camp Lejeune, North Carolina: A Case Control Study." *Environmental Health* 14(74). doi: 10.1186/s12940-015-0061-4.

Rudel, Thomas K. 2009. "How Do People Transform Landscapes? A

Sociological Perspective on Suburban Sprawl and Tropical Deforestation." *American Journal of Sociology* 115(1): 129–54.

Rugh, Jacob S., Len Albright, and Douglas S. Massey. 2015. "Race, Space, and Cumulative Disadvantage: A Case Study of the Subprime Lending Collapse." *Social Problems* 62(2): 186–218.

Rumpler, John. 2010. "Corporate Agribusiness and America's Waterways Report Highlights 8 Companies' Role in Pollution." http://www.environmentamerica.org/news/ame/corporate-agribusiness-and-america%E2%80%99s-waterways-report-highlights-8-companies%E2%80%99-role.

Runyon, Luke. 2016. "How Colorado Is Turning Food Waste into Electricity." NPR.org, April 5.

Sabeti, Heerad. 2011. "The For-Benefit Enterprise." *Harvard Business Review* 89(11): 98–104.

Sanborn, Margaret D., Alan Abelsohn, Monica Campbell, and Erica Weir. 2002. "Identifying and Managing Adverse Environmental Health Effects: 3. Lead Exposure." *Canadian Medical Association Journal* 166(10): 1287–92.

Sapolsky, Robert. 2005. "Sick of Poverty." *Scientific American* 293(6): 92–9.

Sass, Jennifer Beth, Barry Castleman, and David Wallinga. 2005. "Vinyl Chloride: A Case Study of Data Suppression and Misrepresentation." *Environmental Health Perspectives* 113(7): 809–12.

Satcher, David et al. 2005. "What If We Were Equal? A Comparison of the Black–White Mortality Gap in 1960 and 2000." *Health Affairs* 24(2): 459–64.

Schantz, Susan L., John J. Widholm, and Deborah C. Rice. 2003. "Effects of PCB Exposure on Neuropsychological Function in Children." *Environmental Health Perspectives* 111(3): 357–576.

Schmidt, Charles W. 2002. "Debate Percolates over CAFE Standards." *Environmental Health Perspectives* 110(8): A466–8.

Schmidt, Charles W. 2011. "Blind Rush? Shale Gas Boom Proceeds amid Human Health Questions." *Environmental Health Perspectives* 119(8): 348–53.

Schnall, Peter L., Karen L. Belkić, Paul Landsbergis, and Dean Baker. 2000. "Why the Workplace and Cardiovascular Disease?" *Occupational Medicine* 15(1): 97–122.

Schneider, Andrew and David McCumber. 2004. *An Air That Kills: How the Asbestos Poisoning of Libby, Montana, Uncovered a National Scandal.* New York: G. P. Putnam's Sons.

Schrag, Zachary M. 2004. "The Freeway Fight in Washington, DC: The Three Sisters Bridge in Three Administrations." *Journal of Urban History* 30(5): 648–73.

Schwartz, John. 2015. "On Tether to Fossil Fuels, Nations Speak with Money." *New York Times*, December 5.

Schwarzenbach, René P., Thomas Egli, Thomas B. Hofstetter, Urs von

Gunten, and Bernhard Wehrli. 2010. "Global Water Pollution and Human Health." *Annual Review of Environment and Resources* 35(1): 109–36.

Scott-Samuel, Alex and Katherine Elizabeth Smith. 2015. "Fantasy Paradigms of Health Inequalities: Utopian Thinking?" *Social Theory & Health* 13(3–4): 418–36.

Scudellari, Megan. 2015. "Drugging the Environment." *The Scientist.* http://www.the-scientist.com/?articles.view/articleNo/43615/title/Drugging-the-Environment.

Seavey, Dorie and Abby Marquand. 2011. *Caring in America: A Comprehensive Analysis of the Nation's Fastest-Growing Jobs: Home Health and Personal Care Aides.* PHI Policy Works. http://phinational.org/research-reports/caring-america-comprehensive-analysis-nations-fastest-growing-jobs-home-health-and.

Sered, Susan and Rushika Fernandopulle. 2007. *Uninsured in America: Life and Death in the Land of Opportunity.* Berkeley: University of California Press.

Shelley, Donna, Gbenga Ogedegbe, and Brian Elbel. 2014. "Same Strategy Different Industry: Corporate Influence on Public Policy." *American Journal of Public Health* 104(4): e9–11.

Shiva, Vandana. 2000. *Stolen Harvest: The Hijacking of the Global Food Supply.* Cambridge, MA: South End Press.

Shonkoff, Jack P. et al. 2012. "The Lifelong Effects of Early Childhood Adversity and Toxic Stress." *Pediatrics* 129(1): 232–46.

Shor, Glenn. 2014. "The 1980 OSHA Cotton Dust Standard Brochure." *New Solutions* 24(3): 435–47.

Shostak, Sara Naomi. 2013. *Exposed Science: Genes, the Environment, and the Politics of Population Health.* Berkeley: University of California Press.

Sierra Club. 2013. "Coulda Woulda Shoulda." Poster. *Sierra Club Magazine,* July–August. http://www.sierraclub.org/sierra/2013-4-july-august/last-words/coulda-woulda-shoulda.

Silverstein, Jason. 2015. "Genes Don't Cause Racial-Health Disparities, Society Does." *The Atlantic.* http://www.theatlantic.com/health/archive/2015/04/genes-dont-cause-racial-health-disparities-society-does/389637.

Silverstein, Michael. 2008. "Getting Home Safe and Sound: Occupational Safety and Health Administration at 38." *American Journal of Public Health* 98(3): 416–23.

Silverstone, Allen E. et al. 2012. "Polychlorinated Biphenyl (PCB) Exposure and Diabetes: Results from the Anniston Community Health Survey." *Environmental Health Perspectives* 120(5). http://escholarship.org/uc/item/0q31d2vp.

Simon, David R. 2000. "Corporate Environmental Crimes and Social Inequality: New Directions for Environmental Justice Research." *American Behavioral Scientist* 43(4): 633–45.

Simon, Michele. 2013. *And Now a Word from Our Sponsors: Are America's Nutrition Professionals in the Pocket of Big Food?* Academy of Nutrition and

Dietetics. http://www.eatdrinkpolitics.com/wp-content/uploads/AND_Co rporate_Sponsorship_Report.pdf.

Simonton, D. Scott and Stephen King. 2013. "Hydrogen Sulfide Formation and Potential Health Consequences in Coal Mining Regions." *Water Quality, Exposure and Health* 5(2): 85–92.

Skrzycki, Cindy. 2006. "OSHA Does The Darndest Things." *Washington Post*, May 23.

Slaper, Timothy F. and Tanya J. Hall. 2011. "The Triple Bottom Line: What Is It and How Does It Work?" *Indiana Business Review* 86(1): 4–8.

Smelser, Neil J. 1997. *Problematics of Sociology: The Georg Simmel Lectures, 1995.* Berkeley: University of California Press.

Smith, Barbara Ellen. 1981. "Black Lung: The Social Production of Disease." *International Journal of Health Services* 11(3): 343–59.

Smith, Katherine E. et al. 2010. "'Working the System'—British American Tobacco's Influence on the European Union Treaty and Its Implications for Policy: An Analysis of Internal Tobacco Industry Documents." *Public Library of Science Medicine* 7(1). doi: 10.1371/journal.pmed.1000202.

Snell, Bradford C. 1974. *American Ground Transport: A Proposal for Restructuring the Automobile, Truck, Bus and Rail Industries.* Washington, DC: US Government Printing Office.

Sollinger, Marc. 2015. "Building Sustainably... the Ancient Way." Innovation Hub. http://blogs.wgbh.org/innovation-hub/2015/7/31/ochsen dorf-architecture.

Soraghan, Mike. 2011. "Baffled about Fracking? You're Not Alone." May 13. http://www.nytimes.com/gwire/2011/05/13/13greenwire-baffled-about-fracking-youre-not-alone-44383.html.

Sorenson, Susan B., Christiaan Morssink, and Paola Abril Campos. 2011. "Safe Access to Safe Water in Low Income Countries: Water Fetching in Current Times." *Social Science & Medicine* 72(9): 1522–6.

Stahl, Lesley. 2014. *60 Minutes Video: Lesley Stahl Reports on How Duke Energy Is Handling over 100 Million Tons of Coal Ash Waste in North Carolina.* CBS. http://www.cbs.com/shows/60_minutes/video/mMNh MyK3d3Qkaaq15NvLHMvP2rlEMvgV/the-spill-at-dan-river.

Steele, Eurídice Martínez et al. 2016. "Ultra-Processed Foods and Added Sugars in the US Diet: Evidence from a Nationally Representative Cross-Sectional Study." *British Medical Journal* 6(3): e009892. doi: 10.1136/ bmjopen-2015-009892.

Steier, Gabriela. 2012. "Dead People Don't Eat: Food Governmentenomics and Conflicts-of-Interest in the USDA and FDA." *Pittsburgh Journal of Environmental and Public Health Law* 7(1): 1–58.

Stein, Leon. 1962. *The Triangle Fire.* Ithaca, NY: Cornell University Press.

Stolz, Rich. 2005. "A National Transportation Equity Movement for Real Human Needs." *Race, Poverty & the Environment* 12(1): 64–6.

Story, Mary and Simone French. 2004. "Food Advertising and Marketing Directed at Children and Adolescents in the US." *International Journal of*

Behavioral Nutrition and Physical Activity 1(3). doi: 10.1186/1479-5868-1-3.

Stranahan, Susan Q. 2002. "The Clean Room's Dirty Secret." *Mother Jones*, March–April. http://www.motherjones.com/politics/2002/03/clean-rooms-dirty-secret.

Stuckler, David and Marion Nestle. 2012. "Big Food, Food Systems, and Global Health." *PLoS Medicine* 9(6): e1001242.

Stull, Valerie J. and Jonathan Patz. 2015. "Agriculture Policy." In *Climate Change and Public Health*, edited by Bary S. Levy and Jonathan A. Patz, 319–60. Oxford: Oxford University Press.

Syme, S. Leonard. 2004. "Social Determinants of Health: The Community as an Empowered Partner." *Preventing Chronic Disease* 1(1). http://www.cdc.gov/pcd/issues/2004/jan/03_0001.htm.

Taylor, Andrea K. and Linda R. Murray. 2013. "Occupational Safety and Health." In *Social Injustice and Public Health*, edited by Barry S. Levy and Victor W. Sidel, 337–56. New York: Oxford University Press.

Thoits, Peggy A. 2010. "Stress and Health Major Findings and Policy Implications." *Journal of Health and Social Behavior* 51(S1): S41–53.

Tyler, Liz. 2013. "'Small Places Close to Home': Toward a Health and Human Rights Strategy for the US." *Journal of Health and Human Rights* 15(2): 80–96.

UCS (Union of Concerned Scientists). 2004. "Scientific Integrity in Policy Making (2004)." Union of Concerned Scientists. http://www.ucsusa.org/our-work/center-science-and-democracy/promoting-scientific-integrity/reports-scientific-integrity.html.

UCS (Union of Concerned Scientists). 2015. "The Climate Deception Dossiers: *Internal Fossil Fuel Industry Memos Reveal Decade of Corporate Disinformation*." Union of Concerned Scientists. https://docs.google.com/presentation/d/1e6eSs2T5ZcZDA1_699ADpjPwx2hzEhbrR-bXxRt4xb8/embed?start=false&loop=false&delayms=3000&usp=embed_facebook.

UN (United Nations). 2011. "Special Rapporteur on the Human Right to Safe Drinking Water and Sanitation." United Nations Human Rights. http://www.ohchr.org/EN/Issues/WaterAndSanitation/SRWater/Pages/SRWaterIndex.aspx.

UN World Water Report. 2004. *Water for People: Water for Life.* United Nations. http://unesdoc.unesco.org/images/0012/001295/129556e.pdf.

USDA (United States Department of Agriculture). 2003. *Agriculture Fact Book 2001–2002.* USDA. https://www.usda.gov/documents/usda-factbook-2001-2002.pdf.

USDA (United States Department of Agriculture). 2013. "USDA Economic Research Service: Irrigation & Water Use." USDA. http://www.ers.usda.gov/topics/farm-practices-management/irrigation-water-use.aspx.

USDA (United States Department of Agriculture). 2017. "Ag and Food Statistics: Charting the Essentials—Farming and Farm Income."

Subdirectory in *Farming and Farm Income*. http://www.ers.usda.gov/data-products/ag-and-food-statistics-charting-the-essentials/farming-and-farm-income.aspx.

US Department of Commerce. n.d. "Logistics and Transportation Spotlight: The Logistics and Transportation Industry in the United States." Select USA. https://www.selectusa.gov/logistics-and-transportation-industry-united-states.

Vallianatos, E. G. and McKay Jenkins. 2014. *Poison Spring: The Secret History of Pollution and the EPA*. New York: Bloomsbury Press.

Verlicchi, Paola, Alessio Galletti, Mira Petrovic, and Damia Barceló. 2010. "Hospital Effluents as a Source of Emerging Pollutants: An Overview of Micropollutants and Sustainable Treatment Options." *Journal of Hydrology* 389(3–4): 416–28.

Villanueva, Christina M., Gaël Durand, Marie Bénédicte Coutté, Cécile Chevrier, and Sylvaine Cordier. 2005. "Atrazine in Municipal Drinking Water and Risk of Low Birth Weight, Preterm Delivery, and Small-for-Gestational-Age Status." *Occupational and Environmental Medicine* 62(6): 400–5.

Virginia Tech. 2014. "West Virginia Chemical Spill into Elk River Contaminating Air and Water Quality." *ScienceDaily*. http://www.sciencedaily.com/releases/2014/03/140326092040.htm.

Virnig, Beth A., Nancy N. Baxter, Elizabeth B. Habermann, Roger D. Feldman, and Cathy J. Bradley. 2009. "A Matter of Race: Early- versus Late-Stage Cancer Diagnosis." *Health Affairs* 28(1): 160–8.

Vock, Daniel C. 2014. "Why Would You Have a Highway Run through a City?" http://www.governing.com/topics/transportation-infrastructure/gov-highway-through-city.html.

Wall, Kim. 2015. "This Dome in the Pacific Houses Tons of Radioactive Waste: And It's Leaking." *The Guardian*, July 3. http://www.theguardian.com/world/2015/jul/03/runit-dome-pacific-radioactive-waste.

Wang, Lucy. 2014. "Baltimore's Solar-Powered Water Wheel Can Devour 50,000 Pounds of Harbor Trash Every Day." *Inhabitat*. http://inhabitat.com/baltimores-solar-powered-water-wheel-devours-50000-pounds-of-harbor-trash-every-day.

Washburn, Jennifer. 2011. "Academic Freedom and the Corporate University." *Academe* 97(1): 8–13.

Watts, Nick et al. 2015. "Health and Climate Change: Policy Responses to Protect Public Health." *Lancet* 386(10006): 1861–914.

Weiss, Christopher C. et al. 2011. "Reconsidering Access: Park Facilities and Neighborhood Disamenities in New York City." *Journal of Urban Health* 88(2): 297–310.

Welch, John F. and Patricia Daly. 1998. "God versus GE." *Harper's Magazine*, August. http://harpers.org/archive/1998/08/god-versus-g-e.

Welsh-Huggins, Andrew. 2015. "Woman Awarded $1.6 Million over DuPont Chemical in Water." AP: The Big Story. http://bigstory.ap.org/art

icle/56d83a4005184a36b1ec018fb2ed1b7a/woman-awarded-16-million-over-dupont-chemical-water.

WHO (World Health Organization). 2003. *The Right to Water*. WHO. http://www.who.int/water_sanitation_health/en/righttowater.pdf.

WHO (World Health Organization). 2008a. *Closing the Health Gap in a Generation*. Commission on Social Determinants of Health. http://www.who.int/social_determinants/final_report/csdh_finalreport_2008_execsumm.pdf.

WHO (World Health Organization). 2008b. *The Right to Health* (Fact Sheet No. 31). Office of the United Nations, High Commissioner for Human Rights. http://www.ohchr.org/Documents/Publications/Factsheet31.pdf.

WHO (World Health Organization). 2012. *WHO Global Report: Mortality Attributable to Tobacco*. WHO. http://www.who.int/tobacco/publications/surveillance/rep_mortality_attributable/en.

WHO (World Health Organization). 2013. "Diarrhoeal Disease." WHO. http://www.who.int/mediacentre/factsheets/fs330/en.

Wier, Megan, Charlie Sciammas, Edmund Seto, Rajiv Bhatia, and Tom Rivard. 2009. "Health, Traffic, and Environmental Justice: Collaborative Research and Community Action in San Francisco, California." *American Journal of Public Health* 99(S3): S499–504.

Wiist, William H. 2011. "Citizens United, Public Health, and Democracy: The Supreme Court Ruling, Its Implications, and Proposed Action." *American Journal of Public Health* 101(7): 1172–9.

Wilde, Parke E. 2013. "The New Normal: The Supplemental Nutrition Assistance Program (SNAP)." *American Journal of Agricultural Economics* 95(2): 325–31.

Wilkinson, James. 2001. "Community Supported Agriculture." *OCD Technote* 20: 1–2.

Wilkinson, Richard G. 2006. *The Impact of Inequality: How to Make Sick Societies Healthier*. New York: New Press.

Willet, Walter C. and Meir J. Stampfer. 2003. "Rebuilding the Food Pyramid." *Scientific American* 288(1): 64–71.

Williams, David R. and Michelle Sternthal. 2010. "Understanding Racial–Ethnic Disparities in Health Sociological Contributions." *Journal of Health and Social Behavior* 51(1): S15–27.

Williams, David R., Michelle Sternthal, and Rosalind J. Wright. 2009. "Social Determinants: Taking the Social Context of Asthma Seriously." *Pediatrics* 123(S3): S174–84.

Williams, Lauren and John Germov. 2009. "The Social Appetite: A Sociological Approach to Food and Nutrition." In *A Sociology of Food and Nutrition: The Social Appetite*, edited by John Germov and Lauren Williams, 221–35. Melbourne: Oxford University Press.

Williams, Terry Tempest. 1991. *Refuge: An Unnatural History of Family and Place*. New York: Vintage.

Wilper, Andrew P. et al. 2009. "Hypertension, Diabetes, and Elevated

Cholesterol among Insured and Uninsured US Adults." *Health Affairs* 28(6): w1151–9.

Wilson, Sacoby M., Frank Howell, Steve Wing, and Mark Sobsey. 2002. "Environmental Injustice and the Mississippi Hog Industry." *Environmental Health Perspectives* 110 (Suppl. 2): 195–201.

Wines, Michael. 2013. "Genetically Altered Crop in Oregon No Surprise." *New York Times*, June 5.

Wing, Steve and Susanne Wolf. 2000. "Intensive Livestock Operations, Health, and Quality of Life among Eastern North Carolina Residents." *Environmental Health Perspectives* 108(3): 233–8.

Woodcock, James and Rachel Aldred. 2008. "Cars, Corporations, and Commodities: Consequences for the Social Determinants of Health." *Emerging Themes in Epidemiology* 5(4): 1742–53.

Woodhouse, Edward J. 2003. "Change of State? The Greening of Chemistry." In *Synthetic Planet: Chemical Politics and the Hazards of Modern Life*, edited by Monica J. Casper, 177–97. New York: Routledge.

Woolf, Steven H. and Paula Braveman. 2011. "Where Health Disparities Begin: The Role of Social and Economic Determinants—And Why Current Policies May Make Matters Worse." *Health Affairs* 30(10): 1852–9.

Wooters, Monica. 2008. "Coca Cola and Water Resources in Chiapas." *Colectivos de Apoyo, Solidaridad y Acción*. http://www.casacollective.org/index.php.

Worthy, Kenneth A., Richard C. Strohman, Paul R. Billings, and Berkeley Biotechnology Working Group. 2005. "Agricultural Biotechnology Science Compromised." In *Controversies in Science and Technology: From Maize to Menopause*, edited by Daniel Lee Kleinman, Abby J. Kinchy, and Jo Handelsman, 135–39. Madison: University of Wisconsin Press.

Wu, Xun and Nepomuceno Malaluan. 2008. "A Tale of Two Concessionaires: A Natural Experiment of Water Privatization in Metro Manila." *Urban Studies* 45(1). http://papers.ssrn.com/abstract=2336807.

Yang, Quanhe et al. 2014. "Added Sugar Intake and Cardiovascular Diseases Mortality among US Adults." *Journal of the American Medical Association Internal Medicine* 174(4): 516–24.

Young, Robin and Jeremy Hobson. 2013. "Eric Garcetti Takes Over as LA's New Mayor." *Here and Now*. http://hereandnow.wbur.org/2013/07/01/la-mayor-garcetti.

Yu, Chu-Ling et al. 2006. "Residential Exposure to Petrochemicals and the Risk of Leukemia: Using Geographic Information System Tools to Estimate Individual-Level Residential Exposure." *American Journal of Epidemiology* 164(3): 200–7.

Zuckerman, Diana M. 2010. "Reasonably Safe? Breast Implants and Informed Consent." *Reproductive Health Matters* 18(35): 94–102.

Index

Note: page numbers in *italics* denote figures or tables